Evolutionary Perspectives Social Psychology

ABOUT THE AUTHOR

Dr. Faith Onyango, (Ph.D) specializes in research on Language and Cultures and the ways in which second language teching and learning is Influenced by Groplitics. A key areas of interest in particular is how sociolinguistic factors impact the acquisition of language and creole studies. He is bilingual in both English and French and currently resides in France where he is an adjunct professor at the Essex Business School and the University of Cergy-Pontoise.

ABOUT THE BOOK

Social psychology is the scientific study of how people's thoughts, feelings, and behaviours are influenced by the actual, imagined, or implied presence of others. Today scientific psychology is generally defined as the science of behaviour. The term 'behaviour' is employed in a very inclusive and comprehensive sense. We may now see the difference between the layperson's definition of psychology as the science of the mind and the scientific definition of psychology as a science of behaviour. A few decades ago even scientific psychologists defined psychology as the study of the mind. Soon, however, it was found that defining psychology as the field concerned with the study of the mind created certain problems. Social psychologists have studied attitude formation, the structure of attitudes, attitude change, the function of attitudes, and the relationship between attitudes and Behaviour. Because people are influenced by the situation, general attitudes are not always good predictors of specific Behaviour. For a variety of reasons, a person may value the environment and not recycle a can on a particular day. This book materials are used to theoretical and practical significant of students and researchers, teachers and sociologists.

EVOLUTIONARY PERSPECTIVES SOCIAL PSYCHOLOGY

Dr. Faith Onyango

AMIGA PRESS. INC
Delhi -110051

AMIGA PRESS. INC
H.O :- 28-A, Indra Park, Chander Nagar
Delhi :- 110051 (India)
Tel :- 011-22504028, +91-98736-57000
Email :- info@amigapress.co.in
amigapub@gmail.com
Website :- www.amigapress@co.in

This edition is published by Amiga Press.Inc

ISBN : 978-93-87295-23-0

First Published 2019

Printed and bound in India by Replika Press Pvt. Ltd.

Preface

Social Psychology is the study of the nature and causes of human social behaviour, with an emphasis on how people think towards each other and how they relate to each other. As the mind is the axis around which social behaviour pivots, social psychologists tend to study the relationship between mind(s) and social behaviours.

Social psychology reached maturity in both theory and method during the 1980s and 1990s. Careful ethical standards now regulate research, and greater pluralism and multiculturalism perspectives have emerged. Modern researchers are interested in a many phenomena, but attribution, social cognition, and the self-concept are perhaps the greatest areas of growth in recent years. Social psychologists have also maintained their applied interests with contributions in health and environmental psychology, as well as the psychology of the legal system.

In contemporary psychology, unconscious processes are emphasized by a large number of psychologists. The emphasis on unconscious processes was first laid by Sigmund Freud. But one can refer to many more controversies and divergences of opinion which over the years have become narrow as research and understanding has increased. Today there is sufficient agreement, if not unanimity, in defining psychology as the science of behaviour as also in the understanding of the term behaviour, which is now used to include the observable, unobservable and inferred behaviour of the organism. It is difficult to define behaviour briefly. It is easier to describe the nature and characteristics of behaviour.

Most psychologists have, therefore, concentrated on the description of behaviour rather than on its definition, and at this point we could consider some of the characteristics of behaviour. This may help us to understand what is the nature and scope of psychology. Definitions of psychology can be left to a later stage or to the reader himself to evolve his or her own definition because ultimately definitions can never be complete or perhaps are not even necessary.

In social psychology, attitudes are defined as learned, global evaluations of a person, object, place, or issue that influence thought and action. Put more simply, attitudes are basic expressions of approval or disapproval, favorability or unfavorability, or as Bem put it, likes and dislikes. Examples would include liking chocolate ice cream, being against abortion, or endorsing the values of a particular political party. Attitudes that are well remembered and central to our self-concept, however, are more likely to lead to Behaviour, and measures of general attitudes do predict patterns of Behaviour over time. Large amount of recent research on attitudes is on the distinction between traditional, self-report attitude measures and "implicit" or unconscious attitudes. For example, experiments using the Implicit Association Test have found that people often demonstrate bias against other races, even when their questionnaire responses reveal equal mindedness. One study found that explicit attitudes correlate with verbal Behaviour in interracial interactions, whereas implicit attitudes correlate with nonverbal Behaviour. Attitudes are also involved in several other areas of the discipline, such as the following;conformity, interpersonal attraction, social perception, and prejudice.

In social psychology, attitudes are defined as learned, global evaluations of a person, object, place, or issue that influence thought and action. Put more simply, attitudes are basic expressions of approval or disapproval, favourability or unfavourability, or as Bem put it, likes and dislikes.

Examples would include liking chocolate ice cream, being against abortion, or endorsing the values of a particular political party. Social psychologists have studied attitude formation, the structure of attitudes, attitude change, the function of attitudes, and the relationship between attitudes and behaviour.

Because people are influenced by the situation, general attitudes are not always good predictors of specific behaviour. For a variety of reasons, a person may value the environment and not recycle a can on a particular day.

Attitudes that are well remembered and central to our self-concept, however, are more likely to lead to behaviour, and measures of general attitudes do predict patterns of behaviour over time. Large amount of recent research on attitudes is on the distinction between traditional, self-report attitude measures and "implicit" or unconscious attitudes.

This is a reference book. All the matter is just compiled and edited in nature, taken from the various sources which are in public domain.

This book gives an insight into the social processes and its impact on social development.

—*Editor*

Contents

1

Introduction

Social psychology is the scientific study of how people's thoughts, feelings, and behaviours are influenced by the actual, imagined, or implied presence of others. By this definition, *scientific* refers to the empirical method of investigation. The terms *thoughts, feelings,* and *behaviours* include all of the psychological variables that are measurable in a human being. The statement that others may be *imagined* or *implied* suggests that we are prone to social influence even when no other people are present, such as when watching television, or following internalized cultural norms. Social psychologists typically explain human behaviour as a result of the interaction of mental states and immediate social situations. In Kurt Lewin's famous heuristic formula, behaviour can be viewed as a function of the person and the environment, $B = f(P, E)$. In general, social psychologists have a preference for laboratory based, empirical findings. Social psychology theories tend to be specific and focused, rather than global and general. Social psychology is an interdisciplinary domain that bridges the gap between psychology and sociology. During the years immediately following World War II, there was frequent collaboration between psychologists and sociologists. However, the two disciplines have become increasingly specialized and isolated from each other in recent years, with sociologists focusing on "macro variables" (e.g. social structure) to a much greater extent. Nevertheless, sociological approaches to social psychology remain an important counterpart to psychological research in this area. In addition to the split between psychology and sociology, there has been a somewhat less pronounced difference in emphasis between American social psychologists and European social psychologists. As a broad generalization, American researchers traditionally have focused more on the individual, whereas Europeans have paid more attention to group level phenomena.

The discipline of social psychology began in the United States at the dawn of the 20th century. The first published study in this area was an experiment in 1898 by Norman Triplett on the phenomenon of social facilitation. During the

1930s, many Gestalt psychologists, most notably Kurt Lewin, fled to the United States from Nazi Germany. They were instrumental in developing the field as something separate from the behavioural and psychoanalytic schools that were dominant during that time, and social psychology has always maintained the legacy of their interests in perception and cognition. Attitudes and small group phenomena were the most commonly studied topics in this era. During WWII, social psychologists studied persuasion and propaganda for the U.S. military.

After the war, researchers became interested in a variety of social problems, including gender issues and racial prejudice. In the sixties, there was growing interest in new topics, such as cognitive dissonance, bystander intervention, and aggression. By the 1970s, however, social psychology in America had reached a crisis. There was heated debate over the ethics of laboratory experimentation, whether or not attitudes really predicted behaviour, and how much science could be done in a cultural context. This was also the time when a radical situationist approach challenged the relevance of self and personality in psychology. Social psychology reached maturity in both theory and method during the 1980s and 1990s. Careful ethical standards now regulate research, and greater pluralism and multiculturalism perspectives have emerged. Modern researchers are interested in a many phenomena, but attribution, social cognition, and the self-concept are perhaps the greatestareas of growth in recent years. Social psychologists have also maintained their applied interests with contributions in health and environmental psychology, as well as the psychology of the legal system.

Self-concept

The fields of social psychology and personality have merged over the years, and social psychologists have developed an interest in self-related phenomena. In contrast with traditional personality theory, however, social psychologists place a greater emphasis on cognitions than on traits. Much research focuses on the self-concept, which is a person's understanding of his or her self. The self-concept is often divided into a cognitive component, known as the *self-schema,* and an evaluative component, the *self-esteem*. The need to maintain a healthy self-esteem is recognized as a central human motivation in the field of social psychology. Self-efficacy beliefs are cognitions that are associated with the self-schema. These are expectations that performance on some task will be effective and successful. Social psychologists also study such self-related processes as self-control and self-presentation. People develop their self-concepts by varied means, including introspection, feedback from others, self-perception, and social comparison. By comparison to relevant others, people gain information about themselves, and they make inferences that are relevant to self-esteem. Social comparisons can be either "upward" or "downward," that is, comparisons to people who are either higher in status or ability, or lower in status or ability. Downward comparisons are often made in order to elevate self-esteem. Self-perception is a specialized form of attribution that involves making inferences about oneself after observing one's own behaviour. Psychologists have found that too many extrinsic rewards (e.g. money) tend to reduce intrinsic motivation through the self-perception process, a phenomenon known as overjustification. People's attention is directed to the reward and they lose interest in the task when the reward is no longer offered. This is an important exception to reinforcement theory.

Interpersonal Phenomena

Social Influence: Social influence refers to the way people affect the thoughts, feelings, and behaviours of others. Like the study of attitudes, it is a traditional, core topic in social psychology. In fact, research on social influence overlaps considerably with research on attitudes and persuasion. Social influence is also closely related to the study of group dynamics, as most of the principles of influence are strongest when they take place in social groups. Conformity is the most common and pervasive form of social influence. It is generally defined as the tendency to act or think like other members of a group. Group size, unanimity, cohesion, status, and prior commitment all help to determine the level of conformity in an individual. Conformity is usually viewed as a negative tendency in American culture, but a certain amount of conformity is not only necessary and normal, but probably essential for a community to function. The two major motives in conformity are *normative* influence, the tendency to conform in order to gain social acceptance, and avoid social rejection or conflict, as in peer pressure; and *informational* influence, which is based on the desire to obtain useful information through conformity, and thereby achieve a correct or appropriate result. Minority influence is the degree to which a smaller faction within the group influences the group during decision making.

Note that this refers to a minority position on some issue, not an ethnic minority. Their influence is primarily informational and depends on consistent adherence to a position, degree of defection from the majority, and the status and self-confidence of the minority members. Reactance is a tendency to assert oneself by doing the opposite of what is expected.

This phenomenon is also known as *anticonformity* and it appears to be more common in men than in women. There are two other major areas of social influence research. Compliance refers to any change in behaviour that is due to a request or suggestion from another person. The Foot-in-the-door technique is a compliance method in which the persuader requests a small favour and then follows up with a larger favour, e.g. asking for the time, and then asking for ten dollars. A related trick is the Bait and switch. The third major form of social influence is obedience. This is a change in behaviour that is the result of a direct order or command from another person. A different kind of social influence is the self-fulfilling prophecy. This is a prediction that, in being made, actually causes itself to become true. For example, in the stock market, if it is widely believed that a crash is imminent, investors may lose confidence, sell most of their stock, and actually cause the crash. Likewise, people may expect hostility in others and actually induce this hostility by their own behaviour.

Cognitive Dissonance

Cognitive dissonance is a feeling of unpleasant arousal caused by noticing an inconsistency among one's cognition. These contradictory cognitions may be attitudes, beliefs, or ones awareness of his or her behaviour. The theory of cognitive dissonance proposes that people have a motivational drive to reduce dissonance by changing their attitudes, beliefs, and behaviours, or by justifying or rationalizing their attitudes, beliefs, and behaviours. Cognitive dissonance theory is one of the most influential and extensively studied theories in social psychology. Cognitive dissonance theory was originally developed as a theory of attitude change, but it is now considered to be a theory of the self-concept by many social psychologists. Dissonance is strongest when a discrepancy has been noticed between one's self-concept and one's behaviour, e.g. doing something that makes one ashamed. This can result in self-justification as the individual attempts to deal with the threat. Cognitive dissonance typically leads to a change in attitude, a change in behaviour, a self-affirmation, or a rationalization of the behaviour. An example of cognitive dissonance is smoking. Smoking cigarettes increases the risk of cancer, which is threatening to the self-concept of the individual who smokes. Most of us believe ourselves to be intelligent and rational, and the idea of doing something foolish and self-destructive causes dissonance. To reduce this uncomfortable tension, smokers tend to make excuses for themselves, such as "I'm going to die anyway, so it doesn't matter."

Intrapersonal Phenomena

Attitudes: In social psychology, attitudes are defined as learned, global evaluations of a person, object, place, or issue that influence thought and action. Put more simply, attitudes are basic expressions of approval or disapproval, favourability or unfavourability, or as Bem put it, likes and dislikes. Examples would include liking chocolate ice cream, being against abortion, or endorsing the values of a particular political party. Social psychologists have studied attitude formation, the structure of attitudes, attitude change, the function of attitudes, and the relationship between attitudes and behaviour. Because people are influenced by the situation, general attitudes are not always good predictors of specific behaviour. For a variety of reasons, a person may value the environment and not recycle a can on a particular day. Attitudes that are well remembered and central to our self-concept, however, are more likely to lead to behaviour, and measures of general attitudes do predict patterns of behaviour over time. Large amount of recent research on attitudes is on the distinction between traditional, self-report attitude measures and "implicit" or unconscious attitudes. For example, experiments using the Implicit Association Test have found that people often demonstrate bias against other races, even when their questionnaire responses reveal equal mindedness. One study found that explicit attitudes correlate with verbal behaviour in interracial interactions, whereas implicit attitudes correlate with nonverbal behaviour. Attitudes are also involved in several other areas of the discipline, such as the following;conformity, interpersonal attraction, social perception, and prejudice.

Persuasion

The topic of persuasion has received a great deal of attention in recent years. Persuasion is an active method of influence that attempts to guide people toward the adoption of an attitude, idea, or behaviour by rational or emotive means. Persuasion relies on "appeals" rather than strong pressure or coercion. Numerous variables have been found to influence the persuasion process, and these are normally presented in five major categories: *who* said *what* to *whom* and *how*.

1. The Communicator, including credibility, expertise, trustworthiness, and attractiveness.
2. The Message, including varying degrees of reason, emotion (such as fear), one-sided or two sided arguments, and other types of informational content.
3. The Audience, including a variety of demographics, personality traits, and preferences.
4. The Channel, including the printed word, radio, television, the internet, or face-to-face interactions.
5. The Context, including the environment, group dynamics, pre-amble to the message

Dual process theories of persuasion (such as the elaboration likelihood model) maintain that the persuasive process is mediated by two separate routes. Persuasion can be accomplished by either superficial aspects of the communication or the internal logic and evidence of the message. Whether someone is persuaded by a popular celebrity or factual arguments is largely determined by the ability and motivation of the audience. Persuasion attempts that rely on the mass media frequently result in failure. This is because people's attitudes and behaviours are often established habits that tend to be resistant to change. Communication campaigns are most likely to succeed when they use entertaining characters and messages, tailor the message to fit the audience, and repeat messages across relevant media channels. An example of a highly effective mass media campaign is the Got Milk campaign.

Social Cognition

Social cognition is a growing area of social psychology that studies how people perceive, think about, and remember information about others. Person perception is the study of how people form impressions of others. The study of how people form beliefs about each other while interacting is known as interpersonal perception. A major research topic in social cognition is attribution. Attributions are the explanations we make for people's behaviour, either our own behaviour or the behaviour of others. We can ascribe the locus of a behaviour to either internal or external factors. An *internal*, or dispositional, locus of causality involves factors within the person, such as ability or personality. An *external*, or situational, locus involves outside factors, such as the weather. A second element of attribution ascribes the cause of behaviour to either stable or unstable factors. Finally, we also attribute causes of behaviour to either controllable or uncontrollable factors. Numerous biases in the attribution process have been discovered. The fundamental attribution error is the tendency to make dispositional attributions for behaviour. The actor-observer effect is a refinement of this bias, the tendency to make dispositional attributions for other people's behaviour and situational attributions for our own. The just-world phenomenon is the tendency to blame victims (a dispositional attribution) for their suffering. This is believed to be motivated by people's anxiety that good people, including themselves, could be victimized in an unjust world. Finally, the self-serving bias is the tendency to take credit for successes, and blame others for failure. Researchers have found that depressed individuals often lack this bias and actually have more realistic perceptions of reality.

Heuristics are cognitive short cuts. Instead of weighing all the evidence when making a decision, people rely on heuristics to save time and energy. The availability heuristic occurs when people estimate the probability of an outcome based on how easy that outcome is to imagine. As such, vivid or highly memorable possibilities will be perceived as more likely than those that are harder to picture or are difficult to understand, resulting in a corresponding cognitive bias. Numerous other biases have been found by social cognition researchers. The hindsight bias is a false memory of having predicted events, or an exaggeration of actual predictions, after becoming aware of the outcome. The confirmation bias is a type of bias leading to the tendency to search for, or interpret information in a way that confirms one's preconceptions.

Another key concept in social cognition is the assumption that reality is too complex to easily discern. As a result, we tend to see the world according to simplified schemas or images of reality. Schemas are generalized mental representations that organize knowledge and guide information processing. Schemas often operate automatically and unintentionally, and can lead to biases in perception and memory. Expectations from schemas may lead us to see something that is not there. One experiment found that people are more likely to misperceive a weapon in the hands of a black man than a white man. This type of schema is actually a stereotype, a generalized set of beliefs about a particular group of people. Stereotypes are often related to negative or preferential attitudes (prejudice) and behaviour (discrimination). Schemas for types of events (e.g. going to McDonalds, doing laundry) are known as *scripts*.

APPLIED SOCIAL PSYCHOLOGY

The continuous integration of theory, research, and practice. Lewin's vision called for elegant theories that have practical benefits and for theory-relevant research and practice. This prescription appears to he followed in the fields of small-group processes and organisational psychology, but ignored in mainstream social psychology. Many people trained in social psychology contribute to these and other areas in ways that further Lewin's prescription.

A central focus on fundamental social problems at all levels of analysis. The quality of life should be the top priority of applied social psychology. This is operationalised through a consistent focus on social problems, from the mundane (e.g., poor interpersonal communication, ineffective organisational decision making) to the dramatic (e.g., crime, racism). Bickman (1980a) clearly establishes applied social psychology as a problem oriented social psychology that seeks to deal with real-world issues. Mayo and La France's (1980) model sees improving the quality of life as a central element of an applicable social psychology. To increase our social utility, we must move away from the strong emphasis on intrapersonal processes that characterises much contemporary social psychology (Cartwright, 1978). While dissonance and attribution theory help us understand how individuals process information, they give insufficient attention to other influences at higher levels of analysis such as groups, organisations, and society's distribution of economic resources. Recent developments show a rapid expansion in research areas relating to crime, health care, environmental, and other social issues.

The development of middle-range theories stressing the reciprocal interaction of the person and the environment Contemporary social psychological theories represent minitheories of individual functioning rather than middle-range theories of social interaction. Numerous commentrators have lamented over the lack of substance in social psychology's most popular theories. Stephen (1980) points to minitheories of limited scope and notes that even our broadest theories (e.g., social exchange, social learning) are not well validated across populations or settings and yield little that is useful in understanding and promoting social change. In Gergen's (1978) terms, we lack "generative theory" that challenges assumptions and patterns social behaviour and that offers fresh alternatives for social life.

The expansion of practice expertise partly through interdisciplinary collaboration. Mayo and La France (1980) include utilisation/intervention as a central element in their model of an applicable social psychology. Deliberate application must be an integral part of the discipline. Only some of us may become involved in social action, "but all of us need to be concerned about the potential uses of our research" (p. 89). In addition to methodological reform, we need to develop a complex understanding of utilisation and intervention.

The application of a variety of complementary research methods. Experimentation offers precision and control and the almost unique capacity to establish causal relationships. In our view the highest forms of action research and evaluation research involve experimental designs. However, the heavy reliance by contemporary social psychology on the laboratory experiment has led to sterility and constriction in our research efforts. The focus needs to shift, and is shifting, to a wider variety of designs with an emphasis on multimethod, longitudinal research in natural settings.

The adherence to a clearly articulated humanistic value base and a professional code of ethics. Applied social psychology must be grounded in a humanistic value base that affirms the dignity, respect, and enhancement of individuals within a democratic and humanitarian society (Fisher, 1982). Stephen (1980) sees social psychology as having a scientific mind and a humanistic heart, and suggests we needn't lose the former in order to gain the latter; even though the choice is often cast in these terms. The humanistic value base demands adherence to a professional code of ethics for research and practice.

A commitment to continuous profession at development and role versatility. The shift to an applied emphasis will not be easy for individuals or institutions.

Bickman (1980b) speaks of the need for retraining faculty. We would cast this as continuous professional development in the scientist/ practitioner mold. Concurrently, undergraduate courses in social psychology should expand their coverage beyond the minitheories of theoretical experimental social psychology. Graduate training is already responding to the applied shift by providing the conceptual and experiential base required for professional functioning. A general competence along with multiple specialisations will enable individuals to enact a variety of challenging research and practice roles.

THE AIMING OF APPLIED SOCIAL PSYCHOLOGISTS

Given the evolving identity and the challenging roles of applied social psychology the crucial question becomes how to train new professionals for the field (Bickman, 1980b). It is important to first distinguish limited from substantial-training in applied social psychology. Some number of traditional programmes in social psychology have taken initial steps toward applied training. They may have added a course or two, a faculty member with applied interests, and possibly a practicum or other field research experience. At the same time, the majority of faculty members remain committed to a traditional definition of the field. According to Bickman:

> *From our experience, it appears that, in many cases, the title is changed but the programme has not. Many graduate programmes have simply added a new course in field research or a visiting professor who has some sort of "applied" interests. This is understandable, given the dearth of experienced individuals in this field. In many cases, graduate students would have to strike out on their own and create opportunities for training and experience [1980b, p. 179].*

While such efforts certainly expand the scope of training in social psychology, they should not be regarded as substantial training in applied social psychology. In fact, if such efforts are presented as training in applied social psychology, they may do a disservice to both their students and the public.

Constricted training efforts may flow from a limited conception of applied social psychology as given by the traditional response defined above. Limited graduate training would be compatible with a definition of applied social psychologists as primarily experimental researchers who happen to work in field settings. This approach is presented by Kidd and Saks (1980):

> *The applied social psychologist is most often a rather traditional, experimental social psychologist who finds him/herself in contact with settings outside the micro-cosm of the laboratory. Armed with the assumptions, concepts, and methods the discipline, the applied social psychologist carries a point of view*

into a real-world setting and tries to reconcile his/her background and knowledge to the problem at hand [p. 3].

An applied social psychologist is someone trained in the social-psychological point of view who finds him/herself acting as a problem solver outside the laboratory'. The particular problem, role, or theoretical perspective is a function of the operational setting, and only to a minor degree a function of the psychologist's graduate experiences [p. 10].

The social-psychological perspective identified by Kidd and Saks is essentially the phenomenological study of social perception and cognition as exemplified by mainstream laboratory research.

It is true that some of the conceptual and methodological skills of the experimental social psychologist transfer to field settings. To acknowledge this reality may help us to maintain an integrated discipline of social psychology. However, to suggest that traditional training with some minor additions is all that is required to develop an applied social psychologist will likely lead to both frustration and eventual disillusionment. We need to look for new approaches and new combinations of experiences in the training of applied social psychologists.

PROFESSIONAL CERTIFICATION IN SOCIAL PSYCHOLOGY

As social psychology moves toward a more professional identity, the question arises as to whether and how scientist/practitioners should be certified to offer applied research and practice services to the public. Questions on the accreditation of training programmes and internships also arise. To is section will briefly examine the advantages and disadvantages of certification and speculate on potential mechanisms. Three levels of professional accreditation—registration, certification, and licensing — are usually distinguished, although there is no consistency in terminology. The term "registration" will be used here to designate the process by which individual professionals may voluntarily register as members of fraternal and educational associations that have no statutory mechanisms for supporting their determinations of competence. "Certification" refers to the statutory registration and regulation of professionals who may use the title of the profession as determined by a professional association recognised in legislation. "Licensing" extends certification so that both title and practice (the activities in which registered members engage) are legally restricted in usage to members of the association. Practitioners using the title of the profession or engaging in prescribed activities and who are not members of the association (or covered by legislation governing another profession) are open to legal prosecution. Certification will be used here to refer to both certification and/or licensing unless otherwise noted.

Advantages and Disadvantages of Certification

The primary advantage of certification is protection of the public. A professional association composed of one's peers makes the judgment that the individual scientist/practitioner is competent to offer services at large, and this judgment has legal standing. Furthermore, any professional association regardless of whether it provides registration, certification, or licensing, can enhance the personal and professional development of its membership. Peer review of credentials, opportunities for continuing education, and increasing the public's understanding of the profession are all benefits. In addition members may gain greater economic rewards through personal recognition that increases public perception of competence and desirability. Fringe benefits—liability insurance, reduced rates on publications, or work-shops—may also be derived from a professional association. The major criticisms of certification flow not against the benefits of professional affiliation but from the legal pact between the profession and the state, which limits practice to those who are certified. Based mainly on the history of licensing in the medical field, Gross (1978) offers a stinging indictment of what he perceives as primarily an exclusionary process. He suggests that professional associations backed by legislation take on a guild quality that restricts competition, arbitrarily sets prices, controls entry and training, and defines quality only in terms of minimal entrance requirements. Furthermore, certification does not appear to be effective in preventing incompetence, largely because it is in the self-interest of the profession to obscure such problems. Essentially, Gross (1978) sees certification as serving the self-interests of the service providers, especially in terms of economic rewards, and not as protecting of the public welfare. The process actually *institutionalises* a lack of accountability to the public.

A related problem is raised by Koocher (1979), who questions the validity of credentials used for certification in psychology. Whatever existing credentials, such as degrees or state licensure, do measure, they are clearly not highly valid measures of competence. Some emerging trends such as peer review and continuing education requirements may enhance the validity of credentials, but Koocher (1979) does not look for quick improvements. In the meantime, credentials provide some useful information to the public, but the phrase "let the buyer beware" maintains its relevance.

Alternate Mechanisms for Certification

If applied social psychologists decided that the advantages of accreditation outweighed the disadvantages, where might they look for registration, certification, or licensing mechanisms? First, registration in a professional association is provided at the national level by the American Psychological

Association, the Canadian Psychological Association, and so oil. 'These associations require minimal credentials in the profession and offer many of the fraternal and educational benefits cited above. Public accountability is also enhanced by vehicles such as the APA Committee on Scientific and Professional Ethics, which renders judgments on alleged violations of the ethical code. The *Casebook on Ethical Standards of Psychologists* (APA, 1967) illustrates the type of questionable practices and judgments that such committees are concerned with. Applied social psychologists interested in professional affiliation related to specific roles can look to a number of different associations that vary in the credentials they require for registration. For those interested in programme evaluation or programme development consultation, the Evaluation Research Society is an international organisation designed to improve the theory and practice of evaluation for public service. Membership is open to anyone engaged in evaluation research regardless of discipline or profession. In addition to educational functions, mainly an annual convention, the society is working on a number of professional issues including ethics and standards for evaluation. For applied social psychologists interested in the role of organisational consultant, organisation development networks in both the United States and Canada provide a similar fraternal and educational function. As with the national psychological associations, these organisations offer a number of benefits of affiliation without the disadvantages that accrue through legal certification.

The International Association of Applied Social Scientists (IAASS) was formed in 1971 to provide for the accreditation of social science practitioners in the areas of training and consultation. It currently offers accreditation of consultants in five divisions: (1) personal/professional development, (2) group development, (3) internal organisation development, (4) external organisation development, and (5) societal change (formerly community development). As of 1981, the association changed its name to Certified Consultants International (CCI) to fit more closely its major function. Accreditation is based primarily on an intensive peer review of practice activity and is rereviewed every five years. IAASS/CCI offers many of the individual and collective benefits noted above in an area of practice where legislation is problematic due to a lack of standards and measures of competence. However, as with all attempts at some form of accreditation, IAASS/CCI is seen *as* having both advantages (Hogan, 1976) and disadvantages (Jones, 1977).

At present, there exist no statutory mechanisms for the explicit certification or licensing of applied social psychologists. The clearest avenue for this possibility would be through the American Association of State Psychology Boards (Hess, 1977). The AASPB was formed in 1971 to facilitate communication and provide coordination among the state psychology boards throughout North America. Fifty state boards in the United States and eight provincial associations in Canada provide for the practice of professional psychology through statutory regulation. The majority of states have licensing legislation, while the majority of provinces have certification. In all cases, the major functions are to set standards of admission into the profession, to administer selection and examination procedures, to regulate practice, and to discipline violations of professional conduct. The power to carry out these functions is embodied in state or provincial legislation.

The typical requirements for certification include a doctoral degree, one year of supervised experience, and the passing of the Examination of Professional Practice in Psychology (EPPP). Some jurisdictions require additional written and oral examinations, and specialty examinations in such areas as clinical, counselling, school, and industrial psychology may soon become common. The EPPP covers basic knowledge in psychology, methodology, and professional practice (including clinical and other specialties, e.g., industrial and organisational and social psychology and ethical conduct).

In principle it appears that these general certification requirements would be appropriate for applied social psychologists wishing to enter professional practice with legal sanction. This possibility would require the operationalisation of each of the certification requirements in ways that are appropriate to the training and practice of applied social psychology. However, until the field has coalesced to a greater degree, it would be difficult to provide a consensual operationalisation of each requirement. Nonetheless, as Bickman (1980b) points out, certification would help to more firmly establish the field and to create a greater sense of legitimacy.

One area to begin looking for commonality in applied social psychology is that of training programmes and internships. As more programmes are developed, we should continue to ask what the core elements of training are. We should ask what constitutes an acceptable internship in applied social psychology. As answers to these questions become apparent, we might consider the accreditation of both training programmes and internships. Bickman (1980b) notes that internships vary from university to university and that applied social psychology could benefit from a national internship programme. Again, the national associations would be the most obvious mechanism. As with certification, however, we should be aware of the potential constricting effects of programme and internship accreditation. The legitimate forum for the discussion of such issues lies with the national associations and their divisions (e.g., APA's Divisions 8 and 9, CPA's Applied Division, and related interest groups) and with voluntary associations such as the Society for the

Advancement of Social Psychology. Only through continuing discussion can the place of applied social psychology as a profession be satisfactorily established

THE ETHICS OF PRACTICE OF SOCIAL PYSCHOLOGY

As social psychology shifts in the applied direction, ethical concerns will become more salient (Deutsch, 1975). While it is recognised that basic research entails significant ethical issues, it is rarely if ever designed to produce more than temporary effects in the subjects. In applied research and consultation, ethical issues take on a more complex and problematic form. Informed consent, for example, is not as easy to operationalise in an organisational change effort as it is in a laboratory experiment. The complexity and potential impact of applied work necessitates a careful and detailed consideration of ethical issues. Increased concern regarding ethics is based in a view of social psychology as a *profession* and not simply as a scientific discipline. According to Lippitt and Lippitt (1978), in all standard definitions of a profession there are "elements of dedication, of giving one's ethical position a place of extreme importance, of taking pride in applying one's knowledge and skills, and of functioning with integrity" (p. 58). Working as a professional requires sensitivity and a willingness to anticipate and deal with ethical issues.

Codes of ethics have been established in numerous professions in order to protect the welfare of the individual subject or client in relation to the benefits of the research or practice to the discipline, the organisation, or the society. Applied social psychologists as either applied researchers or as social consultants have a number of excellent sources of ethical guidelines upon which to draw.

For research purposes, the most relevant code of ethics is the American Psychological Association's *Ethical Principles in the Conduct of Research and Human Participants* (1973). Stuart Cook (1976), who helped develop the APA code, provides a detailed discussion of the major ethical concerns and questionable practices. Of particular importance are the issues of informed consent, invasion of privacy, deception, and disrespectful treatment. A more specific discussion of ethical issues involved in social experimentation is provided by Rivlin and Timpane (1975) and Warwick (1978). Thus, social psychologists have shown considerable sensitivity to ethical concerns related to both basic and applied research.'

In the area of consultation, several societies provide guidelines: the American Psychological Association, the American Society for Training and Development, the Academy of Management, and the International Association of Applied Social Scientists (Certified Consultants International as of 1981). Lippitt and Lippitt (1978) provide a set of ethical principles synthesised from a number of these sources. This generalised code covers the responsibility and competence of the consultant, moral and legal standards, client welfare, confidentiality, and other aspects such as misrepresentation, remuneration, and promotional activities. As with applied research, ethical issues in different forms of social intervention are no simple matter. Bermant, Kelman, & Warwick (1978) discuss such issues in several different contexts including encounter groups, organisation development, community intervention, and national programme development.

For applied social psychologists, many of whom would be members of APA or similar national associations, the *Ethical Standards of Psychologists* (APA, 1979) and the *Standards for Providers of Psychological Services* (APA, 1977) are particularly relevant. The former deals with the ethical conduct of psychologists as scientists, teachers, and practitioners. The latter specifies the minimal acceptable levels of quality assurance and performance that psychologists as practitioners are expected to provide. The *Standards* covers the provision of human services ordinarily involved in the practice of specialists in clinical, counselling, industrial-organisational, and school psychology. Most of these standards would be appropriate to the services offered by applied social psychologists.

THE DEVELOPMENT SOCIAL BEHAVIOUR

Growing up entails a series of group memberships which begin in the family and continuously expand. A secure early home environment is helpful to the development of social skills. when values in the home are not taught consistently and the child discovers a disparity between what the parents teach and how they behave, the development of internal controls and conscience is established more slowly. It has actually been demonstrated that parents who are accepting during infancy tend to make it easier for the child to relate effectively with his peers.

The Preschool Child

From birth each child has individual characteristics and a unique rate of growth. Each child interprets social events about him in accordance with his developing style of life and thus experiences his environment uniquely. Although the characteristics of age groups may be described, this is merely normative behaviour. Developmental sequences may be anticipated, but the rate at which they are experienced varies among children.

Maturation is basic to the socialisation process. The child's development of motor skills must precede some social skills. A considerable amount of play is based upon the child's mobility. Choice may be a factor in his proceeding socially at a slower pace, but his overall social development is limited by certain maturational factors.

From Havighurst's developmental tasks of infancy and early childhood the following three tasks appear to have significance in social development:

1. Forming simple concepts of social and physical reality.
2. Learning to relate oneself emotionally to parents, siblings, and other people.
3. Learning to distinguish right and wrong; developing a conscience.

The new-born infant is aware only of his needs and makes them known by his increased activity level. As he grows physically, he grows in awareness of the environment around him. This physical growth is accompanied by increased social awareness and a developing capacity for social interaction.

The interaction of the mother with the child during these early weeks does not affect the developing infant's physical needs only; adequate mothering means satisfying the child's social and emotional needs as well. Joyce Robertson, in a study of twenty-five infant-mother pairs at a Child-Therapy Clinic in London, observed the development of the babies in bodily tonus, muscular activity and achievements, quality and quantity of responsiveness to both the mother and the wider environment, communication, and expression of feeling. Robertson found that the twenty babies who were adequately mothered were satisfactorily developed at the age of twelve months, while none of the five inadequately mothered babies was. This study is another indication of the significance of developmental interrelationships physically, socially, and emotionally. The developing infant who is cared for physically but otherwise ignored may at first show signs of distress and later become apathetic and autistic.

Gradually the developing child takes more interest in the people around him. He enjoys watching other children. If his family has been responsive to him, he anticipates friendly relationships. He comes to enjoy social interaction.

By two years of age the child usually plays well with older children. He is happy to watch others, but has not yet learned to play with children his own age. This is a period of parallel play. Children of this age like to be together, but each plays with his own toys. They may exchange toys, but they do not play together.

The child moves from parallel play to playing with one other child and then to group play for short periods of time. He adjusts to children outside the family. Play is the fundamental arena in which children experiment with their social relations. In periods of neighborhood free play, the child acquires a new idea of his place in the world. He must adapt to group requirements or be excluded.

Thus, the family is the first step in the socialisation process for the young child. Within the confines if the family the child gets his first experience in living with other people and making adjustments to them. The family selects what shall be passed on to the child; it also evaluates many of the experiences to which the child is exposed. However, the child's primary reaction pattern and his capacity' for selective response are also influential upon the course of his early social development.

How, specifically, can a child's motor skills affect his social development? Can advanced motor development occasionally serve as a deterrent to social development?

Middle Childhood

The importance of the peers increases in the period of middle childhood. while deference is still paid adults, parental domination is resented when peers are present. By the time the child enters school, a number of the developmental tasks should be accomplished. The child's interests and activities broaden in number and complexity, and he learns to adjust to a number of formal and informal groups.

School becomes a laboratory for expanded experiences in social living. In the school setting the child is for the first time intensively introduced to gaining recognition on his own merits outside the family circle.

When children enter kindergarten, many attitudes and beliefs have already been formed, some of which may have to be unlearned. In the new setting, opportunities are present to help shape the child's social attitudes. The child can benefit greatly from being in a social group. The presence of all kinds of children may be quite upsetting at first, but it creates exactly the kind of situation in which he can come to understand social relationships. It is here that mutual respect, rights, and obligations—can be taught most effectively. The child is helped to develop self-control and is encouraged and guided to make desirable emotional responses and to express his feelings through manipulation, language, or rhythmic expression. The social developmental tasks of middle childhood are:

1. Learning to get along with age-mates.
2. Learning an appropriate sex role.
3. Developing concepts necessary for everyday living.

4. Developing conscience, morality, and a scale of values.
5. Developing attitudes toward social groups and institutions.

When the child goes to school, he encounters a world vastly different from that to which he has been accustomed. He enters a new environment containing many more people than previously. Freedom has to be curtailed; contacts are multiplied, more adjustments to other persons are necessary. In addition to encountering more rivals, the child learns that competition may take one form in the schoolroom, another on the playground, and still another on the way to and from school.

Throughout the elementary school years, the child's behaviour is increasingly affected by what other children think and do. Their habits, interests, likes, and dislikes become most influential. Beginning with the middle elementary school grades, many children develop what appears to be a behaviour pattern quite dominated by the peers. Peer identification is wholesome for the child's development and indicative of normal personal- social development. Although peer influence may be disturbing to adults at this period, it is a sign of social growth.

Acceptance by the peer group is important to the child, as lowered social status may cause him to feel inferior. Not being accepted by a group is the greatest hardship a human being can endure. Inferiority feelings may result in the inadequate development of a feeling of belonging to a group which is expressed through a voluntary desire to participate and contribute. The child at this tune is getting his first extensive exposure to subcultures other than his own.

An important learning derived from the peer group is the discipline of the group. The discipline acquired at home or at school is frequently one of respect for authority. The same children who at home and at school will not take any part in establishing or enforcing rules often voluntarily develop in their peer groups a rigorous code of conduct and methods of enforcing them.

Teachers often overlook the significance to children of peer acceptance and peer group pressure. These relationships can be disruptive and disturbing, or they may make positive contributions to good learning situations. With increasing maturity the child becomes less egocentric and learns to subordinate his own desires so that group goals may be reached. The relationships a child has with his peers determine to a great extent how he views the world around him and how he views himself.

Mr. Carvon, seventh-grade teacher, is especially impressed with Robert's work in science. He frequently calls the attention of the class to how well Robert does the work and suggests that other students might profit from his example.

He notices that Robert is not accepted socially by the other boys and decides to intervene and point out Robert's fine qualities to the group. Evaluate the teacher's effect on Robert's total development. What suggestions would you have for Mr. Carvon?

Give examples of inappropriate parental domination when peers are present. How can the parent deal effectively with the child's relationship to the peer group? What are the ways in which peer influence can be beneficial to development?

Preadolescence

Preadolescence, as the name implies, is the period immediately preceding adolescence. For girls, typically, it comes between the eleventh and thirteenth year, for boys between the ages of twelve and fourteen. In the American school programme it corresponds with the seventh, eighth, and ninth grades.

The developmental tasks of the preadolescents are concerned with preparation for adult life. Among them are:

1. Achieving new and more mature relations with age-mates of both sexes.
2. Achieving a masculine or feminine social role.
3. Accepting one's physique and using the body effectively.
4. Achieving emotional independence of parents and other adults.
5. Developing intellectual skills and concepts necessary for civic competence.
6. Achieving socially responsible behaviour.

In the American culture. preadolescence is the period when children are expected to learn appropriate sex roles. Tomboy activities of girls are now less acceptable in the eyes of both child and adult society. Effeminate behaviour patterns of boys are viewed with disapproval by both peers and adults. The sex differentiation results in an apparent antagonism between the sexes, and is characterised by the formation of age-sex groups. Both boys and girls tend to reject standards set by adults—standards which had been largely accepted by the children prior to this time. The preadolescent school group is the most heterogeneous of all the elementary groupings, so heterogeneous that it can hardly be considered a social group. The chronological age span may be from eleven to fourteen in grade seven, while the social-maturity age span may be even greater. Because of laws which keep many children in school until they reach their sixteenth birthday, the span of intellectual ability in the seventh grade may be from fourth to twelfth grade.

Preadolescents tend to choose friends and form groups on the basis of common interests, but with a distinct separation of boys and girls, even though their interests may be the same. They wonder about many things, but have not always reached the point of discussing their problems even with their peers. In his contacts with others of various backgrounds the child is exposed to ideas that are different from his family's. He discovers that parents are not all alike, and, noting differences in parental requirements, he begins to question the policies of his own parents.

The preadolescent is beginning to learn that he has different roles to play in different groups and must find his place in each of the groups of which he is a member. He now has increased opportunity to choose the groups to which he wishes to belong.

How is failure in the developmental tasks of preadolescence related to the developmental tasks of middle childhood? Take one of the preadolescent developmental tasks, and from your observations illustrate its importance at this stage.

Friendships

The highest level of social development lies in the child's ability to satisfy his social needs by selecting certain individuals for more intense social contacts. These individuals are usually children whose qualities furnish the basis for mutual satisfaction of interpersonal needs. In some instances, the child may be similar in personality make-up; in other instances the traits of the friend will serve to complement the traits of the child.

Most evidence indicates that friends have similar traits. The similarity is probably basic to adequate interaction. Friends tend to be from approximately the same chronological age, socioeconomic status, grade in school, and IQ. During childhood a preference for children of the same age level is usually strong. It is interesting to note that friends usually have a similar level of skill in interpersonal relationships.

Horrocks and Buker did an intensive study of friendship patterns and friendship fluctuations during childhood. Their study indicates that the capacity for lasting friendships gradually increases during childhood and adolescence. They did indicate that some children did not seem to learn how to maintain friendships as adequately as others.

However, it was their opinion that the skills necessary for forming adequate friendships were teachable. Their data reveal a trend toward greater stability of friendship with increasing chronological age and corresponding higher grade placement in school. Data analysis of the average of friendship fluctuation indices for the various chronological age groups form a continuous downward trend in friendship fluctuation from the year five to year eighteen. This is evidence of the average increase in stability of friend ships in children as they grow older.

Girls are more socially active than boys throughout the entire elementary school period, and they tend to establish more intimate and confidential relationships with each other. The capacity of the child to form friendships and to maintain them on the basis of meeting others' needs as well as his own is a strong indication of the development of social maturity.

The Need for Achievement

A characteristic of the child which plays an important role in his social development is the relative amount of achievement motivation he evidences. For our purposes, achievement motivation is evidenced when a child has strong feelings about the process of evaluation and is concerned with approval and disapproval, whether it be of self or others. The child who is achievement-motivated produces behaviour which receives the approval of others.

Adler suggested the satisfaction of achievement needs is one of the significant goals of human behaviour. Certainly feelings of inferiority and the striving for superiority point to the significance of achievement as basic to satisfactory and secure human experiences. The person who cannot achieve, or who does not feel accepted on the basis of his achievements, is not secure in his interpersonal relationships.

Kurt Lewin also emphasised the importance of achievement motivation. He was one of the first to investigate the concepts of human achievement and level of aspiration. Lewin found that successful goal attainment often produced renewed and increased goal striving.

Research studies consistently indicate that achievement is more often stressed in the training of American boys than American girls. Achievement motivation is also influenced by the child's social class. Some studies have indicated that while the father's occupation is not important and has little effect on school performance in the early grades, it seems to have a significant effect on achievement after the fourth-grade level

2

Developmental Method in Social Psychology

DISCIPLINE OF SOCIAL PSYCHOLOGY

The discipline of social psychology began in the United States at the dawn of the 20th century. The first published study in this area was an experiment in 1898 by Norman Triplett on the phenomenon of social facilitation. During the 1930s, many Gestalt psychologists, most notably Kurt Lewin, fled to the United States from Nazi Germany.

They were instrumental in developing the field as something separate from the behavioural and psychoanalytic schools that were dominant during that time, and social psychology has always maintained the legacy of their interests in perception and cognition. Attitudes and small group phenomena were the most commonly studied topics in this era.

During WWII, social psychologists studied persuasion and propaganda for the U.S. military. After the war, researchers became interested in a variety of social problems, including gender issues and racial prejudice. In the sixties, there was growing interest in new topics, such as cognitive dissonance, bystander intervention, and aggression.

By the 1970s, however, social psychology in America had reached a crisis. There was heated debate over the ethics of laboratory experimentation, whether or not attitudes really predicted behaviour, and how much science could be done in a cultural context. This was also the time when a radical situationist approach challenged the relevance of self and personality in psychology.

Social psychology reached maturity in both theory and method during the 1980s and 1990s. Careful ethical standards now regulate research, and greater pluralism and multiculturalism perspectives have emerged. Modern researchers are interested in a many phenomena, but attribution, social cognition, and the self-concept are perhaps the greatest areas of growth in recent years. Social psychologists have also maintained their applied interests with contributions in health and environmental psychology, as well as the psychology of the legal system.

RESEARCH METHODS IN DEVELOPMENTAL PSYCHOLOGY

As with most research, the study of developmental psychology begins with a hypothesis. A hypothesis is a testable statement that reflects what the researcher expects to find in a study. For example, a study on gender and learning disabilities might begin with a hypothesis that one gender will be more impacted by learning disorders. The goal of research is to analyse the area of interest, collect information and data about topic, draw conclusions based upon this research and data, and then add or expand upon previously existing theories of development.

Types of Research

There are a number of different ways to conduct psychological research. The two major types of research are:

Cross-sectional Research

Cross-sectional research involves looking at different groups of people of different ages. For example, a researcher might measure or observe a group of young adults and compare this data with information gathered about a group of elderly participants. The benefit of this type of research is that it can be done relatively quickly; the research data is all gathered at the same point in time. However, because data is gathered from generations of people who share the same cultural experiences, these shared events may play a role in development. This makes it difficult to determine if something is caused by experience or the aging process.

Longitudinal Research

Longitudinal research involves studying the same group of individuals over an extended period of time. Data is first collected at the outset of the study, and may then be gathered repeatedly throughout the length of the study. In some cases, longitudinal studies can last several decades.

The benefit of this type of research is that it allows researchers to look at changes over time. However, longitudinal studies require enormous amounts of time and are often quite expensive. Because of this, these studies often have only a small group of subjects, which makes it difficult to apply the results to a larger population. Another problem is that participants sometimes drop out of the study, shrinking the sample size and decreasing the amount of data collected.

Data Collection

Once it has been decided which type of research to use, the next step is to determine how the information will be gathered. There are a number of different research methods that are used in the study of developmental psychology, each with its own strengths and weaknesses. Some common approaches include observation, case studies, questionnaires, and experimentation.

Observation

There are two different types of observation. The first involves viewing the subject of interest in a laboratory setting. The benefit of this is that the situation can be controlled by the experimental. The drawbacks of lab observation are that the setting can be unnatural and the subject is aware that they are being studied. Both of these factors can have an impact on results of the study. Naturalistic observation allows researchers to observe participants in real-world settings. The strength of this method is that it allows researchers to view behaviour as it really happens in a natural setting. The drawback is that the researcher cannot control outside variables that might impact behaviour.

Questionnaires

Questionnaires offer researchers a quick, easy way to collect a great deal of information. One weakness of this method is that it reduces variety, creativity, and individuality of responses. In cases where the subject is unable to fill out a questionnaire, with very young children for example, questions are often posed through a structured interview.

Experimentation

Experiments involve the manipulation and measurement of variables. This research method is the most scientific, but it can be difficult to use if the variables of interest are abstract or internal concepts. Another problem is that some variables of interest cannot be studied through experimentation for ethical reasons. Examples of this would be research on the effects of child abuse on development.

METHODS OF SOCIAL PSYCHOLOGY

Social-psychological research varies by location, how we measure variables, and how we analyse the data we obtain. It can take place in the *laboratory* (a controlled situation) or in the *field* (everyday situations). Studies can use *observational methods* (simply observing and recording people in social situations) *surveys* (questionnaires specifically designed to get at particular issues which are administered to individuals) or a variety of other techniques to explore the relationships between variables. Furthermore, social psychologists use both quantitative methods (*i.e.*, using statistics to analyse numeric data) as well as qualitative methods (*e.g.*, looking for themes in narrative responses given by participants). Thus the variety of methods and procedures used by social psychologists is wide, and we will encounter all of these approaches in this text.

Correlational Research: Detecting Natural Associations

How we approach social psychological questions varies by method—correlational research asks whether two or more factors are naturally associated, and experimental research manipulates one or more factors to see if they exert a causal impact on another. If you want to be a critical reader of research reported in newspapers and magazines (or even this text), it pays to understand the difference between correlational and experimental research.

There are some features of correlations we need to understand. Sometimes we will have a positive correlation, indicating that as one variable increases, so does the other (such as age and weight gain in childhood—as we get older, we get heavier). Alternatively, there are many negative correlations, which indicate that as levels of one variable increase, the levels of the other variable decrease.

For example, we might observe that people who eat more, are healthy. Although both these relationships are correlations, the direction of the relationship differs (*i.e.*, positive versus negative). Correlations also vary in strength, from a perfect negative correlation (–1.0; meaning that as one factor increases, the other factor always decreases) to a perfectly positive correlation, and every number in between (*e.g.*, –.60,.10,.78, etc). The closer the number is to 1 or –1, the stronger the correlation. There are also situations where two variables are completely unrelated. This would be called a "zero" correlation. The closer the relationship is to 0, the weaker the correlation. For example, we might expect that age and height in children would be strongly correlated, whereas age and athletic performance might show a meaningful but weaker correlation (as children grow they become somewhat more coordinated). But what is the value of correlational research? Using some real examples, let's first consider the advantages of correlational research (often involving important variables in natural settings) and the disadvantages (ambiguous interpretation of cause and effect). Today's psychologists often relate personal and social factors to human health. By using various research methods, social psychologists systematically examine situational and personal *variables*—influential, measurable factors that can take on different values—whose change can affect social perception, judgment, and interaction when people think about one another or gather together. Variables vary in value, which allows social psychologists the opportunity to introduce the presence of a variable in one setting to see how people react and to then compare the effects of its absence on other people in a similar setting.

Situational variables are literally outside people, often in the environment, serving as tangible (*e.g.*, rules, physical boundaries), intangible (*e.g.*, roles, cultural norms, expectations), and even transient (*e.g.*, crowding, temperature, deadlines) influences. In contrast, personal variables include people's physical (*e.g.*, race, gender, height, weight) and dispositional (*e.g.*, a shy or outgoing personality) characteristics, their affective states (*i.e.*, emotions, such as happiness or sadness), and whether they are perceivers (the judges) or being perceived (the judged) by others. On occasion, social psychologists study groups and group processes, how the thought and behaviour of individuals is affected by collections of people who share some common quality or interest.

Despite limitations, LaPiere's (1934) pioneering study led to a great deal of subsequent research on how, why, and when attitudes do or do not predict behaviour. To his credit, LaPiere used two research methods—observation and questionnaires—in a real life situation which revealed some interesting findings but did not allow him to determine why a given establishment's attitudes did not predict the behaviour of its employees. Both these research methods are considered later in this book. What could LaPiere have done to better determine what caused the lack of consistency between attitudes and behaviour?

Establishing Causality: The Importance of Experimentation in Social Psychology

Determining causality—what event led to what outcome—seems simple enough. For centuries, scientists argued that a presumed cause must precede any observed effect. Further, a cause must be demonstrated to occur before an effect in such a way that alternative accounts for the effect are unlikely to be true. These simple statements summarize the basic goal of controlled experiments, which are often easier to describe than to satisfactorily craft and carry out. An *experiment* is a trial or test designed to prove that one explanation for what causes some behaviour is superior to others. To do so, key aspects of the phenomena under study are systematically varied in order to determine how their presence or absence affects behaviour.

LaPiere (1934) could have relied on a more experimental approach to learn why almost no prejudice or discrimination occurred during the actual trip but a considerable amount was disclosed on paper, in the returned questionnaires. Experimental research in social psychology starts with a specific *hypothesis* indicating how one variable causes a change in another variable. The causal variable is called the *independent variable* and the effected variable is labelled the *dependent variable*. Social psychologists create a situation in which to test whether a given independent variable causes change in a given dependent variable. The researcher manipulates the independent variable by creating two or more *conditions*, distinct experiences corresponding to different qualities of that variable. Unlike other research approaches, experiments possess one defining feature: Participants are assigned at random to one and only one condition, and each person has the same chance as all the others of ending up in any of the conditions.

Let's leave the LaPiere (1934) study's causal uncertainty for a bit and review a recent study on a different topic, an aggression experiment illustrating clear causal connections among a hypothesis, an independent variable, and a dependent variable. Klinesmith, Kasser, and McAndrew (2006) hypothesized that men who hold guns experience a hormonal reaction that primes them to behave aggressively. A group of men gave saliva samples from which their testosterone levels were measured. Working alone, each man was seated at a table with paper and either a big handgun or the children's board game Mouse Trap. They were told to take apart the gun or the game and to write directions for disassembly and assembly on the paper.

After 15 minutes, the men's saliva was again collected, revealing that testosterone levels spiked in those who handled the gun but remained the same in those taking apart the game. Aggressiveness was measured in the last part of the experiment, where the men's "taste sensitivity" was examined. Specifically, they were asked to evaluate the taste of a glass of water with a drop of hot sauce in it. They were asked to make a similar drink for the next person in the study, using as much or as little hot sauce as they wished.

What did Klinesmith and colleagues (2006) find? The men who held the gun added three times as much hot sauce to the water for the next person—an aggressive act—compared to those who worked with the game. In other words, higher levels of testosterone caused more hot sauce to be added to the drink to be given to another person. What were the variables in this study? How did they relate to the hypothesis? The independent variable—the observable cause of the aggression—was the object the men took apart and put back together, and it had two conditions: the gun and the game. By chance, each man either ended up with the gun or the game. Touching the gun was expected to heighten the hormone levels, whereas handling the game was not. The dependent variable was the relative amount of hot sauce put in the glass of water; more sauce (hence, more aggression) was dropped by the high testosterone men who had held the gun. Klinesmith and colleagues (2006) used the first samples of saliva to demonstrate that all the men had similar levels of testosterone prior to handling the gun or the game, but not after. Thus they ruled out a major alternative explanation for the results, namely that the men had different levels of hormones before the experiment began. The second saliva sample demonstrated that only those men who worked with the gun subsequently displayed higher levels of testosterone. The researchers also made certain that all the men had similar experiences in the same setting. The only thing that ever differed was whether a man was given the gun or the game.

Now that you understand the importance of experiments in social psychology, can you see the problem in determining cause and effect in the now historic attitude study reported by LaPiere (1934)? Although it is still an important milestone report in the study of attitudes, LaPiere's study was not an experiment. His research lacked the causal clarity associated with experiments like the one reported by Klinesmith and colleagues (2006). LaPiere did not manipulate and measure any variables, nor did he have a working hypothesis that he tried to test. Unfortunately, we know what happened but not necessarily why; put another way, we cannot clearly identity the root cause of why little prejudiced behaviour occurred on the cross-country trip although a considerable amount of prejudiced attitudes were revealed following the trip. Note that we are not criticizing LaPiere's work; rather, we are highlighting the fact that social psychologists prefer to use experiments rather than simple observations or other approaches to form coherent, compelling explanations for the occurrence (or absence) of prejudice and discriminatory behaviour. Experiments represent an ideal, one that sometimes cannot be met due to particular circumstances, the availability of resources, time constraints, or even ethical issues.

Thus far we have considered a definition for social psychology and reviewed some illustrative research. Besides defining what social psychology *is*, we also need to know what it is *not*; that is, we need to compare its research focus with some of the other branches of psychology and the social sciences.

Levels of Explanation: Social Psychology's Relation to Other Fields of Inquiry

Social psychology is one field of scientific inquiry. Whether within or outside of psychology, different fields rely on different *levels of explanation*. Different levels of explanation tell us different things about people's behaviour. The following table lists several fields of inquiry ranging from those with a more *collective* focus (a larger group or groups) to the more *individual* (solitary person or process) level of analysis. The focus becomes narrower and the phenomena of interest become more internal and distinct to individuals. Moving upward in the table, the research emphasis becomes broader and more inclusive, increasingly involving both individuals and their relations to groups, as well as within- and between-group processes.

Social psychologists are generally interested in the experience of people as individuals, notably how real or imagined others influence them in terms of affect (emotions, feelings), cognition (thoughts, beliefs), and behaviour (actions, intentions). After learning about LaPiere's work, for example, most people are curious to know about the nature of the interactions between the travellers and the people they met. What, for example, were the innkeepers and waiters thinking and feeling when they served the travellers? Similarly, we would like to know the thoughts and feelings of the respondents who later indicated on paper that Chinese guests were unwelcome.

By comparison, psychologists interested in the emerging areas of neuroscience would want to examine the electrochemical activity in the brain during social encounters with minority group members or when thinking about minority groups. Neuroscientists study neurochemical processes and how these processes affect the cognitive and behavioural responses of individuals. In contrast, a cognitive psychologist would be curious about a slightly higher level of analysis than a neuroscientist. What is the nature of the mental structures, for example, that leads someone to categorize a person as a member of a minority rather than a majority group? Developmental psychologists, in turn, examine social, cognitive, and emotional changes that occur at different ages and stages of development.

Sociologists are often interested in some of the same issues that attract the attention of social psychologists. Yet sociologists would be likely to take a different, more collective approach, one involving a search for the general laws of behaviour that are based on the nature of social structures and groups. In the context of LaPiere's research, instead of focusing on the experience of individual service providers, a sociologist would be interested in the nature of relations between different racial or ethnic groups, the effects of socioeconomic class, and possibly in the ways that owner-managers as a group held different beliefs than hired workers. Thus sociology's level of analysis is more societal, aimed at the effect of social institutions and customs on groups of people rather than individuals. Finally, an anthropologist would want to examine the origins and the physical, cultural, and social development of groups of people. In our current example, an anthropologist could examine how perceived differences between racial groups originated and influenced social interaction across time.

Not all academic fields relevant to social psychology. Instead, my purpose here is to identify social psychology's unique place as a bridge between individual and collective levels of explanation. Thus social psychological research examines individual processes that people have in common with others, and how those processes regulate a person's interactions with other people, including groups. But what about processes unique to each person—in other words, how does social psychology relate to the discipline of personality psychology?

Personality Psychology's Relation to Social Psychology

Their personalities, were often considered by social psychologists. That is true, and social psychologists often consider the role of personality in their work. Personality psychologists often work closely with social psychologists; indeed, many researchers identify themselves as "social-personality psychologists" and many academic organizations and journals serve as common resources for both types of researchers. Still, personality psychology adopts a somewhat different level of analysis than social psychology. Personality psychologists are interested in the private psychological functions of individuals and how these functions lead to differences between individuals. The term "individual differences" refers to those qualities found in one person's personality that causes him or her to be different than other people. One personality psychologist might want to know which of the people LaPiere and his friends encountered were naturally more helpful than the others; another personality researcher would be interested in knowing who among the people who answered LaPiere's (1934) survey had a truly prejudiced personality. In contrast, a social psychologist is focused on the common experience of all the individuals who encountered the travellers, as well as the shared qualities of those who returned the surveys. In short, what led *most* people to offer LaPiere and the couple a place to stay, what led *most* survey respondents to later say Chinese guests were unwelcome?

You may be thinking, "Now wait a minute, isn't it the case that your personality determines whether your prejudiced feelings lead to a discriminatory action, like denying a couple a place to stay or eat because of their race?" Sometimes, yes; but not always. Social psychologists believe that situations often matter much more when it comes to causing behaviour than do people's personalities, especially at a common level of analysis. This view may initially seem hard to believe. Yet ample research demonstrates that the power of situations often overrides the effects or role of personality. Indeed, in everyday life, people are repeatedly found to overestimate the influence of personality while underemphasizing the effects of situations as the causes of behaviour. Whether they possessed any number of personality types linked with prejudiced feelings, such as authoritarianism or social dominance, for example, the business owners may not have turned away the travellers for sheer economic reasons—money was to be made by housing or feeding them at that moment in time. Alternatively, perhaps the hotel restaurant workers simply did not have the authority to deny anyone service, thus their personalities, prejudiced or otherwise, had no role in guiding their actions. Again, we will never really know what the actual causal factors involved were because LaPiere's (1934) study was not an experiment.

Whether an investigation is an experiment or another approach to research, the social psychologist doing the research is apt to follow an established procedure.

RESEARCH METHODS IN SOCIAL PSYCHOLOGY

Social psychology is an empirical science that attempts to answer questions about human behaviour by testing hypotheses, both in the laboratory and in the field. Careful attention to sampling, research design, and statistical analysis is important, and results are published in peer reviewed journals such as the Journal of Experimental Social Psychology, Personality and Social Psychology Bulletin and the Journal of Personality and Social Psychology. Social psychology studies also appear in general science journals such as Psychological Science and Science.

Experimental methods involve the researcher altering a variable in the environment and measuring the effect on another variable. An example would be allowing two groups of children to play violent or nonviolent videogames, and then observing their subsequent level of aggression during free-play period. A valid experiment is controlled and uses random assignment. Correlational methods examine the statistical association between two naturally occurring variables. For example, one could correlate the amount of violent television children watch at home with the number of violent incidents the children participate in at school. Note that this study would *not* prove that violent TV causes aggression in children. It's quite possible that aggressive children choose to watch more violent TV.

Observational methods are purely descriptive and include naturalistic observation, "contrived" observation, participant observation, and archival analysis. These are less common in social psychology but are sometimes used when first investigating a phenomenon.

An example would be to unobtrusively observe children on a playground (with a videocamera, perhaps) and record the number and types of aggressive actions displayed. Whenever possible, social psychologists rely on controlled experimentation. Controlled experiments require the manipulation of one or more independent variables in order to examine the effect on a dependent variable. Experiments are useful in social psychology because they are high in internal validity, meaning that they are free from the influence of confounding or extraneous variables, and so are more likely to accurately indicate a causal relationship. However, the small samples used in controlled experiments are typically low in external validity, or the degree to which the results can be generalized the larger population. There is usually a trade-off between experimental control (internal validity) and being able to generalize to the population (external validity).

Because it is usually impossible to test everyone, research tends to be conducted on a sample of persons from the wider population. Social psychologists frequently use survey research when they are interested in results that are high in external validity. Surveys use various forms of random sampling to obtain a sample of respondents that are representative of a population. This type of research is usually descriptive or correlational because there is no experimental control over variables.

However, new statistical methods like structural equation modeling are being used to test for potential causal relationships in this type of data. Regardless of which method is used, it is important to evaluate the research hypothesis in light of the results, either confirming or rejecting the original prediction. Social psychologists use statistics and probability testing to judge their results, which define a significant finding as less than 5% likely to be due to chance. Replications are important, to ensure that the result is valid and not due to chance, or some feature of a particular sample.

Ethics

The goal of social psychology is to understand cognition and behaviour as they naturally occur in a social context, but the very act of observing people can influence and alter their behaviour. For this reason, many social psychology experiments utilize deception to conceal or distort certain aspects of the study. Deception may include false cover stories, false participants (known as confederates or stooges), false feedback given to the participants, and so on. The practice of deception has been challenged by some psychologists who maintain that deception under any circumstances is unethical, and that other research strategies (e.g. roleplaying) should be used instead. Unfortunately, research has shown that role-playing studies do not produce the same results as deception studies and this has cast doubt on their validity. In addition to deception, experimenters have at times put people into potentially uncomfortable or embarrassing situations (e.g. the Milgram experiment, Stanford prison experiment), and this has also been criticized for ethical reasons. To protect the rights and well-being of research participants, and at the same time discover meaningful results and insights into human behaviour, virtually all social psychology research must pass an ethical review process.

At most colleges and universities, this is conducted by an ethics committee or Institutional Review Board. This group examines the proposed research to make sure that no harm is done to the participants, and that the benefits of the study outweigh any possible risks or discomforts to people taking part in the study.

Furthermore, a process of informed consent is often used to make sure that volunteers know what will happen in the experiment and understand that they are allowed to quit the experiment at any time. A debriefing is typically done at the conclusion of the experiment in order to reveal any deceptions used and generally make sure that the participants are unharmed by the procedures. Today, most research in social psychology involves no more risk of harm than can be expected from routine psychological testing or normal daily activities.

Famous Experiments

The Asch conformity experiments demonstrated the power of conformity in small groups with a line estimation task that was designed to be extremely easy. On over a third of the trials, participants conformed to the majority, even though the majority judgment was clearly wrong. Seventy-five percent of the participants conformed at least once during the experiment. Muzafer Sherif's Robbers' Cave Experiment divided boys into two competing groups to explore how much hostility and aggression would emerge. Sherif's explanation of the results became known as realistic group conflict theory, because the intergroup conflict was induced through competition over resources. Inducing cooperation and [superordinate goals] later reversed this effect. In Leon Festinger's cognitive dissonance experiment, participants were asked to perform a boring task. They were divided into 2 groups and given two different pay scales.

At the end of the study, some participants were paid $1 to say that they enjoyed the task and another group of participants was paid $20 to say the same lie. The first group ($1) later reported liking the task better than the second group ($20). Festinger's explanation was that people justified their lies by changing their previously unfavourable attitudes about the task.

One of the most infamous experiments in social psychology was the Milgram experiment, which studied how far people would go to obey an authority figure. Following the events of The Holocaust in World War II, the experiment showed that normal American citizens were capable of following orders from an authority even when they believed they were causing an innocent person to suffer. Albert Bandura's Bobo doll experiment demonstrated how aggression is learned by imitation. This was one of the first studies in a long line of research showing how exposure to media violence leads to aggressive behaviour in the observers. In the Stanford prison experiment, by Philip Zimbardo, a simulated exercise between student prisoners and guards showed how far people would follow an adopted role. In just a few days, the "guards" became brutal and cruel, and the prisoners became miserable and compliant. This was an important demonstration of the power of the immediate social situation, and its capacity to overwhelm normal personality traits.

INTERPERSONAL PHENOMENA

Social Influence

Social influence refers to the way people affect the thoughts, feelings, and Behaviours of others. Like the study of attitudes, it is a traditional, core topic in social psychology. In fact, research on social influence overlaps considerably with research on attitudes and persuasion. Social influence is also closely related to the study of group dynamics, as most of the principles of influence are strongest when they take place in social groups.

Conformity is the most common and pervasive form of social influence. It is generally defined as the tendency to act or think like other members of a group. Group size, unanimity, cohesion, status, and prior commitment all help to determine the level of conformity in an individual. Conformity is usually viewed as a negative tendency in American culture, but a certain amount of conformity is not only necessary and normal, but probably essential for a community to function.

The two major motives in conformity are *normative* influence, the tendency to conform in order to gain social acceptance, and avoid social rejection or conflict, as in peer pressure; and *informational* influence, which is based on the desire to obtain useful information through conformity, and thereby achieve a correct or appropriate result.

Minority influence is the degree to which a smaller faction within the group influences the group during decision making. Note that this refers to a minority position on some issue, not an ethnic minority. Their influence is primarily informational and depends on consistent adherence to a position, degree of defection from the majority, and the status and self-confidence of the minority members. Reactance is a tendency to assert oneself by doing the opposite of what is expected. This phenomenon is also known as *anticonformity* and it appears to be more common in men than in women.

There are two other major areas of social influence research. Compliance refers to any change in Behaviour that is due to a request or suggestion from another person. The Foot-in-the-door technique is a compliance method in which the persuader requests a small favor and then follows up with a larger favor, e.g. asking for the time, and then asking for ten dollars. A related trick is the Bait and switch. The third major form of social influence is obedience. This is a change in Behaviour that is the result of a direct order or command from another person.

A different kind of social influence is the self-fulfilling prophecy. This is a prediction that, in being made, actually causes itself to become true. For example, in the stock market, if it is widely believed that a crash is imminent, investors may lose confidence, sell most of their stock, and actually cause the crash. Likewise, people may expect hostility in others and actually induce this hostility by their own Behaviour.

Group Dynamics

A group can be defined as two or more individuals that are connected to each another by social relationships. Groups tend to interact, influence each other, and share a common identity. They have a number of emergent qualities that distinguish them from aggregates:

- Norms-implicit rules and expectations for group members to follow, e.g. saying thank you, shaking hands.
- Roles-implicit rules and expectations for specific members within the group, e.g. the oldest sibling, who may have additional responsibilities in the family.
- Relations-patterns of liking within the group, and also differences in prestige or status, e.g. leaders, popular people.

Temporary groups and aggregates share few or none of these features, and do not qualify as true social groups. People waiting in line to get on a bus, for example, do not constitute a group.

Groups are important not only because they offer social support, resources, and a feeling of belonging, but because they supplement an individual's self-concept. To a large extent, humans define themselves by the group memberships which form their social identity. The shared social identity of individuals within a group influences intergroup Behaviour, the way in which groups behave towards and perceive each other. These perceptions and Behaviours in turn define the social identity of individuals within the interacting groups. The tendency to define oneself by membership of a group leads to intergroup discrimination, which involves favourable perceptions and Behaviours directed towards the in-group, but negative perceptions and Behaviours directed towards the out-group. Intergroup discrimination leads to prejudice and stereotyping, while the processes of social facilitation and group polarization encourage extreme Behaviours towards the out-group.

Groups often moderate and improve decision making, and are frequently relied upon for these benefits, such as committees and juries. A number of group biases, however, can interfere with effective decision making. For example, group polarization, formerly known as the "risky shift," occurs when people polarize their views in a more extreme direction after group discussion. More problematic is the phenomenon of groupthink. This is a collective thinking defect that is characterized by a premature consensus or an incorrect assumption of consensus, caused by members of a group failing to promote views which are not consistent with the views of other members. Groupthink occurs in a variety of situations, including isolation of a group and the presence of a highly directive leader. Janis offered the 1961 Bay of Pigs Invasion as a historical case of groupthink.

Groups also affect performance and productivity. Social facilitation, for example, is a tendency to work harder and faster in the presence of others. Social facilitation increases the likelihood of the *dominant response*, which tends to improve performance on simple tasks and reduce it on complex tasks. In contrast, social loafing is the tendency of individuals to slack when working in a group. Social loafing is common when the task is considered unimportant and individual contributions are not easy to see.

Social psychologists study group-related (collective) phenomena such as the Behaviour of crowds. An important concept in this area is deindividuation, a reduced state of self-awareness that can be caused by feelings of anonymity. Deindividuation is associated with uninhibited and sometimes dangerous Behaviour. It is common in crowds and mobs, but it can also be caused by a disguise, a uniform, alcohol, dark environments, or online anonymity.

Relations with Others

Social psychologists are interested in the question of why people sometimes act in a prosocial way (helping, liking, or loving others), but at other times act in an antisocial way (hostility, aggression, or prejudice against others).

Aggression can be defined as any Behaviour that is intended to harm another human being. *Hostile* aggression is accompanied by strong emotions, particularly anger. Harming the other person is the goal. *Instrumental* aggression is only a means to an end. Harming the person is used to obtain some other goal, such as money. Research indicates that there are many causes of aggression, including biological factors like testosterone and environmental factors, such as social learning. Immediate situational factors such as frustration are also important in triggering an aggressive response.

Although violence is a fact of life, people are also capable of helping each other, even complete strangers in emergencies. Research indicates that altruism occurs when a person feels empathy for another individual, even in the absence of other motives. However, according to the bystander effect, the probability of receiving help in an emergency situation drops as the number of bystanders increases. This is due to both conformity and diffusion of responsibility, the tendency for people to feel less personally responsible when other people are around.

Interpersonal Attraction

A major area in the study of people's relations to each other is interpersonal attraction. This refers to all of the forces that lead people to like each other, establish relationships, and in some cases, fall in love. Several general principles of attraction have been discovered by social psychologists. For example, physical proximity tends to increases attraction, whereas long distances make relationships difficult to form and maintain. Even very small differences in distance—such as the case of a next door neighbour versus someone who lives down the block—can make a significant difference in friendship patterns. Familiarity, or "mere exposure," also increases attraction, influencing people even if the familiarity is not consciously noticed. One of the most important factors in interpersonal attraction is similarity: the more similar two people are in attitudes, background, and other traits, the more probable it is that they will like each other. Contrary to popular opinion, opposites do not usually attract.

Physical attractiveness is an important element of romantic relationships, particularly in the early stages characterized by high levels of passion. Later on, similarity and other compatibility factors become more important, and the type of love people experience shifts from *passionate* to *companionate*. Robert Sternberg has suggested that there are actually three components of love: intimacy, passion, and commitment. When two people experience all three, they are said to be in a state of consummate love; this condition is relatively rare and difficult to maintain for a long period of time.

According to social exchange theory, relationships are based on rational choice and cost-benefit analysis. If one partner's costs begin to outweigh his or her benefits, that person may leave the relationship, especially if there are good alternatives available. This theory is similar to the minimax principle proposed by mathematicians and economists. With time, long term relationships tend to become communal rather than simply based on exchange.

RESEARCH AREAS IN SOCIAL PSYCHOLOGY

Social psychology research topics including social influence, social perception, social interaction and group Behaviour.

Now that you have a better understanding of what social psychology is, we are going to look at some of the major topics that social psychologists investigate in their research. Many of these topics are related to social influence, social perception and social interaction. The following are just a few of the areas of interest within social psychology.

Social Cognition

Social cognition is concerned with the processing, storage and application of social information. This research area is closely related to the field of cognitive psychology, this research area focuses largely on the concept of schemas. Schemas are our general ideas about the world, how things are and how things work. These mental shortcuts allow us to function without constantly stopping to interpret everything around us. We also develop associations between related schemas, which plays an important role in the thought process and social Behaviour.

Attitudes and Attitude Change

Another major research area in social psychology involves the study of attitudes. Social psychologists are interested in the components of attitudes, how attitudes develop and how attitudes change. Researchers have described three core components of attitude: an affective component, a behavioural component and a cognitive component. Often referred to as the "ABC's of attitude," these elements describe how we feel, behave and understand.

Violence and Aggression

What causes violence and aggression? Social psychologists are interested in how and why people engage in violence or act aggressively. Research in this area looks at numerous factors that may cause aggression including social variables and media influences. Researchers often look at the role social learning plays in producing aggressive Behaviours and actions.

Prosocial Behaviour

Prosocial Behaviour is another major research area in social psychology. What is prosocial Behaviour? Prosocial Behaviours are those that involve helping and cooperating. Researchers often look at why people help others, as well as why they sometimes refuse to help or cooperate.

Much of the research in this area was prompted by the murder of a young woman named Kitty Genovese. This case captured national attention when reports revealed that neighbors had witnessed her attack and murder, but failed to call the police for help. Research inspired by the case produced a great deal of information on prosocial Behaviour and how and why people choose-or sometimes refuse-to help others.

Prejudice and Discrimination

Prejudice, discrimination and stereotypes exist in any social group. Social psychologists are interested in the origins, causes and effects of these types of attitudes and social categorizations. How does prejudice develop? Why are stereotypes maintained in the face of contrary evidence? These are just a few of the questions social psychologists seek to answer.

Self and Social Identity

Our perceptions of social identities and ourselves are another important research area in social psychology. How do people come to know and understand themselves? How do these self-perceptions affect our social interactions? Social psychologists are interested in learning more about how this inner life influences our outer lives and social world. Self-awareness, self-esteem and self-expression are just a few of the factors that influence our social experience.

Group Behaviour

The Behaviour of groups is one of the largest research areas in social psychology. Most people realize that groups tend to behave differently than individuals. These group Behaviours are sometimes beneficial and positive, but they can also be detrimental and negative. Social psychologists often look at topics such as group dynamics, leadership, group decision-making, conflicts, cooperation and group influence.

Social Influence

Social psychologists are also interested in the role that social influence has on Behaviour and decision-making. Topics such as the psychology of persuasion, peer pressure, conformity and obedience are just a few of those studied in this area of social psychology. Research has helped reveal the power of social influence and has uncovered ways to help people resist influence.

3

Attitudes and Behavioural Control in Social Psychology

IMPLICIT AND EXPLICIT ATTITUDES

There is also considerable research on implicit attitudes, which are generally unacknowledged or outside of awareness, but have effects that are measurable through sophisticated methods using people's response times to stimuli. Implicit and explicit attitudes seem to affect people's behaviour, though in different ways. They tend not to be strongly associated with each other, although in some cases they are. The relationship between them is poorly understood.

Jung's Definition: Attitude is one of Jung's 57 definitions in Chapter XI of *Psychological Types*. Jung's definition of attitude is a "readiness of the psyche to act or react in a certain way" (Jung, [1921] 1971:par. 687). Attitudes very often come in pairs, one conscious and the other unconscious. Within this broad definition Jung defines several attitudes.

The main (but not only) attitude dualities that Jung defines are the following.

- Consciousness and the unconscious. The "presence of two attitudes is extremely frequent, one conscious and the other unconscious. This means that consciousness has a constellation of contents different from that of the unconscious, a duality particularly evident in neurosis" (Jung, [1921] 1971: par. 687).
- Extraversion and introversion. This pair is so elementary to Jung's theory of types that he labeled them the "attitude-types".
- Rational and irrational attitudes. "I conceive reason as an attitude" (Jung, [1921] 1971: par. 785).
- The rational attitude subdivides into the thinking and feeling psychological functions, each with its attitude.

- The irrational attitude subdivides into the sensing and intuition psychological functions, each with its attitude. "There is thus a typical thinking, feeling, sensation, and intuitive attitude" (Jung, [1921] 1971: par. 691).
- Individual and social attitudes. Many of the latter are "isms".

In addition, Jung discusses the abstract attitude. "When I take an abstract attitude..." (Jung, [1921] 1971: par. 679). Abstraction is contrasted with concretism. "CONCRETISM. By this I mean a peculiarity of thinking and feeling which is the antithesis of abstraction" (Jung, [1921] 1971: par. 696). For example "i hate his attitude for being Sarcastic.

MBTI Definition: The MBTI write-ups limit the use of "attitude" to the extraversion-introversion (EI) and judging-perceiving (JP) indexes.

The JP index is sometimes referred to as an orientation to the outer world and sometimes JP is classified as an "attitude." In Jungian terminology the term *attitude* is restricted to EI. In MBTI terminology *attitude* can include EI and also JP. (Myers, 1985:293 note 7).

The above MBTI Manual statement, is restricted to EI," is directly contradicted by Jung's statement above that there is "a typical thinking, feeling, sensation, and intuitive attitude" and by his other uses of the term "attitude".

Regardless of whether the MBTI simplification (or oversimplification) of Jung can be attributed to Myers, *Gifts Differing* refers only to the "EI preference", consistently avoiding the label "attitude". Regarding the JP index, in *Gifts Differing* Myers does use the terms "the *perceptive* attitude and the *judging* attitude" (Myers, 1980:8).

The JP index corresponds to the irrational and rational attitudes Jung describes, except that the MBTI focuses on the preferred orientation in the outer world in order to identify the function hierarchy. To be consistent with Jung, it can be noted that a rational extraverted preference is accompanied by an irrational introverted preference.

ATTITUDE FORMATION

Unlike personality, attitudes are expected to change as a function of experience. Tesser (1993) has argued that hereditary variables may affect attitudes - but believes that they may do so indirectly. For example, consistency theories, which imply that we must be consistent in our beliefs and values. The most famous example of such a theory is Dissonance-reduction theory, associated with Leon Festinger, although there are others, such as the balance theory.

ATTITUDE CHANGE

Attitudes can be changed through persuasion and we should understand attitude change as a response to communication. Experimental research into the factors that can affect the persuasiveness of a message include:

1. *Target Characteristics:* These are characteristics that refer to the person who receives and processes a message. One such trait is intelligence - it seems that more intelligent people are less easily persuaded by one-sided messages. Another variable that has been studied in this category is self-esteem. Although it is sometimes thought that those higher in self-esteem are less easily persuaded, there is some evidence that the relationship between self-esteem and persuasibility is actually curvilinear, with people of moderate self-esteem being more easily persuaded than both those of high and low self-esteem levels (Rhodes & Woods, 1992). The mind frame and mood of the target also plays a role in this process.
2. *Source Characteristics:* The major source characteristics are expertise, trustworthiness and interpersonal attraction or attractiveness. The credibility of a perceived message has been found to be a key variable here; if one reads a report about health and believes it came from a professional medical journal, one may be more easily persuaded than if one believes it is from a popular newspaper. Some psychologists have debated whether this is a long-lasting effect and Hovland and Weiss (1951) found the effect of telling people that a message came from a credible source disappeared after several weeks (the so-called "sleeper effect"). Whether there is a sleeper effect is controversial. Perceived wisdom is that if people are informed of the source of a message before hearing it, there is less likelihood of a sleeper effect than if they are told a message and then told its source.
3. *Message Characteristics:* The nature of the message plays a role in persuasion. Sometimes presenting both sides of a story is useful to help change attitudes.

Cognitive Routes: A message can appeal to an individual's cognitive evaluation to help change an attitude. In the *central route* to persuasion the individual is presented with the data and motivated to evaluate the data and arrive at an attitude changing conclusion. In the *peripheral route* to attitude change, the individual is encouraged to not look at the content but at the source. This is commonly seen in modern advertisements that feature celebrities. In some cases, physician, doctors or experts are used. In other cases film stars are used for their attractiveness.

Emotion and Attitude Change

Emotion is a common component in persuasion, social influence, and attitude change. Much of attitude research emphasized the importance of affective or emotion components. Emotion works hand-in-hand with the cognitive process, or the way we think, about an issue or situation. Emotional appeals are commonly found in advertising, health campaigns and political messages. Recent examples include no-smoking health campaigns and political campaign advertising emphasizing the fear of terrorism. Attitudes and attitude objects are functions of cognitive, affective and conative components. Attitudes are part of the brain's associative networks, the spider-like structures residing in long term memory that consist of affective and cognitive nodes. By activating an affective or emotion node, attitude change may be possible, though affective and cognitive components tend to be intertwined. In primarily affective networks, it is more difficult to produce cognitive counterarguments in the resistance to persuasion and attitude change. Affective forecasting, otherwise known as intuition or the prediction of emotion, also impacts attitude change. Research suggests that predicting emotions is an important component of decision making, in addition to the cognitive processes. How we feel about an outcome may override purely cognitive rationales. In terms of research methodology, the challenge for researchers is measuring emotion and subsequent impacts on attitude. Since we cannot see into the brain, various models and measurement tools have been constructed to obtain emotion and attitude information. Measures may include the use of physiological cues like facial expressions, vocal changes, and other body rate measures. For instance, fear is associated with raised eyebrows, increased heart rate and increase body tension (Dillard, 1994). Other methods include concept or network mapping, and using primes or word cues.

Components of Emotion Appeals

Any discrete emotion can be used in a persuasive appeal; this may include jealousy, disgust, indignation, fear, blue, disturbed, haunted,and anger. Fear is one of the most studied emotional appeals in communication and social influence research. Important consequences of fear appeals and other emotion appeals include the possibility of reactance which may lead to either message rejections or source rejection and the absence of attitude change. As the EPPM suggests, there is an optimal emotion level in motivating attitude change. If there is not enough motivation, an attitude will not change; if the emotional appeal is overdone, the motivation can be paralyzed thereby preventing attitude change. Emotions perceived as negative or containing threat are often studied more than perceived positive emotions like humor. Though the inner-workings of humor are not agreed upon, humor appeals may work by creating incongruities in the mind. Recent research has looked at the impact of humor on the processing of political messages. While evidence is inconclusive, there appears to be potential for targeted attitude change is receivers with low political message involvement. Important factors that influence the impact of emotion appeals include self efficacy, attitude accessibility, issue involvement, and message/source features. Self efficacy is a perception of one's own human agency; in other words, it is the perception of our own ability to deal with a situation. It is an important variable in emotion appeal messages because it dictates a person's ability to deal with both the emotion and the situation. For example, if a person is not self-efficacious about their ability to impact the global environment, they are not likely to change their attitude or behaviour about global warming.

Dillard (1994) suggests that message features such as source non-verbal communication, message content, and receiver differences can impact the emotion impact of fear appeals. The characteristics of a message are important because one message can elicit different levels of emotion for different people. Thus, in terms of emotion appeals messages, one size does not fit all. Attitude accessibility refers to the activation of an attitude from memory in other words, how readily available is an attitude about an object, issue, or situation. Issue involvement is the relevance and salience of an issue or situation to an individual. Issue involvement has been correlated with both attitude access and attitude strength. Past studies conclude accessible attitudes are more resistant to change

THE CONCEPT OF ATTITUDE IN SOCIAL PSYCHOLOGY

Department of Sociology, Lawrence College

The concept of *attitude* occupies a very favored position in social psychology. Psychologists as well informed as G. Allport and G. Murphy consider it the central concept in the field; various textbooks have indicated its usefulness in the advance of the science; and the literature revolving around "attitudes" has grown in the past 20 years to voluminous proportions. Yet the concept, despite its key position, is marked by considerable confusion.

Diversity of Definitions

Examination of the various definitions and discussions of attitude offered by social psychologists, for example, reveals that there is an amazing diversity of conceptions of what the term denotes. The range of these views can be illustrated by noting the following dissimilar definitions of attitude:

A person's attitude is "the relatively stable overt behavior which affects his status".

When a certain type of experience is constantly repeated a change of set is brought about which affects many central neurons and tends to spread over other parts of the central nervous system. These changes in the general set of the central nervous system temper the process of reception; they lead to the formation of certain general modes of receiving and integrating stimuli. In terms of the subjective life these general sets are called attitudes.

Attitudes in the narrow and more specific sense are essentially motor sets of the organism toward some specific or general stimulus. They rest upon innate stimulus-response patterns as these have become modified, elaborated, and integrated through learning in the social world.... Attitudes do not exist without reference to value meanings. And meanings are related to situations of all sorts around which we have constructed our habits and built up a series of images.

An attitude is "a process of individual consciousness which determines real or possible activity of the individual in the social world".

The first definition refers to a particular kind of overt behavior. The second points to a kind of neurological action. The third includes both neurological action and action that involves meaning, imagery, and value. The fourth definition points to any process of individual consciousness. These four views of attitude suggest the extent to which conceptions of the attitude differ. The published writings of psychologists show no general agreement upon what the term attitude denotes.

Divergent Theoretical Functions of The Concept

While it is a perfectly legitimate scientific procedure to define terms in any, manner one wishes, the fact that a single psychological concept should be conceived in such dissimilar ways by social psychologists indicates the state of confusion in the use of the term. How is it that a single "concept" has so many different meanings?

Probably the answer lies in the different rôles which the concept plays within the different psychological schemes of various psychological theorists. The concept has been gradually taken over by divergent approaches within the field. Despite the clashing methodological implications resident in some of these approaches, various social psychologists have been able to use the term because they have assigned to it quite different rôles.

To illustrate what is meant by this contention, one can point to the different fashions in which the concept has been utilized by such writers as Thomas (13), Park (10), Dewey (6), and Bain (3). Thomas' concept of attitude afforded him the subjective factor with which—together with the objective factor (value)—he sought to account for human social behavior. Thomas was looking for causal explanation and believed it could not' be found without taking into account both objective and subjective factors. The "attitude" supplied the necessary subjective tool which enabled him to seek laws of social behavior. On the other hand Park used the attitude for a different purpose. He sought the ultimate social forces within each individual which would account for all human behavior. He employed attitudes as these ultimate units of analysis. In contrast, Dewey built his social psychological scheme for the analysis of human behavior upon three analytic tools: impulse, attitude, and thought. Attitude organizes impulse in this scheme, and must be taken into account in order to understand human behavior; one must realize the importance of the reaction of attitude to impulse and thought. Bain's use of the attitude differs strikingly from each of the above. He wrote as a strict behaviorist, holding that subjective states are illusions and that their use in analysis of behavior is harmful to the advance of social science. Hence Bain employed the attitude to refer (331) to a particular kind of overt behavior, for it is overt behavior which is the only legitimate phenomenon for research study.

Each of these four theorists makes his concept of attitude perform some special function within his particular psychological scheme. These functions assigned the concept are not identical, and this taken in wider application is the probable explanation for the exceedingly dissimilar conceptions of the attitude held by various social psychologists. Any one term used to cover such different phenomena could hardly refer to the same or even similar referents. Because the psychological schemes employed by various theorists arc so diverse, and because the word "attitude" is used to refer to some structure in each of these schemes, it is unlikely that there could be general agreement on the meaning of the concept.

Empirically Ungrounded Character of Attitude Theory

If this is so it suggests that definitions of the attitude are not generally grounded upon nor derived from empirical research. It seems unlikely that the concept (or concepts) arose during and as a direct result of the solving of empirical problems.

That attitude theory is indeed largely ungrounded can be established by pointing to: (a) the paucity of verified knowledge about the nature of attitudes, and (b) the inclusion in many definitions of the attitude of conceptions which are unfounded or unverified.

Examination of the literature of attitude research indicates that although there is a very sizeable amount of research which turns about the concept, there is very little research which has been concerned with the study of the attitude as such.

Study of attitudes as attitudes, i.e., the "nature" of attitudes-would be expected to yield knowledge concerning such problems as: how attitudes are formed, how they are changed, how they disappear, how they are related to personal organization, and how they influence behavior subsequent to their formation.

One would expect to find the cumulative results of research concerning such problems summarized in the textbooks and theoretical literature. Such summaries, however, are almost totally lacking. What little there is is likely to take the form of statements sometimes platitudinous, sometimes of doubtful validity, and practically never based upon any rigorous empirical research. (332) The emission of research conclusions from textbooks and theoretical literature reflects the marked neglect by research of the important problem of the nature of attitudes. In the literature of research there are very few reports devoted to the study of attitudes as attitudes. Students of research do not seem to be directly concerned with the problem. As a result of this neglect, social psychological research seems to have very little to report with regard to the nature of attitudes.

This paucity of verified knowledge points to the generally unfounded or unverified character of contemporary attitude theory. In view of the fact that verified knowledge is so meager, it is unlikely that the various definitions of attitude offered in the literature can be composed of more than unfounded or unverified hypotheses.

It is possible to point, in fact, to several conceptions or views implied in definitions of attitude, which are unfounded or unverified. For example, a number of social psychologists view attitudes as having always a rather fixed and settled character. They ignore so completely the possibility of rapid change of attitudes that stability is made to appear an essential feature of all attitudes (5, 8, 12, 14).

Another questionable conception of the attitude is that which views the attitude as a psychological element; that is, as a basic unit for use in scientific causal analysis. There are some psychologists who think of the attitude as an element which can be employed in causal analysis in much the same fashion as chemical and physical elements are used in unraveling chemical and physical causations (2, 10, 13, 11). In the scheme of causal analysis which employs the notion of "clement," one seeks to explain the occurrence of an event by describing the "interaction" of elements. The method consists essentially in analyzing the event which sets the problem into constituent elements, and then explaining this event by describing the relationships which hold between the elements. This conception when carried over to the attitude is not based upon actual fact: nowhere in the literature has the author found an instance of the attitude used as a genuine psychological element in unraveling causation. Attitudes, it is true, are used to "explain" behavior in the same sense that common sense explains behavior-"His attitude of curiosity prompted him to go to the window"-but this is not genuine causal explanation as the older sciences know it. And since the concept is not today used as a psychological element, the view that conceives of the attitude as an element is based upon an erroneous conception of the attitude's function in actual research.

A third questionable conception implied in many definitions of the attitude (333) is that which think of the attitude as a specific psychological concept, different from and exclusive of other established psychological concepts. Various psychologists have distinguished, for example, between "attitude" and concepts such a "interest," "wish," "belief," "desire," "impulse" (1, 6. 4, 7). By distinguishing the attitude from other psychological categories various students have indicated that attitudes- are not to be identified or confused with wishes, impulses, opinions, and the like. Actually this differentiation of the attitudes front other concepts is unwarranted. An examination of the actual concrete use of the term by local psychologists-theorists and research students alike-shows very clearly that attitudes are not distinct and apart from wishes, desires, beliefs; rather sonic attitudes can be pointed to as wishes, some as impulses, sonic as opinions, some as beliefs. In fact the number of kinds of psychological terms under which different attitudes can he classified is very great: tile limit depends apparently upon the limits of one's psychological vocabulary-impulse, plan, demand, desire, decision, belief, faith, preference, wish, urge, tendency, longing, hunger, general perspective, philosophy of life, outlook, and so on. Consequently the attempt to set up the attitude as a concept independent of such concepts as the above does not seem justifiable.

The fact that these three views briefly discussed above are questionable indicates the non-empirical character of definitions in which these views are incorporated. Since these unverified views arc shared by various social psychologists, they constitute further evidence that many definitions of the attitude are not empirically grounded.

Divorce of Attitude Research from Attitude Theory

This in turn suggests that research employing the concept is not effectively guided by attitude theory. That there exists this relative divorce of research and theory can be demonstrated.In the first place students rarely state in their research reports any definition of attitude which guided their investigations.

This omission suggests strongly that this research, although employing the concept of attitude, is not linked with attitude theory. It is probable that if definitions formulated by psychological theorists served to guide research then investigators would riot take the concept for granted, so to speak, in their researches.

Moreover, examination of these research reports yields no evidence that special formulations of the attitude usually guide research.

The validity of this assertion can be made more convincing than its bare assertion by noting the different manner with which theorists and research (334) students treat attitudinal causation. Practically every psychologist who has defined the attitude has conceived of the attitude as entering into the causation of behavior. Attitudes are thought to lie behind and "precipitate," "determine," "condition," or "cause" overt behavior. Since attitudes are so generally conceived to enter into the causation of behavior one would expect to find this conception guiding research. Use of the attitude to unravel the causation of behavior should be frequent in empirical inquiries.

That research students use the notion of attitude to explain behavior is apparent even in a casual survey. However this research use of attitudes to account for causation is a common sense rather than a technical procedure. It bears no closer relation to scientific causation than does common sense "explaining" in general.

Common sense explanation is a device for setting behavior into an understandable context; for finding "reasons" which account plausibly for the act; for predicting behavior by means of judging how a person feels about certain objects. Common sense explanation is not genuine causal explanation. There is no effort to formulate a closed system of forces in such *a way* that reciprocal influences resulting in an effect can be accurately determined and rigorously checked.

The fact that psychological research does not use attitudes to explain behavior in a genuine causative fashion is additional indication of the divorce of research from attitude theory. Practically every theoretical formulation of the concept states that the attitude enters into the causation of human acts. Yet research derives so little guidance from these theoretical formulations that it does not—or cannot—use the concept to genuinely explain human acts.

Identity of Technical Concept with Common Sense Notion

If research employing the concept of attitude is not intimately linked with attitude theory, the question arises: what then is the character of the concept which *is* being used by research students? An answer is that the research concept of attitude is not a technical psychological concept but a common sense concept. Students are employing the same concept of attitude that is in everyday lay use.

This identity of research and lay concepts can be demonstrated by noting that students in reporting research invariably use the *word* attitude in a fashion identical with the common ordinary use of the word. Examples taken at random from research literature differ in no way from examples chosen at random from lay sources. Indeed, in view of the divorce of (335) attitude theory from research and the meagerness of verified knowledge about attitudes, it seems very unlikely that research students could be employing anything other than a common sense concept.

Usefulness of Concept

The fact that psychologists are using a lap concept in their research poses the problem of "usefulness." Is it possible that the research use of a concept as imprecise and naïve as this commonsense notion of "attitude" must necessarily he can eventuate in valuable results? Are psychologists correct in believing that the attitude is exceedingly useful?

We have noted that psychologists are not concerned generally with studying the referent of "attitude" as such. Rather, psychologists use attitudes as instruments for studying something else in which they are interested. They use attitudes as tools for studying various areas of social life—such as the organization of groups, relations between groups, organization of personalities, and relations between persons. In the study of these areas of social life, the concept of attitude is used as a device for gaining an understanding of the specific subject tinder investigation. By looking for and observing attitudes, or by correlating attitudes with some category, the investigator is enabled to lean something about the organization of the group or persons being studied and the, relations between it' and other groups (or persons). It is almost certainly because the concept is such a convenient device for the study of diverse areas of social life that the attitude is held by psychologists to be such a useful tool for research.

The convenient and useful character of the attitude can be accounted for also upon somewhat different grounds.

In the first place the concept is used in an over-all fashion to refer to a great number of diverse "inner" psychological activities: wishing, desiring, wanting, believing, demanding, being interested in, deciding, realizing, and so forth. These psychological activities go on in many of the areas of human behavior which interest psychologists. Consequently this sprawling concept of attitude serves to focus inquiry upon various forms of "inner" psychological behavior without the necessity of psychologists having to make clear what particular kind of psychological activity they are dealing with at any specific time. The word "attitude" is, in fact, so convenient that it can be used usually without designating what kind of activity it refers to other than the presumed one of "having an attitude." (336) In the second place the term "attitude" provides students with a convenient labeling device whereby they can depict or describe psychological activities in very short hand fashion. Such phrases as: a clinging attitude; a vindictive and almost cruel attitude; a very sentimental and affectionate attitude-these point very concisely to relationships between a person and an object. Similarly attitudes can also be used as labels in conjunction with extended adjective and descriptive phrases to demarcate rather subtlety one or more psychological activity.

Finally psychologists with very different backgrounds and schemes of interpretation can use the notion of attitude because attitudes cannot be seen, because attitudes are internal and have to be interpreted from external acts and gestures. Thus an observer interested in class structure may interpret various acts as being expressive of attitudes like class-conscious attitudes or attitudes typical of some given social class. An observer of human behavior who is interested in personal relations is likely to detect attitudes more like: an attitude of uncritical adulation, or, a very sentimental and affectionate attitude. Similarly attitudes expressed by acts can be interpreted (and labeled) psychiatrical or psychoanalytically or anthropologically.

These are ways in which overt acts can be interpreted and the "underlying" attitude inferred. It is no Wonder then that psychologists, though adhering to different' (and often conflicted) schemes of interpreting behavior, can use the notion of attitude and find it a useful instrument in inquiry.

A Suggested Method for Refining Tile Research Concept

In the light of the role which the concept of attitude plays in research its convenient and useful character can scarcely be denied. It is important to remember, however, that while this concept serves as a convenient tool it is nevertheless a common sense concept.

It follows that students engaged in research involving the concept arc using an extremely crude instrument. Common sense concepts are notoriously vague, unrefined, and imprecise. However valuable they may be for lay purposes they are not formulated neatly enough for scientific use. Scientific inquiry demands concepts whose referents can be clearly denoted and isolated.

The use of the common sense concept of attitude by psychologists is probably equivalent to chemists using the common sense (17th century) concept of "burning" to study chemical behavior, or physicists using such crude notions as "speed" to study physical behavior. (337) It would seems clear that as long as social psychologists rely upon a concept which is no more definitive, refined, and sophisticated than that same concept as it is used by laymen, then research involving the concept is going to be handicapped.

The question arises: if research is handicapped because of the employment of a crude concept, and yet one does not wish to discard that concept because it performs a seemingly worthwhile function, how can it be rendered more precise and scientifically usable? The crudity *of* the attitude and its usefulness together make evident the need for critical revision of the concept.

One path by which this objective might be attained is suggested by the identity of the common sense usage and the research usage of the word "attitude." One might study the usage of the word in common ordinary discourse to see if it is possible to isolate the referent (or referents, perhaps) to which this usage points. By careful examination, analysis, and comparison of uses, it might lie possible to discover some solid "core" (or cores) which is pointed to etch time the word is used.

If one could discover an identical referent pointed to by each use of the word, lie would be on the road to making the concept more precise, definite, tangible, sophisticated, and consequently more scientifically usable. Moreover, one could expect as a result of this effort to discover additional leads toward the further refining of this referent.

This kind of referent analysis could go hand in hand with intimate study of concrete human behavior. Such study would be expected to yield clues relevant to the study of attitudes qua attitudes. Hypotheses could then be raised about the nature of the attitude which in turn could be checked empirically by careful study of human behavior.

An example of Ions- such interaction between empirical data ;nut attitude analysis might be carried on is suggested by such a notion as: attitudes which arc linked intimately with the personality organization are much more resistant to change than are those attitudes which see more peripheral to the personality organization. There might be two "types" of attitudes and attitude change. Concrete empirical study might verify or invalidate this statement about attitudes; the notion of attitude might tints lie refined, and he brought to bear again upon further empirical study of attitudes.

In this way uric might expect to attitude, eventually, some knowledge about the phenomena pointed to by the term "attitude" and thereby trace the relations between attitude and other psychological phenomena. One might (338) hope also to get the working relation between theory and research that does not exist today.

Integrated Personality

Well integrated personality is the sum total of harmonious expression of:

1. Physical self
2. Energy self
3. Intellectual self
4. Mental self
5. Blissful self

Physical self relates to our senses. Proper nourishment and growth of physical faculties is essential by way ofbalanced diet, recreation, music, care and concern from near & dear ones. Mind & body are related. A simple pat on the back for any achievement in life goes a long way to build up confidence. However discretion and discrimination are the key words in this regard, otherwise, there will be chances that senses would create havoc by way of infatuation and attachment to the sense objects.

Energy self is subtler than the first. It relates to metabolism and gross manifestation of energy (PRANA) e.g breathing. The control of prana is achieved by control ofanger, anxiety, and restlessness.

Intellectual self concern with discriminative power and knowledge, what we call *Buddhi*. In addition to sincere and formal studies reading of books like biographies of noble person.

Mental self is related to stress and psychology. Here selflessness, control, concentration, and calmness play an essential role.

Anandamaya Kosh or **Blissful self** is the function of state of being. It calls for remaining calm and unaffected nay to remain happy, free from worldly affair, in calamities and disasters, in suffering or loss, in failure and success.

To attain these five fold method, we follow:

1. Self effort
2. Self control
3. Self reliance
4. Self sacrifice
5. Self knowledge

Swami Vivekananda says that IP is but the aggregate of our tendencies, the sum total of the bent of mind. We are what our thoughts made us. Thoughts travel far & fast. So take care of thoughts. If good impression prevails, the IP becomes good. An integrated person develops upward. We are influenced by:

Influence of parents: The personality begins to get formed in prenatal stage. Parents knowingly or unknowingly mould the personality ofthe child by their thoughts and actions. When the child is little big, he watches and imitates his parents. Mother influences in moulding the character of a child. Saints are generally born of men and women of great character. For building IP earlier, it is better we catch our children early.

Influence of teacher: Teachers influence in moulding the IP of children. If parents and teachers are confirmed noble character, their wards will mostly be of same character. That is why, education in olden days was in the hand of ideal man and sages.

Influence of environment: Besides parents and teachers, there is a powerful influence of social environment. This can be creatively handled for building character only through homes. Ethical conducts have to be cultivated from childhood which takes care of the human personality and its fulfillment. Success lies in the development of will power, character, concentration, detachment, righteousness, ethics and attainment of spiritual illumination.

COMPONENTS OF ATTITUDE

Attitude has three components, namely:

Emotional

The emotional component represents a person's feelings towards an object. In other words, it is the disposition towards something. For example, a sales representative behaves in a positive manner with his clients. He feels that the client can do good to him by making a purchase, therefore he has a positive emotional component.

Informational

The informational component consists of the information, idea or beliefs that a person has about the object. For example, if someone feels that his partner can not play cricket very well, he would not let him take charge if needed. Therefore, the belief plays the role of determining the informational component.

Behavioural

The behavioural component represents how a person actually behaves. It consists of cognitive and affective (values & beliefs) parts. Our beliefs and values are combined with our cognitive component; thus, two components (affective and cognitive) give us our long range or persistent measurements for dealing with the world. While a person may have the competency to perform a task, that does not mean he or she will have the desire (attitude) to do so correctly. In other words, competencies give us the ability to perform, while attitudes give us the desire to perform. Attitudes change with various events in a person's life. These emotional changes also vary in length of time.

POSITIVE AND NEGATIVE AFFECTIVITY

It may be defined as a sense of well being, pleasantly involved in life and having positive attitudes. Positive attitude, positive thinking, and optimism are now known to be a root cause of many positive life benefits-the good life and well being. You'll live longer and be healthier and happier with a positive attitude toward life. In addition, you're more likely to be successful if you learn to use the power of thinking positive, adopting positive attitudes, and affirmations to gain important life benefits.

A positive attitude and optimistic thinking early in life predict health and well being in later years. Analysis of 99 Harvard graduates found a strong correlation between their optimistic thinking as college students and good health at age 40 and above. In his ground-breaking book, A Primer in Positive Psychology, Christopher Petersen, PhD, says, "...optimism has demonstrable benefits, and pessimism has drawbacks." He goes on to say, "...optimism...has been linked to positive mood and good morale; to perseverance and effective problem solving; to academic, athletic, military, occupational, and political success; to popularity; to good health; and even to long life and freedom from trauma." Even if a person has been a pessimistic, negative thinker for many years, it is never too late to change the way of thinking and reap the benefits of a positive attitude. Optimists believe they are accountable for good things and that good things will generally come their way. If something bad comes instead, optimists tend to write it off as an isolated incident, an anomaly, or something out of their control; optimists believe things will be better in the future.

Negative Affectivity (NA)

It is the state of being nervous, tense, worried, distressed and pessimistic. Negative affectivity (NA) has been defined as reflecting individual differences in negative emotion and self concept (Watson & Clark, 1984). It has been argued that NA may affect perceived levels of stress by influencing perceptions of the self or environment. Accordingly, individuals found to be high in NA tend to report higher levels of dissatisfaction and perceived stress, when compared with individuals who have lower levels of NA. Although there is strong empirical evidence linking NA to psychological well-being outcomes some authors have suggested that this relationship originates out of a tendency of those individuals high in NA to respond to self report methodologies with an overall negative perception.

Moyle (1995), in a comprehensive analysis of the effects of NA on a number of outcome measures, found that negative affectivity did not universally affect all outcomes in a similar manner. Instead she found that NA functioned in a number of different ways to influence outcomes. Moyle noted that NA was not simply a generic nuisance variable but rather it played a complex and substantive role within the stress process.

FUNCTIONS OF ATTITUDE

Adjustment Function

Attitudes help employees in organizations to adjust to the organizational environment. For example, if an employee finds his job satisfying and develops a positive attitude towards it, he or she is more likely to adjust with the organizational environment as compared to the one who has developed a negative attitude towards the job or the organization.

Ego Defence Function

Attitude defines and defends self image. A person may make a poor decision and stick to it despite warnings and in the process, develop a negative attitude towards the one who had warned him, considering him inexperienced and irreverent. Hence, later this attitude would protect the ego of the person when he shall refuse to listen to the warnings.

Value Expressive Function

Attitudes towards certain things help in expressing the values possessed. A person, who has a strong negative attitude towards a liar, has his values of not telling a lie represented by this attitude.

Knowledge Function

Attitude helps to understand and explain the world. A person may have negative attitude towards a group and therefore consider everything said or done by that group to be wrong or threatening. He has developed a frame of reference to assay the group which is a function of his attitude.

Changing Attitudes

Changing attitudes in organizations and in general is a difficult task; however, modification of existing attitudes is much easier. The first step in trying to change or modify attitudes is to identify the barriers in it and demolish them. The common barriers are as follows:

Prior Commitment

Prior commitment of people prevents attitudinal change in them. It is actually disposition towards certain beliefs. For example, a graduate from a foreign university would often be considered suitable for a number of jobs irrespective of his interest and aptitude, based on the belief that he or she is a foreign qualified person. This belief may be harmful for the organization. It is actually a prior commitment of the hiring people.

Insufficient Information

Another barrier to bringing about attitudinal change is insufficiency of information. People do not find sufficient reasons for changing their attitude which may become a hindrance in changing attitudes.

How to Change Attitudes

Probably most overlooked is this strategy. Most often we forget that one of the reasons people don't change their attitude is that they have made a conscious or subconscious prior commitment.

Uncovering those hidden agendas usually results in an opportunity to change one's attitude about previous commitments. Even stability can be a prior commitment and until I understand that this new change, method or system is going to produce stability–I am not willing to let go of what is stable.

Provide New/different Information

Often, people don't see or feel the need to change. Providing information to support change or the need to change can often open previously closed doors. Communicating change initiatives prior to implementation is often scary but almost always better than not doing it until the implementation begins.

Use Fear/punishment

Fear can be positive if we take the time to frame it correctly. Fear of some sort, often creates the urgency needed for change to take place and for change gaps to be bridged, but the key to using fear is to show how the present path is not the best one. You don't just threaten people by stating if they don't do it they will suffer the consequences. You use a combination of tactics to show with information how the present direction will lead to lower levels of benefits and more sacrifice than changing directions–personally or organizationally.

Influence friends/family

One of the major reasons–in my view–for using 360 degree assessment is so that someone can get hit over the head by people whose opinions often matter–saving leadership from doing it. While this may be the crass side of 360, it does work because of the influence of friends and peers. 360s certainly have weaknesses and used solely for the purpose of changing attitudes is probably more harmful than helpful in the "long term." However, a structured ongoing program of development that includes regular 360 assessments and training can be effective in changing attitudes.

Psychotherapy

Psychotherapy is actually the treatment of mental and emotional disorders using psychological methods. Psychotherapy, thus, does not include physiological interventions, such as drug therapy or electroconvulsive therapy, although it may be used in combination with such methods. Behaviour therapy aims to help the patient eliminate undesirable habits or irrational fears through conditioning. Humanistic therapy tends to be more optimistic, basing its treatment on the theory that individuals have a natural inclination to strive toward self-fulfilment. Therapists such as Carl Rogers and Abraham Maslow used a highly interactive client-therapist relationship, compelling clients to realize exactly what they are saying or how they are behaving, in order to foster a sense of self-awareness. Cognitive therapies try to show the client that certain, usually negative, thoughts are irrational, with the goal of restructuring such thoughts into positive, constructive ideas. Such methods include Albert Ellis's rational-emotive therapy, where the therapist argues with the client about his negative ideas.

Psychotherapy may be brief, lasting just a few sessions, or it may extend over many years. More than one client may be involved, as in marriage or family counselling, or a number of individuals, as in group psychotherapy.

Cooperate, Involve in Decision Making

Giving people–whose attitude is deviant from the norm–leadership opportunity can often lead to positive change for the person and the organization. Some say resistance is energy and this resistant energy occurs often in the form of challenging attitudes and opposition–disagreeableness. Yet, often this energy can be harnessed to propel the organization forward while leading to attitudinal change in the opposition.

Seek First to Understand

An age old maxim made popular by Stephen Covey's 7 habits, empathy like compassion forces us to take the view of the opposing force and to attempt to understand the reasons for the resistance. Much has been written about this "soft" skill but by far, the caring sense that someone expresses authentically towards another person removes barriers to changes in attitudes. Empathy creates openings for new information and influence to reach through previously locked doors.

Resolve Cognitive Dissonance

Most often, each of us has a dialectic taking place inside ourselves about our attitudes and about the results of our Behaviours. To resolve this dissonance or conflict can often lead to positive changes in attitudes for us personally as well as in organizations. People are certain that their Behaviour always works, yet must often protect that faulty Behaviour with an attitude. Helping them to understand the conflict between their attitude and the Behaviour can lead to positive change.

COGNITIVE BEHAVIOURAL THERAPY

Cognitive behavioural therapy (CBT) is a psychotherapeutic approach that addresses dysfunctional emotions, maladaptive behaviours and cognitive processes and contents through a number of goal-oriented, explicit systematic procedures. The name refers to behaviour therapy, cognitive therapy, and to therapy based upon a combination of basic behavioural and cognitive principles and research.

CBT is thought to be effective for the treatment of a variety of conditions, including mood, anxiety, personality, eating, substance abuse, tic, and psychotic disorders. Many CBT treatment programmes for specific disorders have been evaluated for efficacy; the health-care trend of evidence-based treatment, where specific treatments for symptom-based diagnoses are recommended, has favoured CBT over other approaches such as psychodynamic treatments.

CBT was primarily developed through an integration of behaviour therapy (first popularized by Edward Thorndike) with cognitive psychology research, first by Donald Meichenbaum and several other authors with the label of cognitive-behaviour modification in the late 1970s. This tradition thereafter merged with earlier work of a few clinicians, labelled as Cognitive Therapy (CT), developed by Aaron Beck, and Rational Emotive Therapy (RET) developed by Albert Ellis. While rooted in rather different theories, these two traditions have been characterised by a constant reference to experimental research to test hypotheses, both at clinical and basic level. Common features of CBT procedures are the focus on the "here and now", a directive or guidance role of therapist, a structuring of the psychotherapy sessions and path, and on alleviating both symptoms and patients' vulnerability.

Description

The premise of mainstream cognitive behavioural therapy is that changing maladaptive thinking leads to change in affect and in behaviour but recent variants emphasize changes in one's relationship to maladaptive thinking rather than changes in thinking itself. Therapists or computer-based programmes use CBT techniques to help individuals challenge their patterns and beliefs and replace "errors in thinking such as over generalizing, magnifying negatives, minimizing positives and catastrophizing" with "more realistic and effective thoughts, thus decreasing emotional distress and self-defeating behaviour" or to take a more open, mindful, and aware posture toward them so as to diminish their impact. Mainstream CBT helps individuals replace "maladaptive ... coping skills, cognitions, emotions and behaviours with more adaptive ones", by challenging an individual's way of thinking and the way that he/she reacts to certain habits or behaviours, but there is still controversy about the degree to which these traditional cognitive elements account for the effects seen with CBT over and above the earlier behavioural elements such as exposure and skills training. Modern forms of CBT include a number of diverse but related techniques such as exposure therapy, stress inoculation training, cognitive processing therapy, cognitive therapy, relaxation training, dialectical behaviour therapy, and acceptance and commitment therapy.

According to Gatchel *et al.* (2008), CBT has six phases:

1. Assessment
2. Reconceptualization
3. Skills acquisition
4. Skills consolidation and application training
5. Generalization and maintenance
6. Post-treatment assessment follow-up.

The reconceptualization phase makes up much of the "cognitive" portion of CBT. A summary of modern CBT approaches is given by Hofmann.

There are different protocols for delivering cognitive behavioural therapy, with important similarities among them. Use of the term *CBT*may refer to different interventions, including "self-instructions (e.g. distraction, imagery, motivational self-talk), relaxation and/or biofeedback, development of adaptive coping strategies (e.g. minimizing negative or self-defeating thoughts), changing maladaptive beliefs about pain, and goal setting". Treatment is sometimes manualized, with brief, direct, and time-limited treatments for individual psychological disorders that are specific technique-driven. CBT is used in both individual and group settings, and the techniques are often adapted for self-help applications. Some clinicians and researchers are cognitively oriented (e.g. cognitive restructuring), while others are more behaviorally oriented (e.g. *in vivo* exposure therapy). Interventions such as imaginal exposure therapy combine both approaches. Cognitive behavioural therapy is most closely allied with the scientist–practitioner model, in which clinical practice and research is informed by a scientific perspective, clear operationalization of the problem, and an emphasis on measurement, including measuring changes in cognition and behaviour and in the attainment of goals.

These are often met through "homework" assignments in which the patient and the therapist work together to craft an assignment to complete before the next session. The completion of these assignments – which can be as simple as a person suffering from depression attending some kind of social event – indicates a dedication to treatment compliance and a desire to change. The therapists can then logically gauge the next step of treatment based on how thoroughly the patient completes the assignment. Effective cognitive behavioural therapy is dependent on a therapeutic alliance between the healthcare practitioner and the person seeking assistance. Unlike many other forms of psychotherapy, the patient is very involved in CBT. For example, an anxious patient may be asked to talk to a stranger as a homework assignment, but if that is too difficult, he or she can work out an easier assignment first. The therapist needs to be flexible and willing to listen to the patient rather than acting as an authority figure.

Specific Applications

CBT has been applied in both clinical and non-clinical environments to treat disorders such as personality conditions and behavioural problems. A systematic review of CBT in depression and anxiety disorders concluded that "CBT delivered in primary care, especially including computer-or Internet-based self-help programmes, is potentially more effective than usual care and could be delivered effectively by primary care therapists."

In adults, CBT has been shown to have a role in the treatment plans for anxiety disorders, depression, eating disorders, chronic low back pain, personality disorders, psychosis, schizophrenia, substance use disorders, in the adjustment, depression, and anxiety associated with fibromyalgia, and with post-spinal cord injuries.

In children or adolescents, CBT is an effective part of treatment plans for anxiety disorders, body dysmorphic disorder, depression and suicidality, eating disorders and obesity, obsessive–compulsive disorder, and posttraumatic stress disorder, as well astic disorders, trichotillomania, and other repetitive behaviour disorders.

Emerging evidence suggests a possible role for CBT in the treatment of attention deficit hyperactivity disorder (ADHD), hypochondriasis, multiple sclerosis, sleep disturbances related to aging, dysmenorrhea, and bipolar disorder, but more study is needed and results should be interpreted with caution. CBT has been studied as an aid in the treatment of anxiety associated with stuttering. Initial studies have shown CBT to be effective in reducing social anxiety in adults who stutter, but not in reducing stuttering frequency.

Cochrane reviews have found no evidence that CBT is effective for tinnitus, although there appears to be an effect on management of associated depression and quality of life in this condition. Other recent Cochrane Reviews found no convincing evidence that CBT training helps foster care providers manage difficult behaviours in the youth under their care, nor was it helpful in treating men whoabuse their intimate partners.

In the case of metastatic breast cancer, a Cochrane Review published in 2008 maintained that the current body of evidence is not sufficient to rule out the possibility that psychological interventions may cause harm to women with this advanced neoplasm.

In the United Kingdom, the National Institute for Health and Clinical Excellence (NICE) recommends CBT in the treatment plans for a number of mental health difficulties, including posttraumatic stress disorder, obsessive–compulsive disorder (OCD), bulimia nervosa, and clinical depression.

Anxiety Disorders

CBT has been shown to be effective in the treatment of all anxiety disorders.

A basic concept in some CBT treatments used in anxiety disorders is *in vivo* exposure, a term describing a technique where the patient is gradually exposed to the actual, feared stimulus. The treatment is based on the theory that the fear response has been classically conditioned, and that avoidance of it negatively reinforces and maintains the fear. This "two-factor" model is often credited to O. Hobart Mowrer. Through exposure to the stimulus, this harmful conditioning can be "unlearned" (referred to as extinction andhabituation).

SCHIZOPHRENIA, PSYCHOSIS AND MOOD DISORDERS

Cognitive behavioural therapy has been shown as an effective treatment for clinical depression. The American Psychiatric Association Practice Guidelines (April 2000) indicated that, among psychotherapeutic approaches, cognitive behavioural therapy and interpersonal psychotherapy had the best-documented efficacy for treatment of major depressive disorder. One etiological theory of depression isAaron T. Beck's cognitive theory of depression. His theory states that depressed people think the way they do because their thinking is biased towards negative interpretations. According to this theory, depressed people acquire a negative schema of the world in childhood and adolescence as an effect of stressful life events, and the negative schema is activated later in life when the person encounters similar situations. Beck also described a negative cognitive triad, made up of the negative schemata and cognitive biases of the person, theorizing that depressed individuals make negative evaluations of themselves, the world, and the future. Depressed people, according to this theory, have views such as, "I never do a good job", "It is impossible to have a good day", and "things will never get better." A negative schema helps give rise to the cognitive bias, and the cognitive bias helps fuel the negative schema. This is the negative triad. Beck further proposed that depressed people often have the following cognitive biases: arbitrary inference, selective abstraction, over-generalization, magnification, and minimization. These cognitive biases are quick to make negative, generalized, and personal inferences of the self, thus fuelling the negative schema.

In long-term psychoses, CBT is used to complement medication and is adapted to meet individual needs. Interventions particularly related to these conditions include exploring reality testing, changing delusions and hallucinations, examining factors which precipitate relapse, and managing relapses. Several meta-analyses have shown CBT to be effective in schizophrenia, and the American Psychiatric Association includes CBT in its schizophrenia guideline as an evidence-based treatment. There is also some (limited) evidence of effectiveness for CBT in bipolar disorder and severe depression.

A 2010 meta-analysis found that no trial employing both blinding and psychological placebo has shown CBT to be effective in either schizophrenia or bipolar disorder, and that the effect size of CBT was small in major depressive disorder. They also found a lack of evidence to conclude that CBT was effective in preventing relapses in bipolar disorder. Evidence that severe depression is mitigated by CBT is also lacking, with anti-depressant medications still viewed as significantly more effective than CBT, although success with CBT for depression was observed beginning in the 1990s.

Chronic Fatigue Syndrome

CBT has been shown to be moderately effective for treating chronic fatigue syndrome.

VARIATIONS OF VERBAL PSYCHOTHERAPY

Psychotherapy, in one form or another, has probably been practiced since human languages developed. Sympathetic listening, suggestion, exhortation, and confession have all been used throughout history to reduce depression, fear, anxiety, and ambivalence. However, systematic verbal psychotherapy as we now know it can be traced back to she creative genius of Sigmund Freud in the late nineteenth century. Freud began work with Charcot and then Breur, employing hypnotism to alleviate hysterical symptoms. He soon discovered that hypnotism had two major failings. First, many potential patients could not be hypnotised; second, hypnotic "cures" did not prevent the occurrence of new symptoms. In his search for an alternative, Freud discovered that the illness could also be treated by having patients talk freely and extensively about themselves, their feelings, their lives, and anything else that came to mind. This procedure developed into the "talking cure": psychoanalysis.

With psychoanalysis as a model and stimulus, many different forms of psychotherapy have been developed over the years. Like psychoanalysis, most of them have evolved from theories of personality. Most personality theories have different conceptions of human nature, of psychological health, and of psychopathology and its development. These conceptions typically dictate specific goals for treatment, as well as the therapeutic process by which change can be achieved and the goals reached. Thus. Freud viewed early childhood experiences as crucial to further development, and psychoanalysis focuses on uncovering repressed memories of those experiences. Alfred Adler considered feelings of inferiority to be a critical factor in neuroses; his therapy, therefore, aims at rectifying those feelings and altering the life style which evolved to compensate for them. These various theories of personality and therapy are usually referred to as "schools," under the name of its creator—e.g., Rogerian, Adlerian, Sullivanian, Freudian.

Unfortunately, these diverse positions are often viewed as religious, each being seen as the only and final answer to all problems. If one attempted to compare these models based on the writing of their most zealous adherents (who are often the most prolific as well), they would each appear to be quite different in many critical ways. However, the differences are more apparent in terminology than in actual therapeutic practice (Weiner. 1976). Furthermore, the adherents of the various schools do not all practice the same way. Wolberg (1967) has suggested that the variations *within* schools are often greater than those *between* schools. Consequently, these self-applied labels do not reflects real differences between approaches.

Psychoanalysis

Classic psychoanalysis is the model for most current psychotherapies. This approach was developed over many years by Freud as he sought to understand and modify human behaviour. The ideas and procedures of psychoanalysis have remained relatively unchanged since his death in 1939. Despite the incursions and modifications made by the neo-Freudian and psychodynamic therapies, classic psychoanalysis retains much influence, prestige, and something of a mystique.

According to Freud, the seeds of neurosis are planted in childhood, when the child fails to pass successfully through the oral, anal, or phallic stages of development. As a result of conflict, trauma, overindulgence, or underindulgence, the child becomes fixated at some level. Unacceptable impulses are repressed, and various defence mechanisms are employed to keep them under control.

The defensive network gradually expands and solidifies, and it becomes more and more difficult to deal with new life experiences and normal day-to-day environmental stresses. By the time a full-blown neurosis develops, a substantial part of life experience has been repressed, and the individual is still plagued by anxiety, guilt, and the like. The task of psychoanalysis is to make the person aware of the repressed material, recognise that it is a harmless residue of childhood fears and confusion, and thus accept the feelings and end the defensive process. As a result, the person would then be more open to experience and better able to function, while the major symptoms and distress would be eliminated.

Free Association. The primary tool of psychoanalysis is *free association;* the person is told to talk about whatever comes to mind. He or she can follow any train of thought, discuss any experience, person, or feeling. The stream of association moves from one topic to another, sometimes dealing with important issues, other times not. Periodically the person touches on a focal issue which is close to the defensive structure or the depressed material. Early in therapy, these critical associations are infrequent. Also, they produce great distress and can be considered only briefly. However, over time the person becomes more and more capable of considering such highly sensitive material, and the association stream moves closer and closer to deeply repressed issues.

Interpretation. Of course, if the process were limited to free association, the patient could do this therapy alone. The therapist serves two critical functions, without which the treatment could not work. First, he or she helps the associative process along by making periodic *interpretations.* These are statements which relate various aspects of the person's behaviour, explain something, provide new information which helps to clarify the association, or point out something of which the person was unaware. Interpretations can range from simple declarative statements such as, "You're angry about that!" to questions such as, "Is that what you really want to do?" to mini speeches. Regardless of their specific form, they are designed to move the patient in the direction of unconscious material.

The proper use of interpretation is the therapist's greatest and most difficult responsibility. First of all, the interpretation must be *accurate.* The therapist must have tremendous insight into the person's thoughts and feelings, as well as considerable knowledge about behaviour and psychopathology, to know what a particular response means. Second, the interpretation must be *timed* properly. Unless the person is ready to hear and consider the material, it can break a train of thought and temporarily disrupt the whole course of therapy. Finally, the interpretation must be of the right level or *depth.* That is, it must present something that is just slightly beyond the person's current level of understanding. If it deals with material which is still too threatening, it will be ignored or perhaps arouse too much distress and interfere with progress. Conversely, it must do more than repeat what the person already knows. The effective interpretation leads but does not push.

The goal of both free association and interpretation is to promote *insight:* understanding and acceptance of unconscious material. The terms "insight" and "interpretation" are deceptively simple. Many nonprofessionals assume that the therapist sits back "analysing" the patient, and then suddenly makes one brilliant interpretation which gets right to the heart of the problem, such as "Aha, you really hated it when your mother bathed you, and that is why you have a phobia for water!" The patient then has a sudden burst of insight after which all troubles vanish; the so-called "aha" experience makes everything clear. In reality, the process of therapy is exceedingly slow and irregular. It involves many small steps, including frequent dead ends and periods of backsliding, when progress is reversed. A complete analysis can require three to five years of treatment, with five sessions per week.

The session-by-session progress in therapy involves a process known as *working through* (Hartley and Strupp, 1980). The therapist's interpretations are often repeated, rephrased, and directed to different situations, experiences, and associations which have some common element. The person sometimes rejects the interpretation and sometimes accepts part of it; rarely is it totally understood and accepted at any one time. Gradually the person begins to understand, and then to accept what is understood. Even at that point, the process is not complete. At its ultimate, insight involves the ability to generalise and to apply understanding to various new experiences, as well as to be aware of the childhood sources of distress. Thus, by the end of treatment, the person can provide his or her own interpretations, explaining feelings and behaviour and identifying the sources of new distress.

Transference. The therapist, we have said, serves two critical functions, the first being interpretation. The second involves facilitating and helping the person work through a *transference neurosis.* The neurotic person employs various defences to control anxiety, guilt, and id impulses. These defences result in some distortion of reality. This distortion occurs with the analyst in therapy, in the same manner as with other people in other situations. For example, a person who uses projection might see the analyst—rather than the self—as angry. This process is known as *transference.* Transference is not simply recognised by the analyst but is deliberately fostered. The person lies on a couch while the analyst is seated behind, out of sight. (This position is designed to facilitate the associative process.) The analyst remains almost anonymous, avoiding many of the usual social amenities before and after sessions and remaining relatively silent during sessions. Interpretations are made infrequently. The therapist is relatively passive, providing a blank screen for the person to play against. Faced with this relative vacuum, the person is free to create a picture of what the analyst is like. This picture is distorted by the defensive processes. Furthermore, because the person is steeped in associations to unconscious and emotionally charged material, the analyst becomes involved in these matters. Eventually the entire neurosis is re-created with the analyst as focus: the transference neurosis. For example, the person might begin to see the analyst as a rejecting parent, critical of his or her achievements. Or the analyst might become the focus of sexual urges and a fantasied sexual object. It would be difficult for the analyst to get the person to see how he or she is distorting experience outside of sessions; after all, the analyst is not there and does not know the person's family, friends, and other important objects. However, the transference reaction can be interpreted more easily precisely because the person knows that the analyst it not a parent or lover, and is not critical, seductive, angry, and so on. Thus, the person gains insight into the distortion and its motivation by working through the transference neurosis. This insight is then generalised to behaviour and people outside of the analyst's office. This process is the core of psychoanalysis (Wolberg, 1967).

Countertransference. Just as the person brings his or her conflicts, anxieties, and defences to therapy, so too does the therapist come to the office with family problems, financial concerns, and psychological difficulties. While ideally the therapist's personality and problems should remain apart from the therapy, this is not always the case. In a manner analogous to transference, the therapist sometimes distorts the person's behaviour and feelings and responds to things other than the material itself.

This process can be a mild interference with misinterpretation of certain communications, such as failure to perceive anger or inability to recognise certain types of conflicts. Or, at the other extreme, the therapist can develop strong emotional reactions to the patient, including hostility and sexual arousal. In either case, this process is called *Countertransference* and interferes with treatment. The major strategy for dealing with countertransference is for the therapist to have his or her own psychoanalysis. In fact, a personal analysis is a requirement and one of the major training vehicles for prospective analysts. In this way, the therapist eliminates most of his or her own conflicts and defensive blind spots, and is thus more open to the diverse materials presented. In addition, the therapist can examine his or her own emotional reactions to the person and use them as clues to the effect on others.

Resistance. Psychotherapy, of any form, is a necessarily painful and threatening process. The person must continually deal with highly stressful issues: feelings of inadequacy and guilt, terrifying anxiety unacceptable urges, and emotional reactions. In addition, change itself is a terrifying prospect. Even though the person's current adjustment is painful and unsatisfactory, it is nevertheless an adjustment. Things might be worse. And so, persons approach each therapy session with ambivalence and trepidation.

Sometimes they overcome these feelings and come to grips with the difficult issues, but at other times they avoid them. This avoidance, which is largely an unconscious process, is called *resistance.* Resistance can take many forms. The person might miss a session or come late when therapy is focusing on an especially painful issue. Free association can be stymied as the person reports that nothing comes to mind. Conversely, irrelevant material or issues might be raised, including complaints about the therapist. The therapist's bills may go unpaid, or the accuracy of interpretations may be denied. As with transference, resistance is a potential form of interference which can be turned into a valuable therapeutic tool. The therapist carefully monitors resistive behaviour, identifies its source or motivation, and eventually interprets them to the person. Ultimately, the interpretation of resistance and the associated unconscious processes is one of the most important activities of psychoanalysis (Fine, 1973).

Neo-Freudian and Ego Psychology Approaches

Almost from the beginning of the analytic movement, many of Freud's followers began to question his theory and therapeutic strategy. These questions have ranged from rather esoteric points to basic issues, and have led to corresponding changes in theory and technique. In this section, we will consider some of the more important changes which have been adopted by various analytic therapies.

Weiner (1976) has distinguished between therapeutic strategies and tactics. *Strategies* are the guiding principles which determine the direction of therapy: its goals and the plans for reaching them (e.g., stimulating a transference neurosis). *Tactics* are the procedures and techniques used to implement the strategy (e.g., making interpretations, asking questions). We will first consider modifications in strategy and then innovations in tactics.

Therapeutic Strategies. Human behaviour, according to Freud, is rooted in biological factors, especially instinctual (id) drives. The most important of these is Eros: sexuality. The major "psychological" factor in behaviour is the ego, which is more a servant of the id than an independent force. The environment, like the ego is of secondary importance. Its primary influence is negative or repressive and is exerted during childhood. Neurosis is considered to be largely a result of society's inhibition of the expression of sexuality. Thus, the primary therapeutic strategies are designed to uncover and free the instinctual drives. Little attention is paid to the person's current environment or to any nondefensive aspects of the ego. Freud's emphasis on sexuality (and biological factors in general), and his relative neglect of the ego and environmental influences on behaviour, have been the subject of considerable criticism from within the analytic camp (as well as from other orientations).

Two of Freud's earliest critics were Jung and Adler, both of whom felt that he placed far too much emphasis on sexuality. Jung hypothesised that human beings had a *collective or inherited unconscious* in addition to the personal unconscious emphasised by Freud. One of the major goals of Jungian analysis is to foster insight into both types of unconscious forces and facilitate an accommodation between both of them and the environment (Weiner, 1976). Adler argued that all people are born with feelings of *inferiority* and *helplessness.* In an attempt to compensate for these anxiety-provoking feelings, they strive for superiority and develop unique life styles to deal with environmental demands and pressures. Adlerian therapy emphasises the person's current life situation and the way that situation affects and is affected by the life style. Interpretations focus on the ongoing interaction between inferiority feelings, life style, and daily events: accomplishments, failures, relationships with others, and so on.

Among those who criticised Freud for his comparative disregard of social and environmental influences on behaviour, Harry Stack Sullivan, Karen Homey, and Erich Fromm are the most representative. While their particular theories and emphases varied, all three highlighted the central role of *social* factors in shaping adult as well as early childhood behaviour. For example. Homey described how the neurotic adapts a defensive posture characterised by moving toward people away from people, or against people in an effort to curtail and avoid anxiety. Thus, an analysis based on one of these models would emphasise current interpersonal functioning. Interpretations would focus on conflicts between the person, the environment, and defensive interpersonal style, rather than on intrapsychic conflicts and drives.

Probably the most significant modification of Freudian theory has come from the *ego psychologists,* including Erikson, Hartmann, Kris, and Loewenstein. According to these theorists, the ego is independent of the id rather than its servant. The ego has its own energy and functions, including thinking, remembering, perceiving, and conscious awareness. All behaviour is not motivated by drive reduction; instead, the ego has its own sources of gratification and motivation, such as love, creativity, and achievement.

The healthy adult is not bound by unconscious instinctual forces but has a good deal of conscious control over behaviour and strives to grow and improve. The personality is not solidified by puberty; instead, growth and development continue throughout life. The neurotic individual is characterised by poor ego development. Like children, neurotics are much more under the control of instincts and the environment. Thus, they are less capable of determining the course of their lives and fulfilling their potential.

Treatment based on an ego psychology model strives to strengthen the ego and increase the degree of conscious and adaptive control over behaviour. In keeping with the analogy between the neurotic and the child, Hartley and Strupp (1980) have referred to therapy as "reparenting"; the therapist, like the parent, helps the person to become more independent and capable of functioning effectively. Little attention is paid to historical and instinctual influences on development. The emphasis is on current conflicts and anxieties, and the inadequacy of current coping strategies (Weiner, 1976). The ego analysts, like most other neo-Freudians, stress the transference neurosis less than the classic analysts. Transference is either viewed as an impediment to therapy and quickly resolved or it is interpreted as a reflection of current interpersonal style. In neither case is it facilitated by the therapist or viewed as a critical element of therapy.

Therapy Techniques. The theoretical conceptions of the post-Freudian analysts lead to different ways of thinking about behaviour and of understanding patient reports. As a result, their therapeutic strategies differ greatly. Their techniques, however, are quite similar (Weiner, 1976). As stated previously, there is greater variation between individual therapists than between schools.

One reason for this peculiar pattern is that research has failed to identify a set of specific techniques to be applied in a particular way at a particular time with a particular client. Therapists are left to their own experience and "best guess" as to what to do. Thus it would be quite unusual for two therapists to provide the same interpretation at any point. This fact is dramatised at case conferences and supervision sessions, when recordings of therapy sessions are reviewed. While there is often agreement as to very poor and highly effective interpretations, the middle ground is the area where each listener responds differently.

In reviewing the various psychodynamic techniques, it is difficult to even identify their source, let alone tie them to any particular school. The most notable changes from Freudian procedures probably involve the activity and behaviour of the therapist. Without the need to develop a transference neurosis, the therapist became free of the classic need for passivity and anonymity. Therapist and client now sit face-to-face in armchairs.

Some therapists like to sit behind a desk while others prefer a more casual arrangement such as around a coffee table. Style of dress also varies with the person, although coat and tie (for men) and dress or skirt and blouse (for women) predominate. The general tone of the therapist-client relationship is often more relaxed and pleasant. While the use of the title "Dr." is most common, some therapists and clients are on a first name basis. While the therapist's personal life is still usually kept out of the relationship, there is less rigidity about this as well. Pre—and post-session conversation takes on a more social atmosphere, with occasional references to vacation plans, family activities, and attitudes about public events. References to personal experiences (e.g., "You know, I felt that way once") are also sometimes used therapeutically by some therapists. A positive relationship is often attempted, and is used to facilitate therapeutic progress.

Therapy sessions are also marked by greater therapist responsiveness. In addition to interpretations typical responses include questions, clarifications, reflections. exclamations and confrontations (Weiner, 1976). Open-ended and indirect questions are most often employed. Clarifications are responses which move the patient in a certain direction while providing no new information. For example, "That seems to be an important issue; I think we should focus on it some more." Clarifications are similar in effect to indirect questions. Reflections summarise and integrate client responses. They usually involve some feelings the patient has directly or indirectly expressed. Examples include. "You seem to be angry," and "I have the feeling you are afraid of what you might learn." Weiner (1976) defines exclamations as noncommittal response facilitators, including "Mm-hmm," "Uh-huh," and "I see." They convey the therapist's interest and reinforce the topic of conversation. Confrontations give the client new information about his or her behaviour. They typically involve direct, objective statements about specific responses or issues, rather than the non-definitive hypotheses offered in interpretations. For example, "You've been late for the last three sessions, and we need to talk about that," or "You say that it's not important, but I find that hard to believe." Confrontations are used sparingly because of their potentially threatening or conflict producing nature.

They are usually reserved for roadblocks or issues left unresolved by more indirect means.

It is clear that free association is no longer the main form of interaction. The process is much more of a two-way conversation, in contrast to the semimonologue format of classic psychoanalysis. The dialogue moves back and forth between the two participants, although the client still does most of the talking.

The topics covered deal much more with current experiences and interpersonal relationships, and with ego-relevant issues (e.g., feelings of competence, the direction of one's life, sources of pleasure). Some therapists (notably Adlerian) give clients homework assignments—for example, to initiate interpersonal activity (Mosak and Dreikurs, 1973).

The nature of a therapeutic interaction can best be portrayed by an example. The following transcript segments are from Wolberg (1967), a prominent therapist and training analyst. The comments in parentheses indicate the nature and purpose of certain therapist responses. The first segment illustrates transference and its interpretation.

Th. It sounds as if you would like to let loose with me, but you are afraid of what my response would be. *(summarising and restating)*

Pt. I get so excited by what is happening here. I feel I'm being held back by needing to be nice. I'd like to blast loose sometimes, but I don't dare.

Th. Because you fear my reaction?

Pt. The worst thing would be that you wouldn't like me. You wouldn't speak to me friendly; you wouldn't smile, you'd feel you can't treat me and discharge me from treatment. But I know this isn't so, I know it.

Th. Where do you think these attitudes come from?

Pt. When I was nine years old, I read a lot about great men in history. I'd quote them and be dramatic. I'd want a sword at my side; I'd dress like an Indian. Mother would scold me. Don't frown, don't talk so much. Sit on your hands, over and over again. I did all kinds of things. I was a naughty child. She told me I'd be hurt. Then at fourteen I fell off a horse and broke my back. I had to be in bed. Mother then told me on the day I went riding not to, that I'd get hurt because the ground was frozen. I was a stubborn, self-willed child. Then I went against her will and suffered an accident that changed my life, a fractured back. Her attitude was, "I told you so." I was put in a cast and kept in bed for months.

Th. You were punished, so to speak, by this accident.

Pt. But I gained attention and love from mother for the first time. I felt so good. I'm ashamed to tell you this. Before I healed I opened the cast and tried to walk to make myself sick again so I could stay in bed longer.

Th. How does that connect up with your impulse to be sick now and stay in bed so much? *(The patient has these tendencies, of which she is ashamed).*

Pt. Oh...*(pause)*

Th. What do you think?

Pt. Oh, my God, how infantile, how ungrown up. *(pause)* It must be so, I want people to love me and be sorry for me. Oh, my God. How completely childish. It is, *is* that. My mother must have ignored me when I was little, and I wanted so to be loved. *(This sounds like insight.)*

Th. So that it may have been threatening to go back to being self-willed and unloved after you got out of the cast. *(interpretation)*

Pt. It did. My life changed. I became meek and controlled. I couldn't get angry or stubborn afterward.

Th. Perhaps if you go back to being stubborn with *me,* you would be returning to how you were before, that is, active stubborn but unloved.

Pt. *(excitedly)* And, therefore, losing your love. I need you, but after all you aren't going to reject me. The pattern is so established now that the threat of the loss of love is too overwhelming with everybody, and I've got to keep myself from acting selfish or angry.

(Wolberg, 1967, p. 662)

The patient in the next segment is a woman who began to experience a variety of symptoms after becoming pregnant and quitting her job.

Pt. And on Wednesday I began thinking *(laughs)* The funniest thing happened. I was working in the kitchen and suddenly I got that awful feeling. It came on me like a squirmy wave,. I got scared and tense and the muscles back here *(strokes the muscles in the back of her neck)* got tight and my head filled up as if I had a tight bandage around, and queasy feelings in the pit of my stomach.

Th. Mm hmm.

Pt. And there was something else that happened. I knew something was bothering me and I just didn't know what.

Th. Mm hmm.

Pt. Something bothering. It's like something I had to do supposed to do. It was such a frustrating feeling. *(pause)*

Th. A frustrating feeling, as if you just couldn't grasp what was going on?

Pt. Yes, just like that. So out of desperation, I guess, I turned on the radio. The first thing was one of those breakfast Mr. and Mrs. programmes. They were bantering back and forth, and I detected a snide attitude toward the woman. This made me boil. And all of a sudden the thing flashed in mind. It came to me that I promised my husband that I'd buy him several pairs of socks a week ago. I've been putting if off, and putting it off, and not thinking of it. When I'd go out, it wouldn't occur to me to get the socks until I'd remember when I got home. *(laughs)*

Th. *(smiles)* You suspected something was going on inside of you?

Pt. I knew it. As I was listening to the programme, it came to me. I suddenly got mad, furious and said, "Darn him, why doesn't he buy socks for himself? Why should I do his dirty work?" *(laughs)*

Th. You resented his making this demand on you?

Pt. *(laughs)* No question about that. My next thought *(laughs)*...it was, Damn him, why doesn't he buy socks for *himself.* Why do I have to do *all* the dirty work around here. He wants and expects me to be a slave, just tidy up the place and get nowheres. I thought of him in his nice comfortable office. Then I thought of how wonderful I felt when I was working. At least I felt appreciated and didn't get the constant criticism I get now.

Th. This must really burn you up.

Pt. I suppose marriage is a sacrifice. I do love the children, I don't know what they'd do if I went back to work. But it's the noise, noise, the howling of the kids and the criticism of my husband.

Th. When you were working, you felt you were doing something significant that gave you status.

Pt. You know, doctor, I sometimes feel as if I was absolutely crazy to give up my job. I don't know what I imagined marriage was going to be like.

Th. And it turned out to be something where you have to take care of howling kids and buy socks for your husband.

Pt. You know, as soon as I had these thoughts I got very mad. I screamed out loud, "Why doesn't he buy the socks himself." I had a picture of him *(laughs)* this is silly...slipping on, *(laughs)* slipping on a banana peel and turning a half somersault in the air, I started laughing. Doctor, do I want him to break his neck? When this all happened I noticed that I felt better. My headache went away and the stiffness in the neck. *(Apparently, realisation and acknowledgment of her hostility removed the necessity for its repression and its conversion into symptoms.)*

Before concluding this overview of new-Freudian technique, one further contrast with classic psychoanalysis must be mentioned. As indicated above, classic analysis typically requires five (fifty-minute) sessions per week for several years. This type of intervention obviously is extremely costly in terms of money as well as in a patient and therapist time. Many neu-Freudians have argued that such deep, extensive analysis is of intellectual value rather than a necessity for effective treatment. Many of the modified approaches attempt to speed up the process. Sessions are still often fifty minutes, but longer sessions are not uncommon. Sessions typically are held once or (at most) twice a week, and treatment usually lasts from six months to one to two years. It is presumed that the focus on more current issues and greater therapist activity can produce meaningful change with less intensive and extensive treatment.

A related change involves the timing and nature of termination. Classic analysis continues until all major unconscious conflicts are resolved and the client has relatively complete insight into his or her experience. The briefer neo-Freudian approaches often conclude with less than total personality reorganisation. Given the emphasis on current experience, good adjustment with sufficient ego strength to withstand future stress and to grow after treatment are more typical expectations. In any case, termination is always a painful process, much like the adolescent's leaving home for the first time. The client is eager to try to live independently, yet questions his or her ability to function without the therapist. For this reason, termination is usually a gradual weaning process, requiring several sessions and marked by ambivalence and a sense of loss.

4

Emotions and Social Psychology

Emotion is a common component in persuasion, social influence, and attitude change. Much of attitude research emphasized the importance of affective or emotion components. Emotion works hand-in-hand with the cognitive process, or the way we think, about an issue or situation. Emotional appeals are commonly found in advertising, health campaigns and political messages. Recent examples include no-smoking health campaigns and political campaign advertising emphasizing the fear of terrorism. Attitudes and attitude objects are functions of cognitive, affective and conative components. Attitudes are part of the brain's associative networks, the spider-like structures residing in long term memory that consist of affective and cognitive nodes.

By activating an affective or emotion node, attitude change may be possible, though affective and cognitive components tend to be intertwined. In primarily affective networks, it is more difficult to produce cognitive counterarguments in the resistance to persuasion and attitude change.

Affective forecasting, otherwise known as intuition or the prediction of emotion, also impacts attitude change. Research suggests that predicting emotions is an important component of decision making, in addition to the cognitive processes. How we feel about an outcome may override purely cognitive rationales.

In terms of research methodology, the challenge for researchers is measuring emotion and subsequent impacts on attitude. Since we cannot see into the brain, various models and measurement tools have been constructed to obtain emotion and attitude information.

Measures may include the use of physiological cues like facial expressions, vocal changes, and other body rate measures. For instance, fear is associated with raised eyebrows, increased heart rate and increase body tension (Dillard, 1994). Other methods include concept or network mapping, and using primes or word cues.

Classification

There exist basic and complex categories, where some basic emotions can be modified in some way to form complex emotions (e.g. Paul Ekman). In one model, the complex emotions could arise from cultural conditioning or association combined with the basic emotions. Alternatively, analogous to the way primary colors combine, *primary emotions* could blend to form the full spectrum of human emotional experience. For example interpersonal anger and disgust could blend to form contempt.

Robert Plutchik proposed a three-dimensional "circumplex model" which describes the relations among emotions. This model is similar to a colour wheel. The vertical dimension represents intensity, and the circle represents degrees of similarity among the emotions. He posited eight primary emotion dimensions arranged as four pairs of opposites. Some have also argued for the existence of meta-emotions which are emotions about emotions.

Another important means of distinguishing emotions concerns their occurrence in time. Some emotions occur over a period of seconds (e.g. surprise), whereas others can last years (e.g. love). The latter could be regarded as a long term *tendency* to have an emotion regarding a certain object rather than an emotion proper (though this is disputed).

A distinction is then made between emotion episodes and emotional dispositions. Dispositions are also comparable to character traits, where someone may be said to be generally disposed to experience certain emotions, though about different objects. For example an irritable person is generally disposed to feel irritation more easily or quickly than others do. Finally, some theorists (e.g. Klaus Scherer, 2005) place emotions within a more general category of 'affective states' where affective states can also include emotion-related phenomena such as pleasure and pain, motivational states (e.g. hunger or curiosity), moods, dispositions and traits. The neural correlates of hate have been investigated with an fMRI procedure. In this experiment, people had their brains scanned while viewing pictures of people they hated. The results showed increased activity in the medial frontal gyrus, right putamen, bilaterally in the premotor cortex, in the frontal pole, and bilaterally in the medial insula of the human brain. The researchers concluded that there is a distinct pattern of brain activity that occurs when people are experiencing hatred.

Theories

Theories about emotions stretch back at least as far as the Ancient Greek Stoics, as well as Plato and Aristotle. We also see sophisticated theories in the works of philosophers such as Rene Descartes' Baruch Spinoza and David

Hume. Later theories of emotions tend to be informed by advances in empirical research. Often theories are not mutually exclusive and many researchers incorporate multiple perspectives in their work.

Somatic Theories

Somatic theories of emotion claim that bodily responses rather than judgements are essential to emotions. The first modern version of such theories comes from William James in the 1880s. The theory lost favour in the 20th century, but has regained popularity more recently due largely to theorists such as John Cacioppo, Antonio Damasio, Joseph E. LeDoux and Robert Zajonc who are able to appeal to neurological evidence.

James-Lange Theory

William James, in the article 'What is an Emotion?' (*Mind*, 9, 1884: 188-205), argued that emotional experience is largely due to the experience of bodily changes. The Danish psychologist Carl Lange also proposed a similar theory at around the same time, so this position is known as the James-Lange theory. This theory and its derivatives state that a changed situation leads to a changed bodily state. As James says "the perception of bodily changes as they occur *is* the emotion." James further claims that "we feel sad because we cry, angry because we strike, afraid because we tremble, and neither we cry, strike, nor tremble because we are sorry, angry, or fearful, as the case may be."

This theory is supported by experiments in which by manipulating the bodily state, a desired emotion is induced. Such experiments also have therapeutic implications (e.g. in laughter therapy, dance therapy). The James-Lange theory is often misunderstood because it seems counter-intuitive. Most people believe that emotions give rise to emotion-specific actions: i.e. "I'm crying because I'm sad", or "I ran away because I was scared". The James-Lange theory, conversely, asserts that *first* we react to a situation (running away and crying happen before the emotion), and *then* we interpret our actions into an emotional response. In this way, emotions serve to explain and organize our own actions to us.

Neurobiological Theories

Based on discoveries made through neural mapping of the limbic system, the neurobiological explanation of human emotion is that emotion is a pleasant or unpleasant mental state organized in the limbic system of the mammalian brain. If distinguished from reactive responses of reptiles, emotions would then be mammalian elaborations of general vertebrate arousal patterns, in which neuro-chemicals (e.g., dopamine, noradrenaline, and serotonin) step-up or step-down the brain's activity level, as visible in body movements, gestures, and postures. In mammals, primates, and human beings, feelings are displayed as emotion cues. For example, the human emotion of love is proposed to have evolved from paleocircuits of the mammalian brain (specifically, modules of the cingulate gyrus) which facilitate the care, feeding, and grooming of offspring.

Paleocircuits are neural platforms for bodily expression configured millions of years before the advent of cortical circuits for speech. They consist of pre-configured pathways or networks of nerve cells in the forebrain, brain stem and spinal cord. They evolved prior to the earliest mammalian ancestors, as far back as the jawless fish, to control motor function.

Presumably, before the mammalian brain, life in the non-verbal world was automatic, preconscious, and predictable. The motor centres of reptiles react to sensory cues of vision, sound, touch, chemical, gravity, and motion with pre-set body movements and programmed postures.

With the arrival of night-active mammals, circa 180 million years ago, smell replaced vision as the dominant sense, and a different way of responding arose from the olfactory sense, which is proposed to have developed into mammalian emotion and emotional memory. In the Jurassic Period, the mammalian brain invested heavily in olfaction to succeed at night as reptiles slept—one explanation for why olfactory lobes in mammalian brains are proportionally larger than in the reptiles. These odor pathways gradually formed the neural blueprint for what was later to become our limbic brain.

Emotions are thought to be related to activity in brain areas that direct our attention, motivate our behaviour, and determine the significance of what is going on around us. Pioneering work by Broca (1878), Papez (1937), and MacLean (1952) suggested that emotion is related to a group of structures in the center of the brain called the limbic system, which includes the hypothalamus, cingulate cortex, hippocampi, and other structures.

More recent research has shown that some of these limbic structures are not as directly related to emotion as others are, while some non-limbic structures have been found to be of greater emotional relevance.

Prefrontal Cortex

There is ample evidence that the left prefrontal cortex is activated by stimuli that cause positive approach. If attractive stimuli can selectively activate a region of the brain, then logically the converse should hold, that selective activation of that region of the brain should cause a stimulus to be judged more positively. This was demonstrated for moderately attractive visual stimuli and replicated and extended to include negative stimuli. Two neurobiological models of emotion in the prefrontal cortex made opposing predictions. The Valence Model predicted that anger, a negative emotion, would activate the right prefrontal cortex. The Direction Model predicted that anger, an approach emotion, would activate the left prefrontal cortex. The second model was supported. This still left open the question of whether the opposite of approach in the prefrontal cortex is better described as moving away (Direction Model), as unmoving but with strength and resistance (Movement Model), or as unmoving with passive yielding (Action Tendency Model). Support for the Action Tendency Model (passivity related to right prefrontal activity) comes from research on shyness and research on behavioural inhibition. Research that tested the competing hypotheses generated by all four models also supported the Action Tendency Model.

Homeostatic Emotion

Another neurological approach, described by Bud Craig in 2003, distinguishes between two classes of emotion. "Classical emotions" include lust, anger and fear, and they are feelings evoked by *environmental stimuli,* which motivate us (in these examples, respectively, to copulate/fight/flee). "Homeostatic emotions" are feelings evoked by *internal body states*, which modulate our behaviour. Thirst, hunger, feeling hot or cold (core temperature), feeling sleep deprived, salt hunger and air hunger are all examples of homeostatic emotion; each is a signal from a body system saying "Things aren't right down here. Drink/eat/move into the shade/put on something warm/sleep/ lick salty rocks/breathe." We begin to feel a homeostatic emotion when one of these systems drifts out of balance, and the feeling prompts us to do what is necessary to restore that system to balance. Pain is a homeostatic emotion telling us "Things aren't right here. Withdraw and protect."

Cognitive Theories

There are some theories on emotions arguing that cognitive activity in the form of judgements, evaluations, or thoughts is necessary in order for an emotion to occur. This, argued by Richard Lazarus, is necessary to capture the fact that emotions are about something or have intentionality. Such cognitive activity may be conscious or unconscious and may or may not take the form of conceptual processing. An influential theory here is that of Lazarus. A prominent philosophical exponent is Robert C. Solomon (e.g. *The Passions, Emotions and the Meaning of Life*, 1993). The theory proposed by Nico Frijda where appraisal leads to action tendencies is another example. It has also been suggested that emotions (affect heuristics, feelings and gut-feeling reactions) are often used as shortcuts to process information and influence behaviour.

Perceptual Theory

A recent hybrid of the somatic and cognitive theories of emotion is the perceptual theory. This theory is neo-Jamesian in arguing that bodily responses are central to emotions, yet it emphasises the meaningfulness of emotions or the idea that emotions are about something, as is recognised by cognitive theories.

The novel claim of this theory is that conceptually based cognition is unnecessary for such meaning. Rather the bodily changes themselves *perceive* the meaningful content of the emotion because of being causally triggered by certain situations. In this respect, emotions are held to be analogous to faculties such as vision or touch, which provide information about the relation between the subject and the world in various ways. A sophisticated defence of this view is found in philosopher Jesse Prinz's book *Gut Reactions* and psychologist James Laird's book *Feelings.*

Affective Events Theory

This a communication-based theory developed by Howard M. Weiss and Russell Cropanzano (1996), that looks at the causes, structures, and consequences of emotional experience (especially in work contexts). This theory suggests that emotions are influenced and caused by events which in turn influence attitudes and behaviors.

This theoretical frame also emphasizes *time* in that human beings experience what they call emotion episodes—a "series of emotional states extended over time and organized around an underlying theme". This theory has been utilized by numerous researchers to better understand emotion from a communicative lens, and was reviewed further by Howard M. Weiss and Daniel J. Beal in their article, *Reflections on Affective Events Theory* published in *Research on Emotion in Organizations* in 2005.

Cannon-Bard Theory

In the Cannon-Bard theory, Walter Bradford Cannon argued against the dominance of the James-Lange theory regarding the physiological aspects of emotions in the second edition of *Bodily Changes in Pain, Hunger, Fear and Rage.* Where James argued that emotional behaviour often precedes or defines the emotion, Cannon and Bard argued that the emotion arises first and then stimulates typical behaviour.

Two-Factor Theory

Another cognitive theory is the Singer-Schachter theory. This is based on experiments purportedly showing that subjects can have different emotional reactions despite being placed into the same physiological state with an injection of adrenaline. Subjects were observed to express either anger or amusement depending on whether another person in the situation displayed that emotion. Hence, the combination of the appraisal of the situation (cognitive) and the participants' reception of adrenaline or a placebo together determined the response. This experiment has been criticized in Jesse Prinz's (2004) *Gut Reactions*.

Component Process Model

A recent version of the cognitive theory regards emotions more broadly as the synchronization of many different bodily and cognitive components. Emotions are identified with the overall process whereby low-level cognitive appraisals, in particular the processing of relevance, trigger bodily reactions, behaviors, feelings, and actions.

EARLY EMOTIONAL REACTION

Some psychologists hold that cries and thrashes of limbs of a new born infant are emotional in nature. But one cannot assert this fact definitely. When, however, the infant learns to smile at the human face it shows an emotional reaction. Perhaps, this early smile will soon change into hearty laughter at a later age. As a child grows, he may subdue some of his more violent emotions like anger and dislike. This is partly due to his observing his elders whom he finds expressing their feelings in a controlled manner and whom he imitates. Partly it is due to adult resenting any violent display of emotions. Perhaps it is also due to the fact that with increasing age the child gets a greater command over his language and learns other forms of expression through symbols and gestures and hence no longer needs violent bodily demonstration to give vent to his feelings.

Be that as it may, children's display of emotions is more violent and overt than that of an adult. The conditions that provide an outburst of emotion change with growth. An Infant's emotion is aroused by such stimuli as affect him directly, and in which he is vitally concerned. As the child grows older, his world gets larger and his interests also change. It is but natural that he should become impervious to events that produced a more violent emotional response at an earlier period.

During infancy any situation that blocks the natural course of satisfaction or a child's interests or desires may cause an emotional stress. Perhaps the child wants to accompany the parents in their outing, but the latter would not take him out. He starts crying out, as a result of the emotional strain caused by this apparent parental rejection. Perhaps the parents in order to pacify him would give him a doll to play with. At other times the doll would have pleased the infant, but now this would not do. It has become a poor substitute. He was eager to participate in adult activity that was denied him. The child wreaks his vengeance on the doll which becomes an object of parental deception. His vengeance may assume a form of cruelty which the child is not otherwise expected to display. This is gradually formed into a habit and the child gets cross and peevish, and throws up tantrums. To avoid this, we must, understand the child and his needs for the moment. Perhaps we are not able to satisfy his needs, perhaps satisfaction is not always desirable. In such cases we must be able to give him a substitute. When the child wants to go out with adults, he is interested in human company. Let him, if he has to be kept back at all, be given the company of others of his age group, or let someone else take him out to another place.

Emotional Reaction from Weaning to Early Schooling

Weaning is a critical stage for emotional development. As the teeth appear, children often develop symptoms of severe malady, and their good habits change. Breast-feeding has perhaps been stopped, for the child hurts his mother by his teeth. To the child, however, the reason for this stoppage is not clear. He thinks that he is being deprived of a privilege which had been his birth right. Probably, at this time a second baby is born into the family, and seems to monopolise the mother. In such a situation, it is natural for the child to become jealous of the new arrival, thinking it to be responsible for all his losses. This antipathy is often expressed in a violent form, sometimes by hurting the baby.

After weaning, while the child is engaged in individual games, he is somewhat narcissistic and self-centred, and seldom displays violent temper unless he feels that he has been unduly deprived of some of his due or thwarted in his activities. Sickly and underdeveloped children who are unable to engage themselves in play activities are, however, possessive and emotional, perhaps somewhat peevish and self-centred. They will not want adults to pay attention to any one but themselves. They do so, perhaps because they have nothing else to distract them. Perhaps their peevishness is due to ill health.

If a child is sent to school too early, he finds himself confined there for a large part of the day in a new surrounding. The first few days of school are periods of great tension and anxiety for any child, because he does not know how to get along with other children or with the teacher. The boy feels himself removed from the congenial home surroundings which he knew. He compares his situation with that of his younger brother who is happily resting with the members of his family. He feels he has been put into a strange place with strangers under a certain amount of restraint. This makes him feel somewhat jealous and wayward, not unlike the feeling he had experienced during early weaning. Perhaps he would refuse to go to school and play truant. Those more submissive may not dare do so, but they would still in the words of Shakespeare in *As You Like* it, feel like 'Crawling like a snail unwilling to school'. In order to understand this resistance to school, we must take into account his inner conflict and try to resolve it with sympathy and tact. Some of his outward behaviour, although apparently illogical, may he found to have a logic of its own, if examined in the light of the child's inner urge. Perhaps our understanding of the child will make him adjust happily with his own age group, a need that is quite imperative for his socialisation in the world at large.

By and by, the child adjusts himself to his elementary school, his playmates and his teachers. But when he is suddenly forced to leave school which has become a second home for him, and forced to enter a secondary school, new problems may arise, which will bring another set of emotional troubles and need fresh adjustment.

Emotional Conflicts in the Secondary School

Under the present set-up a child enters the secondary school after five years' primary schooling, when he is on the threshold of puberty (adolescence). If the primary and secondary schools are parts of the same institution, the conflict is not very great, for the surroundings are familiar to the child and he goes along with his old classmates. But if the school is a new one, he may not find many of his old mates there.

One must realise that this is a period of adolescence which has problems of its own. The child feels doubly isolated. He is isolated from children and adults, as are adolescents, and he is isolated with his old friends who might have joined other schools. The social isolation associated with the problems of physical growth makes the child somewhat of a withdrawing type who resolve their emotional conflicts mostly in fantasy and daydreams. Breaking of friendship causes emotional stress, and perhaps this may be aggravated for a child whose transfer to a new school is also caused by the transfer of his parents to a new place, when he is totally cut off from his old friends. A quarrel between two friends sometimes causes a severe emotional stress, and its effect should not be overlooked.

Another cause of emotional stress in this period is that social requirements sometimes force an adolescent to appear in the presence of members of the opposite sex. Adolescents, as we have seen, are extremely self-conscious, and girls especially feel highly embarrassed in such situations. This is particularly so at the age of 13 or 14. Whatever may be said in favour of co-educational institutions, and their advantages in socialisation, it is undeniable that unless both the sexes are present in at least equal numbers, the sex that is in a minority suffers a peculiar discomfort, and is subjected to severe emotional stress. Although, an adolescent craves for recognition and praise from members of the other sex, he will find a greater sense of security if the teacher belongs to the same sex. The display of the 'Calf Love' instinct in some of the girls' schools where a young male teacher is employed is fraught with great emotional and sociological dangers, even when the teacher bears an exemplary character and the girls are sobre and sophisticated. Occasional feelings of embarrassment leaving deep impressions in the minds of the young people are by no means uncommon. It is, therefore, necessary that in a secondary institution, the proportion of women teachers and male teachers should be approximately equal, so that the boys may go to an elderly guide for solution of such problems as they cannot confide in a teacher of an opposite sex. The girls, more than the boys, should have access to women teachers, who will look into their personal problems tactfully and sympathetically.

Failure in schools is a common cause of emotional disturbance, for it hurts the newly developed 'ego' (feeling of self-esteem) and makes a child lose his status both at home and in the class. It also frustrates the desire for success. Detention also means staying in the same class, reading the old books with the accompanying boredom, and spending time in the company of students whom the child had not so long ago looked down upon as his juniors. It means parting of old friends. Anyone of these factors, if taken singly, would be enough to cause strain, and the cumulative effect of many factors is most likely to create a sense of frustration and loss of interest in work, which is psychologically known as retardation.

Children are subjected to emotional disturbances in schools in other ways also. Sometimes the moral code followed at home and schools differs, and this causes a feeling of insecurity in a child, if not occasional conflict. Children coming from orthodox and conservative families find the code of conduct followed in a secular and liberal school rather problematic. Likewise, children from secular and liberal families find it hard to adjust themselves properly in a mission school or a school set up by a particular religious denomination. If such children follow their home codes in school, they are likely to be ostracised and feel isolated. If they try to bring the school codes within their family circles they are rebuked. A similar state of affairs is seen when a school is populated by one socio-economic group, and a child belonging to another group enters it. The cultural patterns and codes of conduct followed at home and school act at cross purposes and create severe strain in the child. In India such problems are created by the caste system, for caste is both a religious and a socio-economic institution and the cultural patterns of different castes show considerable variations.

Our secular schools should take note of the possible conflict between home patterns and school patterns and their likely repercussions on children. Reforms are desirable and angularities should be rounded off, no doubt, slowly. Any attempt to hasten the process will make the child a rebel, either in home or in school situations, more often in school situations, for home has imprinted its culture patterns at an early age. This is a possible calamity which we should not overlook.

In later adolescence, in high school, there may be conflicts between the vocational aspirations of the youth and those of the family. The boy may aspire to become a doctor and has acquired an interest in biological studies, but the parents, wishing to make him an engineer instead, force him to study mathematics, a subject which he dislikes. This causes the boy to begin hating studies altogether. It often results in failure with all its attendant problems, all due to the parents' lack of foresight.

Emotional conflicts may also be caused by a difference between the levels of aspiration and achievement. A student having a much higher ambition than justified by his abilities will always have a setback. He hopes to secure a high position in the class, but is disappointed when he finds that the marks obtained by him in examinations are poor. This may make his adjustment to reality rather difficult. To prevent such a state of affairs, teachers would do well by changing their standards of encouragement. Perhaps, instead of encouraging attainment, they should encourage effort. A boy whose previous work merited say, 25 per cent marks and later on 45 per cent, should be given more praise than one who improves his work from 65 per cent to 75 per cent, or is steady at 70 per cent.

Repeated failure in class examinations generally causes frustration and the level of inspiration goes down. The students lose confidence in their efforts. As a rule, whatever may be said about failures being pillars of success, they seldom stimulate a student to a higher level of aspiration. Obviously, a major contribution of the school to the proper emotional development of a child will be to adjust the level of aspiration of the children to the basic facts of reality. Depending on their innate intelligence and personality according to the opportunities available in terms of their socio-economic status, they may find it hard to cross a barrier. A wise teacher can remedy the situation by personal counselling but to succeed he must he able to secure the confidence and trust of his pupils through his superior scholarship, exemplary character, high sense of justice, fairness and sympathy.

Frustrating Emotions and Education

The course of life seldom runs smooth. Very often we come across hurdles on the path of progress. The way in which we react to these hurdles determines the emotional makeup of our pesonalities. Educationally, we are concerned with them because by proper adjustment to the situation, we may mitigate the effects of those emotions which have a frustrating effect and which are thus likely to act as hurdles in the development of a child.

Anger: As a frustrating emotion, anger is perhaps the most common feeling which has its beginnings in infancy. When we feel we are being deprived of our dues on account of somebody's fault, we get angry. Anger may vary in intensity from simple resentment or irritation to an outburst of violent rage. When we feel others are getting what is really our due, anger takes the form of jealousy. The visible signs of anger are a flush on the face and a rise in blood pressure. Its intensity increases when we are tired or hungry. Sometimes instead of being the result of a single thwarting situation, anger may be the effect of piling up of a number of irritating situations. Constantly asking foolish questions when a person is busy can make him get suddenly angry, as if the last straw has broken the camel's back. Sneers and backbites of others may produce as much anger in the mind of a child as a severe thrashing. Sometimes anger takes the form of inward aggression, and an angry child wishes himself to be very sick or even dead in order to retaliate against his father's thrashing. Perhaps subconsciously the feeling within is to cause inconvenience to or hurt the sentiments of persons who have injured his feelings. Sometimes aggression gets transferred. A child hit by the parents cannot hit them back. But he hits his younger brother or a doll, just to provide an outlet for his pent-up feelings. Perhaps, at the back of this lies the subconscious desire to wound the feelings of the aggressive parent, at least indirectly.

Perhaps the best way to prevent this frustrating emotion is to prevent development of situations that may foster in. If the teacher or the parent is impartial, there will be no occasion for jealousy. In cases of punishment, the child should understand why lie is being punished. His moral self, 'Super Ego' as Freud calls it, must be on the side of the elder when the punishment is being inflicted. Thrashing as a rule should be rare, if not banished altogether. Sneers will not make a sluggard work so effectively as a little patting on the back, however insignificant it may otherwise be.

Fear: Sometimes thwarting of an activity may develop a negative situation, and we experience a feeling of insecurity. Fear may assume forms ranging from mild apprehension to paralysing terror. But in all cases, a feeling of haplessness to meet situation seems to be the origin of the fear. The visible signs are trembling (perhaps with accompanying clattering of teeth) of hand and feet, accompanied by perspiration and dry tongue. There is also loss of appetite. A child who is continuously afraid feels more and more helpless and is ultimately unable to accomplish anything. We shall, in a majority of cases, find that the bogey of fear is often planted in the minds of children in early infancy. Some people get afraid at the sight of harmless insects like spiders or cockroaches because of thoughtless actions of the elders. Fear like anger may not be the result of a single situation but may be the cumulative effect or a number or trying situations. A child who is scolded daily in school for instance, may develop a fear about the school itself.

Perhaps, if we teachers are careful, we can cure a child of this emotional complex to a large extent. Many of the fears implanted into the child will appear to be foolish and he will learn to get over them, if the teacher works his way up patiently. Gradually, a spirit of confidence will replace the paralysing state of helplessness in the face of frustrating situations, if the teacher can inspire confidence in the child. But alas! instead of trying to cure it, we often aggravate the situation by providing occasions for frustrations, like failure in examinations, by humiliation and sneers and perhaps rejection. These naturally leave lasting impressions on the personality of the child and, instead of building healthy individuals, we are producing timid and subservient creatures who cannot stand on their own legs and are unable to withstand any shocks in their lives. Let us remember the words of Tagore: "Where the mind is without fear and the head is held high". On this lie the future hopes of a free India.

Emotional Exhaustion: Frustration may sometimes cause a person to be so completely worn out that he reacts to a situation in utter helplessness. He may not be afraid, yet he loses all interest in grappling with the situation, He is too much exhausted or otherwise distracted to concentrate his efforts on solving his difficulties. Such a situation may occur within the school-room. When such children are unable to concentrate on their studies, the quality of their work goes down. When this maladjustment is carried to the point of complete exhaustion, we get a nervous breakdown or neurasthania. This is a common malady among adolescents.

Perhaps, with a little encouragement and timely help, we will be able to solve these difficulties. But if the right time has passed, the malady may become pathological and nothing but clinical treatment and complete rest with the attendant waste of involving the risk of retardation, will cure it.

Escapes and Pseudo-solutions: Perhaps a few individuals will try to avoid danger by pretending that it does not exist, or by escaping from it, without showing the courage to face the reality. They may be compared to rabbits who simply close their eyes in the face of approaching danger. Some run away at the very approach of danger like so many fawns running away from a mere sound. If a child finds the school unwelcome, he may often play truant. More often, the escape is only in fancy, as in the case of an adolescent who tries to compensate for his inadequacy in the real world by daydreaming and creating a world of imagination. A child who is not vigorous and assertive will find daydreaming almost an obsession, a situation which he cannot help falling into. As a result of frustration, whether at home or at school, he will, instead of facing the reality and removing the basic cause of such frustration, try to live in a dreamland of his own fantasies. Such persons, when they grow up, will never be able to face realities squarely, unless they are able to cure themselves of this habit.

It is, therefore, necessary that while constructive imagination should be encouraged, fruitless daydreaming should be cured at all costs. This can only be done by wise guidance. Schools can do so by providing useful alternative choices in cases where a particular line of effort has proved fruitless. Children should also be given opportunities to exercise their imagination along constructive channels.

Over-compensation: Some individuals, however, react to frustrating situations in a different way. Although inwardly conscious of their inadequacy or limitations, they try to show off, assuming a carefree and often a bragging attitude. By this aggressive and over-bearing display of emotion, they are really trying to conceal their inadequacy. This type of emotional maladjustment needs curing, otherwise it may produce undesirable conflicts within the class-room, besides developing the braggat's personality on wrong lines. Perhaps, a wise teacher can do much by individual guidance and showing him how foolish he has been, and how he can achieve eminence in more socially approved ways.

Restoring Emotions

Pleasure: A feeling of pleasure motivates us to push our way forward. Satisfaction gained from an activity serves as a tonic helping us to overcome fresh barriers. To produce this effect we are sometimes tempted to offer rewards and prizes. This stimulates the competitive spirit, but it moves the source of joy away from activity and implants it on an external thing, namely on the reward. Sometimes, it will bring about undesirable results: trying to win the prize by hook or by crook—which becomes the motivating tendency. To be really effective, the source of excitement must be the activity itself. It is the effort that must give the pleasure. This is possible provided the situation offers a challenge to the individual, and its successful outcome provides an individual an opportunity to assert his confidence. The task set up must certainly be within the range of the capacity of the person attempting to perform it.

If we as teachers can set up tasks that are challenging, tasks whose utility is self-evident (they being related to real life situations) and which are within their publics capacity to perform we shall be providing them with an opportunity to derive real pleasure from the effort they are to make. This and this alone will make school tasks worthwhile and pleasant and stimulating.

Humour: Wit is the sauce of life. A sense of humour saves us from many a frustrating situation and keeps our strength intact. It must be cultivated in the child from an early age. It is a false notion that the teacher is likely to lose respect if he displays humour. Of course, he should not seem funny and clownish. A sense of humour expressed at the right place in a right and dignified way will enhance his respect among the children and, at the same time, afford the latter an opportunity to wield a shield with which to ward off approaching difficulties.

Affection and Sympathy: Of all the restoring emotions that a child perhaps heeds most in a teacher is affection. The child comes to school with a certain amount of frustration. He has been snatched away from his home and put in the midst of strange surroundings. He needs a sympathetic teacher to rehabilitate him there, providing him the security of a second home. Perhaps his home conditions are unhappy; he may have a tyrannical father, or a stepmother who shows him no affection. Perhaps the constant quarrels at home Lave made him feel insecure there.

It is the sympathy and affection of the teacher that will provide him the necessary refuge which his home has denied him and will help him develop his personality in the right way. Perhaps, his classmates do not treat him well and instead of looking at his physical disabilities and awkwardness in a kindly and tolerant way, take pleasure in ridiculing him. This makes, the school a hell for him, tempting him to play truant. It is the sympathy and affection of the teacher that will help him to bear these problems. It is the want of affection that makes an unwanted or ugly child wayward. It is, again, the lack of sympathy in broken homes which makes a child delinquent. If children reared in a hostel or in an orphanage are sometimes hardhearted, and self-centred, the fault lies in the fact that they have missed this vital tonic in their upbringing. Of course, just as a mild drizzle rather than a heavy downpour is more conducive to the growth of crops, so is a stream rather than a flood of affection to the development of a child.

Affection of teachers and parents, if wisely bestowed, will be helpful for the normal development of children and such children will, in the long run, be more amenable to discipline than others who are always harshly treated: "It is far better to rule by love than by fear".

COMPONENTS OF EMOTION APPEALS

Any discrete emotion can be used in a persuasive appeal; this may include jealousy, disgust, indignation, fear, and anger. Fear is one of the most studied emotional appeals in communication and social influence research.

Important consequences of fear appeals and other emotion appeals include the possibility of reactance which may lead to either message rejections or source rejection and the absence of attitude change.

As the EPPM suggests, there is an optimal emotion level in motivating attitude change. If there is not enough motivation, an attitude will not change; if the emotional appeal is overdone, the motivation can be paralyzed thereby preventing attitude change.

Emotions perceived as negative or containing threat are often studied more than perceived positive emotions like humour. Though the inner-workings of humour are not agreed upon, humour appeals may work by creating incongruities in the mind.

Recent research has looked at the impact of humour on the processing of political messages. While evidence is inconclusive, there appears to be potential for targeted attitude change is receivers with low political message involvement.

Important factors that influence the impact of emotion appeals include self efficacy, attitude accessibility, issue involvement, and message/source features. Self efficacy is a perception of one's own human agency; in other words, it is the perception of our own ability to deal with a situation. It is an important variable in emotion appeal messages because it dictates a person's ability to deal with both the emotion and the situation.

For example, if a person is not self-efficacious about their ability to impact the global environment, they are not likely to change their attitude or behaviour about global warming.

Dillard (1994) suggests that message features such as source non-verbal communication, message content, and receiver differences can impact the emotion impact of fear appeals. The characteristics of a message are important because one message can elicit different levels of emotion for different people. Thus, in terms of emotion appeals messages, one size does not fit all.

Attitude accessibility refers to the activation of an attitude from memory in other words, how readily available is an attitude about an object, issue, or situation. Issue involvement is the relevance and salience of an issue or situation to an individual. Issue involvement has been correlated with both attitude access and attitude strength. Past studies conclude accessible attitudes are more resistant to change

PLACE OF EMOTIONS IN LIFE

An emotion is the meaning we give to our felt states of arousal. Psychologists consider emotions to be complex states involving diverse aspects. On the one hand an emotion is a physiological state of arousal; on the other, it also involves an object as having a certain significance or value to the individual. Emotions are dynamically fed by our drives and dispositions; they are also interlocked with other emotions, related to an individual's beliefs, a wide-ranging network of symbols and the "cultural ethos" of a society.

Emotions basically involve dispositions to act by way of approach or withdrawal. Let us take an example to illustrate this. A man who walks a long distance across a forest track feels thirsty, he is attracted by the sight of water in a passing stream and he approaches; but there is a fierce animal close to the stream and he is impelled to withdraw or fight; if he withdraws he might then have a general feeling of anxiety, and if he gets back home safely he will be relieved.

Thus perception of objects and situations is followed by a kind of appraisal of them as attractive or harmful. These appraisals initiate tendencies to feel in a certain manner and an impulse to act in a desirable way. All states of appraisal do not initiate action; for instance, in joy we like a passive continuation of the existing state and in grief we generally give up hope.

Though there may be certain biologically built-in patterns of expressing emotions, learning plays a key role. Learning influences both the type and intensity of arousal as well as the control and expression of emotions. The emotional development of people has been the subject of serious study. There are significant differences in the emotional development of people depending on the relevant cultural and social variables. In fact, certain societies are prone to give prominence to certain types of emotions (a dominant social ethos). There are also differences regarding the degree of expressiveness and control of emotions. The important point is that each of us develops a relatively consistent pattern of emotional development, coloured by the individual's style of life.

EMOTIONAL DEVELOPMENT—MEANING—POSITIVE AND NEGATIVE EMOTIONS

Research and theory on the role of emotion and regulation in morality have received considerable attention in the last decade. Much relevant work has concerned the role of moral emotions in moral behaviour. Research on differences between embarrassment, guilt, and shame and their relations to moral behaviour is reviewed, as is research on the association of these emotions with negative emotionality and regulation.

Recent issues concerning the role of such empathy-related responses as sympathy and personal distress to prosocial and antisocial behaviour are discussed, as is the relation of empathy-related responding to situational and dispositional emotionality and regulation. The development and socialization of guilt, shame, and empathy also are discussed briefly. In addition, the role of nonmoral emotions (e.g. anger and sadness), including moods and dispositional differences in negative emotionality and its regulation, in morally relevant behaviour, is reviewed.

Theories of Emotion

Several perspectives help explain the role of emotion in development. Some theorists emphasize that emotions occur during events involving self and environment, but that events must be cognitively appraised before an emotion is experienced; this appraisal occurs with reference to one's goals.

The *social constructivist* approach also highlights appraisal, but focuses on emotions as social products based on cultural beliefs. In contrast, *Differential Emotions Theory* asserts that different emotions are already present at birth. Keith Oatley and Jennifer Jenkins (1996) assimilate these divergent views, holding that emotions derive from a universal biological core, but also contain an appraisal/semantic component that is largely a product of social construction.

Emotional Competence

Both Susanne Denham (1998) and Carolyn Saarni (1990, 1999) have written about children's emotional competence; they agree that, although there are no overarching stages for emotional development, children become increasingly sophisticated in their expression and experience, understanding, and regulation of emotions.

These early foundations of emotional competence contribute to mental health throughout the lifespan.

Socialization of emotional competence: Because emotions are inherently social, skills of emotional competence are vividly played out during interaction and within relationships with others. As noted by Joseph Campos and Karen Barrett (1984), emotions provide useful information for self and others. This entry focuses on the emotional transactions between parent and child and on parents' contributions to emotional competence.

Amy Halberstadt (1991) has highlighted three possible mechanisms of parents' socialization of emotional competence: Modelling, reactions to children's emotions, and teaching about emotions. The theories of psychologists like Sylvan Tomkins (1963, 1991), as well as empirical findings from late twentieth-century research, predict that parents' positive emotional expression

children in experiencing and regulating their own emotions. Children of such parents gradually formulate a coherent body of knowledge about emotional expressions, situations, and causes.

Late twentieth-century research suggests that Japanese mothers also talk to their preschoolers about emotions. They use emotion language for similar reasons as U.S. mothers; what differs is the content of their conversations, which focus on aspects of emotion relevant for Japanese culture.

Thus, positive elements of emotion socialization seem clear. Moreover, there is some evidence that parents' support of one another also helps to ensure such positive elements. However, do beneficial aspects of parents' socialization of emotion differ across children's ages, or across parents? Although more research is needed in this area, it is predicted that these socializing techniques would occur across development and parents, albeit with different emphasized emotions, and different aspects yielding positive child outcomes. In part, however, these questions require an elucidation of children's changing skills of emotional competence.

Expression and experience of emotions: An important element of emotional competence is emotional expressiveness, the sending of affective messages. Emotions must be expressed in keeping with the child's goals, and in accordance with the social context; goals of self and others must be coordinated. Thus, emotional competence includes *expressing emotions* in a way that is advantageous to moment-to-moment interaction and relationships over time.

First, emotionally competent individuals are aware that an affective message needs to be sent in a given context. But what affective message should be sent, for interaction to proceed smoothly? Children slowly learn which expressions of emotion facilitate specific goals. Second, children also come to determine the appropriate affective message, one that works in the setting or with a specific playmate. Third, children must also learn how to send the affective message convincingly. Method, intensity, and timing of an affective message are crucial to its meaning, and eventual success or failure.

After preschool, children learn that their goals are not always met by freely showing their most intense feelings. For example, grade-schoolers regulate anger in anticipation of the negative consequences they expect in specific situations or from specific persons. Along with the *cool rule* mandating more muted emotions within most social settings, older children's emotional messages become more complex, with the use of more blended signals, and better differentiated expressions of social emotions.

These general tenets of competent experience and expression of emotion may be universal, but children from different cultures differ in the emotions they express. For example, Japanese preschoolers show less anger and distress in conflict situations than U.S. children, even though the two groups' prosocial and conflict *behaviours* do not differ. These differences fit the Japanese taboo on publicly displayed negative emotions.

Japanese toddlers and preschoolers' expressiveness is not always different from that of their U.S. peers'. For example, they express empathy in response to others' distress. Even this similarity, however, may arise from differing cultural imperatives.

Japanese youngsters are encouraged to feel as one with their group, whereas Western children are encouraged to feel the state of another as part of their increasingly autonomous regulation of emotional states. The import of these subtle differences needs further exploration.

Understanding Emotions: Emotion knowledge predicts later social functioning, such as social acceptance by peers. By preschool, most children can infer basic emotions from expressions or situations, and understand their consequences. Preschoolers gradually come to differentiate among the negative emotions, and become increasingly capable of using emotional language. Furthermore, young children begin to identify other peoples' emotions, even when they may differ from their own.

Grade-schoolers become more aware of emotional experience, including multiple emotions, and realize that inner and outer emotional states may differ. By middle school, children comprehend the time course of emotions, display rules associated with emotional situations, and moral emotions. They now have an adult-like sense of how different events elicit different emotions in different people, and that enduring personality traits may impact individualized emotional reactions.

These general tenets of competent emotion knowledge seem similar for Japanese children. For example, even two-year-olds use some emotion language; by the end of preschool, their understanding of culturally appropriate emotion language is acute. They begin to understand dissemblance of emotion. As in U.S. research, however, there is a relative dearth of research on older children.

Emotion Regulation: Emotion regulation is necessary when the presence or absence of emotional expression and experience interferes with a person's goals. Negative or positive emotions can need regulating, when they threaten to overwhelm or need to be amplified. Children learn to retain or enhance those emotions that are relevant and helpful, to attenuate those that are relevant but not helpful, and to dampen those that are irrelevant. These skills help them to experience a greater sense of well-being and maintain satisfying relationships with others.

Early in preschool, much of this emotion regulation is biobehavioral (e.g., thumb sucking), and much is supported by adults. Important cognitive foundations of emotion regulation contribute to the developmental changes observed in emotional competence from preschool to adolescence. Preschoolers gradually begin to use independent coping strategies for emotion regulation, and grade-schoolers refine these strategies—problemsolving, support-seeking, distancing, internalizing, externalizing, distraction, reframing/redefining, cognitive "blunting" (i.e., convincing oneself that one's distress is minimal), and denial.

Older children are uniquely aware of the multiple strategies at their command, and know which are adaptive in specific situations. They also use more cognitive and problem-solving, and fewer support-seeking, strategies. Adolescents appraise the controllability of emotional experiences, shift thoughts intentionally, and reframe situations to reach new solutions.

Japanese children, as noted above, are initially very close to their mothers, who assist them in emotion regulation even more than Western mothers. Some researchers have noted, however, that once emotionally distressed, Japanese children find it harder to regain their equilibrium. It could be that extended maternal coregulation, coupled with stricter cultural display rules, make it more difficult for these children to self-regulate once distressed. More research is needed to follow up on these findings.

EMOTIONAL CONTROL AND MATURITY

Controlling your emotion begins with a deliberate decision to keep composure and emotional retrain at all times. You should be very mindful of your feelings in every situation whether it is exuberant or sorrowful. You should avoid the belief that people are entitled to loose control in special occasions or that people have the right to let out their emotions in specific circumstances. You should stop adhering to the belief that "people are just humans" because what makes people humans is their ability to tame their desires and emotions.

You should understand that emotion is actually dependent on your behaviour and not the other way around. To put it simply, you feel sad because you realize that you are frowning, contrary to the popular notion that you frown because you realize that you are sad. In social psychology, it has been discovered behaviour influences emotions, and not the other way around. With this key information at hand, you are empowered with the ability to influence feelings by modifying behaviour.

A common cause of emotional outbursts is having problems. Oftentimes, when people are faced with difficulties, they react by panicking or by being angry. However, these are not solutions to the initial problem; they are sources of problems themselves. When you are in a state of panic or in a rage of anger, your mind is clouded with emotions that the situation is not seen clearly. This does make it harder to think of concrete solutions to the problem being dealt with. Whenever a problem comes, instead of immediately throwing tantrums or pacing restlessly, you should stop, breath, and evaluate the entirety of the circumstance. This way, the problem can be viewed in a clearer perspective, and solutions may be thought out more logically.

One very valuable tool in emotional control is the ability to pause. While there are no pause and play buttons in real life, people have the capability to stop themselves, and take a break in certain situations that usually cause emotional outbursts. Before shouting and screaming out of a disappointing occurrence, you should first take a break to think and reflect. Pausing in itself is a form of emotional control. At this point, you can think if letting go of the emotions is indeed necessary. You should also think of the consequences that the emotional explosion would entail. If the emotions involved in the situation are too strong to withhold, you can think of reasonable emotional expressions such as crying instead of screaming when you are depressed, or smiling instead of jumping around when you are elated.

The problem with most people who are unable to control their emotions is that they dwell too much on the present situation. It is undeniable that the height of emotions experienced in certain circumstances could be overwhelming. However, these are also the times when you are vulnerable to do things that you might regret later on. To avoid this, it is important to examine how things would go in the future. Emotional control is indeed difficult to master. But with will power and determination, it can be possibly achieved. You just have to be aware that emotions do not really have the power to overcome people. On the contrary, people have the ability to watch over their emotions and control them to what they think is necessary.

5

Social, Moral and Cognitive Development

To understand the characteristics of learners in childhood, adolescence, adulthood, and old age, educational psychology develops and applies theories of human development. Often represented as stages through which people pass as they mature, developmental theories describe changes in mental abilities (cognition), social roles, moral reasoning, and beliefs about the nature of knowledge.

For example, educational psychologists have researched the instructional applicability of Jean Piaget's theory of development, according to which children mature through four stages of cognitive capability. Piaget hypothesized that children are not capable of abstract logical thought until they are older than about 11 years, and therefore younger children need to be taught using concrete objects and examples. Researchers have found that transitions, such as from concrete to abstract logical thought, do not occur at the same time in all domains. A child may be able to think abstractly about mathematics, but remain limited to concrete thought when reasoning about human relationships. Perhaps Piaget's most enduring contribution is his insight that people actively construct their understanding through a self-regulatory process.

Piaget proposed a developmental theory of moral reasoning in which children progress from a naïve understanding of morality based on behaviour and outcomes to a more advanced understanding based on intentions. Piaget's views of moral development were elabourated by Kohlberg into a stage theory of moral development. There is evidence that the moral reasoning described in stage theories is not sufficient to account for moral behaviour. For example, other factors such as modeling (as described by the social cognitive theory of morality) are required to explain bullying.

Rudolf Steiner's model of child development interrelates physical, emotional, cognitive, and moral development in developmental stages similar to those later described by Piaget. Developmental theories are sometimes presented not as shifts between qualitatively different stages, but as gradual increments on separate dimensions. Development of epistemological beliefs (beliefs about knowledge) have been described in terms of gradual changes in people's belief in: certainty and permanence of knowledge, fixedness of ability, and credibility of authorities such as teachers and experts. People develop more sophisticated beliefs about knowledge as they gain in education and maturity.

FACTORS OF SOCIAL DEVELOPMENTS

Discrimination: Sometimes there are social or cultural factors that hold back poor countries. Discrimination is one of these. If there are certain people groups that are discriminated against, the country's overall productivity can suffer. This may be a tribe, a caste, a racial category or minority language group. I have already mentioned Cameroon, which has both French speaking and English speaking regions. All the infrastructure happens in the French speaking part. French speakers in Canada complain of the opposite. Welsh speakers in Britain, or Catalans in Spain, have historically faced similar problems. Racial discrimination may be an issue, excluding certain groups from economic activity, either deliberately or not. Racial minorities regularly have poorer exam results and economic prospects than the majority. More serious forms of exclusion would be apartheid South Africa, or the Asian communities driven out of Uganda under Idi Amin, which was disastrous for Uganda's economy.

Another division may be the role of women. Jeffrey Sachs talks about this in The End of Poverty: 'Cultural or religious norms may block the role of women… leaving half the population without economic or political rights and without education, thereby undermining half of the population in its contribution to overall development.' If you don't believe that women should work, you have effectively halved the earning potential of your country.

Population: Closely linked to this is the population issue. If women see staying at home and bringing up children as their chief role, they will have more children than those who work. There is nothing wrong with having lots of children, as long as you can provide for them. Jeffrey Sachs again: 'With fewer children, a poor household can invest more in the health and education of each child, thereby equipping the next generation with the health, nutrition, and education that can lift living standards in future years.'

As Paul has talked about here before, world population has exploded. What is interesting is that the countries where this has happened are often those where women do not play a role in business or society. When women are educated and given a choice, some will stay at home and look after children, and others will pursue careers or start small businesses. This is an important factor, as some countries have seen their population double or triple without their economies keeping pace. That leaves more mouths to feed, and just not enough to go around.

Culture

I've already mentioned the role of women, but culture can have hidden effects in business, trade and development. China may be a major power now, but it was the world's most developed country in the middle ages, and stagnated, or even went backwards, for centuries. Part of this was cultural, a pride and sense of self-sufficiency that led to a closing of China's borders. 'China seems to have long been stationary', Adam Smith wrote in 1776, in his Wealth of Nations. 'A country which neglects or despises foreign commerce... cannot transact the same quantity of business which it might do with different laws and institutions.' That's changed, but nationalism, suspicion, or radical philosophy still has some countries closed down to outside involvement – communism in North Korea, or extremist Islam in Taliban Afghanistan, locking countries out of development.

This the far end of the spectrum, but culture works in subtler ways too. Some cultures believe in a greater good, in unity, in the rule of law. They are optimistic, hopeful, ambitious and ready to pull together. Others can be paranoid, fragmented, uncertain of their place in the modern world, angry, resistant to change.

Rich countries can be overconfident and brash. Poor countries can see themselves as victims and become despondent. In his The Wealth and Poverty of Nations, economic historian David Landes says 'If we learn anything from the history of economic development it is that culture makes all the difference.'

SOCIAL MATURITY: ERIKSON'S STAGES OF SOCIAL DEVELOPMENT

What we've just gone over is a sort of abstracted version of Kegan's social maturity theory without any real detail shown. Of course, it will help to have that detail along with some concrete examples of what he is talking about to make this all comprehensible, so that is what I will now try to supply.

Kegan is suggesting that as babies grow into adults, they develop progressively more objective and accurate appreciations of the social world they inhabit. They do this by progressing through five or more states or periods of development which he labelled as follows:

- Incorporative

- Impulsive
- Imperial
- Interpersonal
- Institutional.

In their beginnings, babies are all subjective and have really no appreciation of anything objective at all, and therefore no real self-awareness. This is to say, at first, babies have little idea how to interpret anything, and the only perspective they have with which to interpret things is their own scarcely developed perspective. They can recognize parent's faces and the like, but this sort of recognition should not be confused with babies being able to appreciate that parents are separate creatures with their own needs. This key recognition doesn't occur for years.

Kegan describes this earliest period as **Incorporative**. The sense of self is not developed at this point in time. There is no self to speak of because there is no distinction occurring yet between self and other. To the baby, there is not any reason to ask the question, "who am I" because the baby's mind is nothing more and nothing less than the experience of its senses as it moves about. In an important sense, the baby is embedded in its sensory experience and has no other awareness.

Babies practice using their senses and reflexes a lot and thus develop mental representations of those reflexes. At some point it occurs to the baby that it *has* reflexes that it can use and senses that it can experience. Reflex and sensation are thus the first mental objects; the first things that are understood to be distinct components of the self. The sense of self emerges from the knowledge that there are things in the world that aren't self (like reflexes and senses); things that I am not. To quote Kegan,

> *"Rather than literally being my reflexes, I now have them, and "I" am something other. "I" am that which coordinates or mediates the reflexes..."*

Kegan correspondingly refers to this second period of social appreciation development as **Impulsive**, to suggest that the child is now embedded in impulses – which are those things that coordinate reflexes. The sense of self at this stage of life would be comfortable saying something like, "hungry", or "sleepy", being fully identified with these hungers. Though babies are now aware that they can take action to fulfil a need, they still are not clear that other people exist yet as independent creatures. From the perspective of the Impulsive mind, a parent is merely another reflex that can be brought to bear to satisfy impulses.

The objectification of what was previously subjective experience continues as development continues. Kegan's next developmental leap is known as the

Imperial self. The child as "little dictator" is born. In the prior impulsive self, the self literally is nothing more and nothing less than a set of needs. *There isn't anyone "there" having those needs yet. The needs alone are all that exists.* As awareness continues to rise, the child now starts to become aware that "it" is the very thing that has the needs. Because the child is now aware that it *has* needs (rather than *is* needs), it also starts to become aware that it can consciously manipulate things to get its needs satisfied. The impulsive child was also manipulative, perhaps, but in a more unaware animal manner. The imperial child is not yet aware that other people have needs too. It only knows at this stage that it has needs, and it doesn't hesitate to express them.

The **Interpersonal** period that follows next starts with the first moment when the child comes to understand that there are actually other people out there in the world whose needs need to be taken into account along side their own. The appreciation of the otherness of other people comes about, as always by a process of expanding perspectives. The child's perspective in this case expands from its own only to later include both its own and those of other important people around it. It is the child's increasingly sophisticated understanding of the idea that people have needs itself which cause the leap to occur. To quote Kegan again,

> *"I" no longer am my needs (no longer the imperial I); rather I have them. In having them I can now coordinate, or integrate, one need system with another, and in so doing, I bring into being that need-mediating reality which we refer to when we speak of mutuality."*

In English then, the interpersonal child becomes aware that "not only do I have needs, *other people do too!*" This moment in time is where conscience is born and the potential for guilt and shame arises, as well as the potential for empathy. Prior to this moment, these important aspects of adult mental life don't exist except as potentials.

The interpersonal child is aware that other people have needs which it needs to be taken into account if it is to best satisfy its own needs. There is no guiding principle that helps the interpersonal child to determine which set of needs is most important – its own, or those of the other people. Some children will conclude that their own needs are most important to satisfy, while others will conclude that other's needs should be prioritized, and some children will move back and forth between the two positions like a crazy monkey.

As the child's sense of self continues to develop, at some point it becomes aware that a guiding principle can be established which helps determine which set of needs should take precedence under particular circumstances. This is the first moment that the child can be said to have values, or commitments to ideas and beliefs and principles which are larger and more permanent than its own passing whims and fears. Kegan refers to this new realization of and commitment to values as the **Institutional** period, noting that in this period, the child's idea of self becomes something which can be, for the first time, described in terms of institutionalized values, such as being honest. "I'm an honest person. I try to be fair. I strive to be brave." are the sorts of things an institutional mind might say. Values, such as the Golden Rule (e.g., "Do unto others as you would have them do unto you"), start to guide the child's appreciation of how to be a member of the family and of society. The moral, ethical and legal foundations of society follow from this basic achievement of an Institutional self. Further, children (or adults) who achieve this level of social maturity understand the need for laws and for ethical codes that work to govern everyone's behaviour. Less socially mature individuals won't grasp why these things are important and cannot and should not simply be disregarded when they are inconvenient.

For many people, social maturity seems to stop here at the Institutional stage. Kegan himself writes that this stage is the stage of conventional adult maturity; one that many (but not all) adults reach, and beyond which most do not progress. However, the potential for continued development continues onwards and upwards.

The next evolution of self understanding occurs when the child (by now probably an adult) starts to realize that there is more than one way of being "fair" or "honest" or "brave" in the world. Whereas before, in the interpersonal mindset, there is only one possible right way to interpret a social event (e.g., in accordance with one's own value system), a newly developed **Inter-industrial** mindset starts to recognize a diversity of ways that someone might act and still be acting in accordance with a coherent value system (though not necessarily one's own value system).

For example, let's consider how someone with an Institutional mindset and someone with an InterIndividual mindset might judge someone who has become a "draft dodger" so as to avoid military duty. There are precisely two ways that an Institutionally minded person might look at such an action. If he or she is of the mainstream institutional mindset, draft dodging is a non-religious sort of heresy and a crime which should be punishable. If, on the other hand, he or she is of a counter-cultural institutional mindset, then judgements are reversed and draft dodging is seen as a brave action which demonstrates individual courage in the face of massive peer pressure to conform. An institutionally minded person can hold *one or the other* of these perspectives but not both, because he or she is literally embedded in one or the other of those perspectives and cannot appreciate the other except as something alien and evil. A person who has achieved InterIndividual social maturity is able to hold both mainstream and counter-cultural value systems in mind at the same time, and to see the problem of draft dodging from both perspectives. This sort of dual-vision will appear to be the worst kind of wishy-washiness and flip-floppery to someone stuck in a conventional Institutional mindset and maturity level. However, if you are following the progression of social maturity states, and how one states' embedded subjective view becomes something which is seem objectively alongside other points of view as social maturity progresses, you will see that such dual-vision is indeed the logical next step; what a more socially mature sort of human being might look like.

Kegan thinks of the achievement of InterIndividual social maturity, what might be considered "post-maturity", as a dubious thing. In a wonderful interview published by "What is Enlightenment Magazine " and available online here, Kegan comments on the danger that this state poses:

> *"... you have to think about what it means to actually be more complex than what your culture is currently demanding. You have to have a name for that, too. It's almost something beyond maturity, and it's usually a very risky state to be in. I mean, we loved Jesus, Socrates, and Gandhi—after we murdered them. While they were alive, they were a tremendous pain in the ass. Jesus, Abraham Lincoln, Martin Luther King, Jr.—these people died relatively young. You don't often live a long life being too far out ahead of your culture."*

I'm not going to comment on whether or not Kegan's social maturity theory is accurate. Whether or not it is accurate, it is still a very useful and interesting way of thinking about how social maturity develops. If we can agree to accept this theory as basically correct, for a moment, a whole lot of mental problems and disorders that are otherwise difficult to talk about suddenly start to make some sense; start to "click into place". This is already a rather long essay and I don't want to belabour it, but I need to give at least one example, and to my mind there is no better example for my purpose than Narcissistic Personality Disorder.

Narcissists are (typically) arrogant, self-important and even grandiose people who consider themselves special and "above the law", lacking in empathy and compassion, willing to exploit innocents, and who are consumed by visions of dramatic personal success and power to which they quite passionately believe they are entitled for no apparent reason. Narcissists use other people if it suits their purpose to use them, and discard or attack them if they are in the way.

Everyone knows a few people who fit the narcissist mold to one degree or another. It is generally not at all clear what the heck is wrong with narcissists that causes them to act in this obnoxious fashion, so most people tend to think of them in more simple terms, as "jerks" or "a holes".

Now, think for a moment what an adult might look like who never left the Imperial self stage of social maturity development. Keep in mind that there are many different types of maturity and that we are only suggesting an adult whose growth has been stunted in this particular social-emotional manner. Other aspects of maturity (e.g., cognitive and intellectual maturity, knowledge, and of course age) are unaffected. That particular hypothetical adult is pretty much going to look like a narcissist, huh? A "little dictator" writ into adult form.

For example, the adult narcissist lacks empathy for the same reason that the normal imperial child lacks empathy; as an Imperially minded individual, he cannot conceive of any perspective that has any meaning other than his own. He or she is literally embedded in an inadequate and inaccurate representation of social reality; one in which only his own needs and impulses are important and no one else is important. The existence of other human beings with separate needs may be partially understood by such a fellow, but there is no recognition that those other people's needs have equivalent weight and reality to the Imperial-minded narcissists' own.

A similar argument can be made to explain how to account for sociopaths; antisocial personality disorders (who similarly lacks in empathy, guilt and remorse for criminal actions which harm other people), and also for the childish, immature and often reckless behaviour that is frequently displayed by otherwise normal people who have been abusing drugs and/or alcohol since they were small and have only recently become sober. Such people's behaviour can be made more comprehensible if you think of them as developmentally delayed in this dimension of social-emotional maturity.

Just because we can use Kegan's theory to explain why people act like jerks, doesn't for a second excuse jerky behaviour. Or criminal behaviour, for that matter. Adult narcissists and antisocials may be akin to little children in terms of their social maturity development, but they are not typically retarded in other aspects of maturity. They often have the full compliment of adult intellectual capabilities and may even have very good social skills. They often know right from wrong in some abstract manner even if they can't conceive it like a more socially mature person might. They are accountable for their actions even if they possess real handicaps that lead them to act in unacceptable ways.

Ask any therapist and he or she will tell you-it is quite difficult to do effective therapy with people who have social immaturity problems. If Kegan is right in his thinking, the reason for this would not be that these people are fundamentally resistant to the therapy process (which is how many therapists see the problem), but rather in large part because they cannot *comprehend* the therapy process, which is after all, very much a social process that requires a certain level of social maturity on the part of patients before they can benefit. It isn't enough to simply teach a set of skills to such people, because all such people will be capable of doing is aping those skills. They won't be able to fully appreciate the meaning of those skills and thus generalize from them to a more abstract (and mature) way of being with other people. Teaching social skills might actually work for some such people. Some people might actually learn the skills and that will be enough to trigger their growth. However, there ought to be a better, more direct way to make this sort of social maturity growth occur.

Actually, the question of how to help adult people become more socially mature when they aren't is a huge unanswered question that this theory leaves us with. Is there a way to help the Narcissists and the Antisocials and the Pedophiles out there? What about the rest of the people out there who are not quite at the level of social maturity that society demands of them? Kegan explores these questions in his follow-on book, In Over Our Heads" which is also very good and worth reading. If there is interest in this essay, I'll find a way to go over his conclusions from that book in a future essay.

Hopefully, those of you who have stuck this out will have comprehended what I've been trying to say and it will have been a worthwhile expenditure of your time. If not, all I can say in my defense is that I tried my best (grin!). My aim is to educate, and this stuff is worth knowing about, even if it isn't something Oprah or Dr. Phil would do a show about. As per usual, I'm happy to answer questions and post non-trollish comments. Be well.

INDIVIDUAL DIFFERENCES AND DISABILITIES

Each person has an individual profile of characteristics, abilities and challenges that result from predisposition, learning and development. These manifest as individual differences in intelligence, creativity, cognitive style, motivation and the capacity to process information, communicate, and relate to others.

The most prevalent disabilities found among school age children are attention-deficit hyperactivity disorder (ADHD), learning disability, dyslexia, and speech disorder. Less common disabilities include mental retardation, hearing impairment, cerebral palsy, epilepsy, and blindness.

Although theories of intelligence have been discussed by philosophers since Plato, intelligence testing is an invention of educational psychology, and is coincident with the development of that discipline. Continuing debates about the nature of intelligence revolve on whether intelligence can be characterized by a single factor known as general intelligence, multiple factors (e.g., Gardner's theory of multiple intelligences), or whether it can be measured at all.

In practice, standardized instruments such as the Stanford-Binet IQ test and the WISC are widely used in economically developed countries to identify children in need of individualized educational treatment. Children classified as gifted are often provided with accelerated or enriched programs. Children with identified deficits may be provided with enhanced education in specific skills such as phonological awareness. In addition to basic abilities, the individual's personality traits are also important, with people higher in conscientiousness and hope attaining superior academic achievements, even after controlling for intelligence and past performance.

Learning and Cognition

Two fundamental assumptions that underlie formal education systems are that students (a) retain knowledge and skills they acquire in school, and (b) can apply them in situations outside the classroom. But are these assumptions accurate? Research has found that, even when students report not using the knowledge acquired in school, a considerable portion is retained for many years and long term retention is strongly dependent on the initial level of mastery. One study found that university students who took a child development course and attained high grades showed, when tested 10 years later, average retention scores of about 30%, whereas those who obtained moderate or lower grades showed average retention scores of about 20%. There is much less consensus on the crucial question of how much knowledge acquired in school transfers to tasks encountered outside formal educational settings, and how such transfer occurs. Some psychologists claim that research evidence for this type of *far transfer* is scarce, while others claim there is abundant evidence of far transfer in specific domains. Several perspectives have been established within which the theories of learning used in educational psychology are formed and contested. These include behaviourism, cognitivism, social cognitive theory, and constructivism. This chapter summarizes how educational psychology has researched and applied theories within each of these perspectives.

Behavioural Perspective

Applied behaviour analysis, a set of techniques based on the behavioural principles of operant conditioning, is effective in a range of educational settings. For example, teachers can alter student behaviour by systematically rewarding students who follow classroom rules with praise, stars, or tokens exchangeable for sundry items. Despite the demonstrated efficacy of awards in changing behaviour, their use in education has been criticized by proponents of self-determination theory, who claim that praise and other rewards undermine intrinsic motivation.

There is evidence that tangible rewards decrease intrinsic motivation in specific situations, such as when the student already has a high level of intrinsic motivation to perform the goal behaviour.

But the results showing detrimental effects are counterbalanced by evidence that, in other situations, such as when rewards are given for attaining a gradually increasing standard of performance, rewards enhance intrinsic motivation. Many effective therapies have been based on the principles of applied behaviour analysis, including pivotal response therapy which is used to treat autism spectrum disorders.

Cognitive Perspective

Among current educational psychologists, the cognitive perspective is more widely held than the behavioural perspective, perhaps because it admits causally related mental constructs such as traits, beliefs, memories, motivations and emotions. Cognitive theories claim that memory structures determine how information is perceived, processed, stored, retrieved and forgotten. Among the memory structures theorized by cognitive psychologists are separate but linked visual and verbal systems described by Allan Paivio's dual coding theory. Educational psychologists have used dual coding theory and cognitive load theory to explain how people learn from multimedia presentations.

The spaced learning effect, a cognitive phenomenon strongly supported by psychological research, has broad applicability within education. For example, students have been found to perform better on a test of knowledge about a text passage when a second reading of the passage is delayed rather than immediate. Educational psychology research has confirmed the applicability to education of other findings from cognitive psychology, such as the benefits of using mnemonics for immediate and delayed retention of information.

Problem solving, regarded by many cognitive psychologists as fundamental to learning, is an important research topic in educational psychology. A student is thought to interpret a problem by assigning it to a schema retrieved from long term memory. When the problem is assigned to the wrong schema, the student's attention is subsequently directed away from features of the problem that are inconsistent with the assigned schema. The critical step of finding a mapping between the problem and a pre-existing schema is often cited as supporting the centrality of analogical thinking to problem solving.

Developmental Perspective

Developmental psychology, and especially the psychology of cognitive development, opens a special perspective for educational psychology. This is so because education and the psychology of cognitive development converge on a number of crucial assumptions. First, the psychology of cognitive development defines human cognitive competence at successive phases of development. Education aims to help students acquire knowledge and develop skills which are compatible with their understanding and problem-solving capabilities at different ages. Thus, knowing the students' level on a developmental sequence provides information on the kind and level of knowledge they can assimilate, which, in turn, can be used as a frame for organizing the subject matter to be taught at different school grades. This is the reason why Piaget's theory of cognitive development was so influential for education, especially mathematics and science education. In the same direction, the neo-Piagetian theories of cognitive development suggest that in addition to the concerns above, sequencing of concepts and skills in teaching must take account of the processing and working memory capacities that characterize successive age levels.

Second, the psychology of cognitive development involves understanding how cognitive change takes place and recognizing the factors and processes which enable cognitive competence to develop. Education also capitalizes on cognitive change, because the construction of knowledge presupposes effective teaching methods that would move the student from a lower to a higher level of understanding. Mechanisms such as reflection on actual or mental actions vis-à-vis alternative solutions to problems, tagging new concepts or solutions to symbols that help one recall and mentally manipulate them are just a few examples of how mechanisms of cognitive development may be used to facilitate learning.

Finally, the psychology of cognitive development is concerned with individual differences in the organization of cognitive processes and abilities, in their rate of change, and in their mechanisms of change. The principles underlying intra-and inter-individual differences could be educationally useful, because knowing how students differ in regard to the various dimensions of cognitive development, such as processing and representational capacity, self-understanding and self-regulation, and the various domains of understanding, such as mathematical, scientific, or verbal abilities, would enable the teacher to cater for the needs of the different students so that no one is left behind.

Social Cognitive Perspective

Social cognitive theory is a highly influential fusion of behavioural, cognitive and social elements that was initially developed by educational psychologist Albert Bandura. In its earlier, neo-behavioural incarnation called *social learning theory*, Bandura emphasized the process of observational learning in which a learner's behaviour changes as a result of observing others' behaviour and its consequences. The theory identified several factors that determine whether observing a model will affect behavioural or cognitive change.

These factors include the learner's developmental status, the perceived prestige and competence of the model, the consequences received by the model, the relevance of the model's behaviours and consequences to the learner's goals, and the learner's self-efficacy. The concept of self-efficacy, which played an important role in later developments of the theory, refers to the learner's belief in his or her ability to perform the modeled behaviour.

An experiment by Schunk and Hanson, that studied grade 2 students who had previously experienced difficulty in learning subtraction, illustrates the type of research stimulated by social learning theory. One group of students observed a subtraction demonstration by a teacher and then participated in an instructional program on subtraction. A second group observed other grade 2 students performing the same subtraction procedures and then participated in the same instructional program. The students who observed peer models scored higher on a subtraction post-test and also reported greater confidence in their subtraction ability. The results were interpreted as supporting the hypothesis that perceived similarity of the model to the learner increases self-efficacy, leading to more effective learning of modeled behaviour. It is supposed that peer modeling is particularly effective for students who have low self-efficacy.

Over the last decade, much research activity in educational psychology has focused on developing theories of self-regulated learning (SRL) and metacognition. These theories work from the central premise that effective learners are active agents who construct knowledge by setting goals, analysing tasks, planning strategies and monitoring their understanding. Research has indicated that learners who are better at goal setting and self-monitoring tend to have greater intrinsic task interest and self-efficacy; and that teaching learning strategies can increase academic achievement.

Constructivist Perspective

Constructivism is a category of learning theory in which emphasis is placed on the agency and prior 'knowing' and experience of the learner, and often on the social and cultural determinants of the learning process. Educational psychologists distinguish individual (or psychological) constructivism, identified with Piaget's theory of cognitive development, from social constructivism. A dominant influence on the latter type is Lev Vygotsky's work on sociocultural learning, describing how interactions with adults, more capable peers, and cognitive tools are internalized to form mental constructs. Elabourating on Vygotsky's theory, Jerome Bruner and other educational psychologists developed the important concept of instructional scaffolding, in which the social or information environment offers supports for learning that are gradually withdrawn as they become internalized.

Motivation

Motivation is an internal state that activates, guides and sustains behaviour. Educational psychology research on motivation is concerned with the volition or will that students bring to a task, their level of interest and intrinsic motivation, the personally held goals that guide their behaviour, and their belief about the causes of their success or failure.

A form of attribution theory developed by Bernard Weiner describes how students' beliefs about the causes of academic success or failure affect their emotions and motivations.

For example, when students attribute failure to lack of ability, and ability is perceived as uncontrollable, they experience the emotions of shame and embarrassment and consequently decrease effort and show poorer performance. In contrast, when students attribute failure to lack of effort, and effort is perceived as controllable, they experience the emotion of guilt and consequently increase effort and show improved performance.

Motivational theories also explain how learners' goals affect the way they engage with academic tasks. Those who have *mastery goals* strive to increase their ability and knowledge. Those who have *performance approach goals* strive for high grades and seek opportunities to demonstrate their abilities. Those who have *performance avoidance* goals are driven by fear of failure and avoid situations where their abilities are exposed.

Research has found that mastery goals are associated with many positive outcomes such as persistence in the face of failure, preference for challenging tasks, creativity and intrinsic motivation. Performance avoidance goals are associated with negative outcomes such as poor concentration while studying, disorganized studying, less self-regulation, shallow information processing and test anxiety. Performance approach goals are associated with positive outcomes, and some negative outcomes such as an unwillingness to seek help and shallow information processing. Locus of control is a salient factor in the successful academic performance of students. During the 1970s and 1980s, Cassandra B. Whyte did significant educational research studying locus of control as related to the academic achievement of students pursuing higher education coursework. Much of her educational research and publications focused upon the theories of Julian B. Rotter in regard to the importance of internal control and successful academic performance. Whyte reported that individuals who perceive and believe that their hard work may lead to more successful academic outcomes, instead of depending on luck or fate, persist and achieve academically at a higher level. Therefore, it is important to provide education and counselling in this regard.

Research Methodology

The research methods used in educational psychology tend to be drawn from psychology and other social sciences. There is also a history of significant methodological innovation by educational psychologists, and psychologists investigating educational problems. Research methods address problems in both research design and data analysis. Research design informs the planning of experiments and observational studies to ensure that their results have internal, external and ecological validity. Data analysis encompasses methods for processing both quantitive (numerical) and qualitative (non-numerical) research data. Although, historically, the use of quantitative methods was often considered an essential mark of scholarship, modern educational psychology research uses both quantitative and qualitative methods.

Quantitative Methods

Perhaps first among the important methodological innovations of educational psychology was the development and application of factor analysis by Charles Spearman. Factor analysis is mentioned here as one example of the many multivariate statistical methods used by educational psychologists. Factor analysis is used to summarize relationships among a large set of variables or test questions, develop theories about mental constructs such as self-efficacy or anxiety, and assess the reliability and validity of test scores. Over one hundred years after its introduction by Spearman, factor analysis has become a research staple figuring prominently in educational psychology journals.

Because educational assessment is fundamental to most quantitative research in the field, educational psychologists have made significant contributions to the field of psychometrics. For example, alpha, the widely used measure of test reliability was developed by educational psychologist Lee Cronbach. The reliability of assessments are routinely reported in quantitative educational research. Although, originally, educational measurement methods were built on classical test theory, item response theory and Rasch models are now used extensively in educational measurement worldwide. These models afford advantages over classical test theory, including the capacity to produce standard errors of measurement for each score or pattern of scores on assessments and the capacity to handle missing responses.

Meta-analysis, the combination of individual research results to produce a quantitative literature review, is another methodological innovation with a close association to educational psychology. In a meta-analysis, effect sizes that represent, for example, the differences between treatment groups in a set of similar experiments, are averaged to obtain a single aggregate value representing the best estimate of the effect of treatment. Several decades after Pearson's work with early versions of meta-analysis, Glass published the first application of modern meta-analytic techniques and triggered their broad application across the social and biomedical sciences. Today, meta-analysis is among the most common types of literature review found in educational psychology research.

Other quantitative research issues associated with educational psychology include the use of nested research designs (e.g., a student nested within a classroom, which is nested within a school, which is nested within a district, etc.) and the use of longitudinal statistical models to measure change.

Qualitative Methods

Qualitative methods are used in educational studies whose purpose is to describe events, processes and situations of theoretical significance. The qualitative methods used in educational psychology often derive from anthropology, sociology or sociolinguistics. For example, the anthropological method of ethnography has been used to describe teaching and learning in classrooms. In studies of this type, the researcher may gather detailed field notes as a participant observer or passive observer. Later, the notes and other data may be categorized and interpreted by methods such as grounded theory. Triangulation, the practice of cross-checking findings with multiple data sources, is highly valued in qualitative research.

Case studies are forms of qualitative research focusing on a single person, organization, event, or other entity. In one case study, researchers conducted a 150-minute, semi-structured interview with a 20-year old woman who had a history of suicidal thinking between the ages of 14 to 18. They analysed an audio-recording of the interview to understand the roles of cognitive development, identity formation and social attachment in ending her suicidal thinking.

Qualitative analysis is most often applied to verbal data from sources such as conversations, interviews, focus groups, and personal journals. Qualitative methods are thus, typically, approaches to gathering, processing and reporting verbal data. One of the most commonly used methods for qualitative research in educational psychology is protocol analysis. In this method the research participant is asked to *think aloud* while performing a task, such as solving a math problem.

In protocol analysis the verbal data is thought to indicate which information the subject is attending to, but is explicitly not interpreted as an explanation or justification for behaviour. In contrast, the method of verbal analysis does admit learners' explanations as a way to reveal their mental model or misconceptions (e.g., of the laws of motion). The most fundamental operations in both protocol and verbal analysis are segmenting (isolating) and categorizing sections of verbal data. Conversation analysis and discourse analysis, sociolinguistic methods that focus more specifically on the structure of conversational interchange (e.g., between a teacher and student), have been used to assess the process of conceptual change in science learning. Qualitative methods are also used to analyse information in a variety of media, such as students' drawings and concept maps, video-recorded interactions, and computer log records.

MORAL DEVELOPMENT

Obviously moral behaviour is a worthwhile goal, assuming the morality upon which it's based is reasonable, self-consistent, and consonant with the fundamental values of everyone involved. Moral systems exist for the purpose of producing a group/society in which the default mode of interaction is optimal for the participants in the system, so clearly the "end state" of such systems is significant. The overall "morality" of a society is both a desirable goal and a partial barometre of the success of a given moral system. Its abilities to measure success, however, must be tempered by an understanding of the distinction between moral reasoning and moral behaviour.

How morality is learned

Religious people have it easy. They don't need morally sound parents to teach them about these rules nor do they have to reflect or ponder on their own as to how they should live their lives morally. Christianity, for example, has the Ten Commandments—laid out right in front of them clearly and concisely. How simple! Just ten simples rules by which to lead your life. No thinking necessary. Evolutionists don't have it that easy. They must deliberate for themselves how to lead their lives by learning from laws, family, and intuition.

For the modern evolutionist, it is not too hard to find places that can be helpful in finding morals that fit a lifestyle. Laws are the easiest to find and follow. It is against the law to kill or steal; so there you have it: an evolutionist can simply follow the laws that the United States has put into place and lead a moral life. You can't lie under oath or rape another human being.

All of these are important morals by which someone should live, in addition to them being basic laws. They force you to treat yourself and others with respect and kindness and have repercussions when not followed—not only legally but also consciously. One might say that by following laws, the evolutionist did not put any thought into what morals she would live by. But neither do people who follow the morals set forth by a religious text. Mere humans created laws, someone may mention, whereas God created the Ten Commandments. Not true. Stories and sessions in religious texts are just that:stories.

They were written down and passed on by "mere humans" thousands of years ago. So, federal law and religious law are actually quite comparable. Morality has a lot to do with the way a person is raised as well. People are usually either raised religiously or evolutionistically. Depending on the family of a person, they learn their morals from a religious text or learn morals from parents, siblings, extended family, and family friends who also follow non-religiously based morals. It's a lifestyle choice: live by God's morals or your own.

For families who believe in a religion, they can pass on the word of their religious text and successfully lead a moral life in that manner. For those that believe in evolution, or don't believe in a religion, they can pass on the morals they have learned from friends or family that holds the same beliefs.

In some families I'm sure evolutionistic morals have been passed down from many generations, while others are just starting their newly found evolutionarily moral lives. Another factor in morality is intuition. Maybe this intuition is from family or community values or maybe it is hardwired. Hardwired meaning that we are born with some sort of basic knowledge of what is right and what is wrong—what is moral and what is immoral. I believe that at least some of our moral values are hardwired, but still influenced by outside values. It seems ingrained in most human beings that when you do something right or "moral", you feel good about yourself. When you do something wrong or "immoral", you feel bad about yourself. As a child growing up, you encounter different experiences that teach what makes you feel great and what makes you feel terrible. As you mature, you turn these sessions into morals by which you can live your life, no Ten Commandments necessary. Some theories agree with this idea of hardwired morality. They essentially say that a human's innate sense of what is right and wrong allows them to survive and reproduce more successfully. Therefore, a greater number of morally sound humans are in existence today due to natural selection.

The innate human ability to have morals seems to play an important role in how evolutionists choose their morals and then live their lives morally. A religion or a religious text is not necessary to lead a morally sound life. Some people may find it easier because the rules are laid out clearly and concisely. Some may find it more reliable since they believe it has the dependability of God within those rules. I believe that the evolutionists have a more sound idea of morality. Because they have to decide what is immoral and moral for themselves, they hold a stronger conviction of this moral. They are therefore more likely to live by their morals on a consistent basis.

In many cases, it seems probable that religious people would go against morality because their morals are not as ingrained or deeply believed by religious people when compared to evolutionists. Many criminals are religious, and many even blame their wrongdoing on the belief that God told them to commit the crime. That's hardly morality. Morality is learned through a lifestyle: either a religious one or and evolutionistic one. Morals are comprised of family history, intuitive senses, and federal laws. For now, that's as far back as the origin of morality can be traced. Even religious morality can only be traced back to religious texts. How did the people who passed on those stories decide what was moral and what was not moral? For modern evolutionists, many different sources can be used to aid in deciding how a life should be lived morally, but finding the foundation of these is a difficult task. Sometimes a beginning just cannot be found.

IMPACTING MORAL AND CHARACTER DEVELOPMENT

Campbell and Bond (1982) state there are four major questions to be addressed when focusing on character development:

1. what is good character;
2. what causes or prevents it;
3. how can it be measured so that efforts at improvement can have corrective feedback;and
4. how can it best be developed?

The good character is defined in terms of one's actions. Character development traditionally has focused on those traits or values appropriate for the industrial age such as obedience to authority, work ethic, working in group under supervision, etc. However, as discussed in the SCANS report (1991) and Huitt's (1997) critique, modern education must promote character based on values appropriate for the information age: truthfulness, honesty, integrity, individual responsibility, humility, wisdom, justice, steadfastness, dependability, etc. In terms of what influences character development, Campbell and Bond (1982) propose the following as major factors in the moral development and behaviour of youth in contemporary America:

1. heredity
2. early childhood experience
3. Modelling by important adults and older youth
4. peer influence
5. the general physical and social environment
6. the communications media
7. what is taught in the schools and other institutions
8. specific situations and roles that elicit corresponding behaviour.

These sources of influence are listed in approximate order of least tractable to most tractable in order to suggest why we often seek solutions to social problems through schools. It is important to realize that while schools do and should play a role in the development of character, families, communities, and society in general also have an important influence.

The measurement of character has proven difficult since character, by definition, involves behaviour, but character is often defined in terms of traits (i.e., honesty, integrity, etc.). Some possible measures suggested by Campbell and Bond (1982) are:

1. student discipline;
2. student suicide rates;
3. crimes: assault, burglary, homicides;
4. pregnancy rates of teenage girls; and
5. prosocial activities.

Bennett (1993) proposed a list of cultural indicators that he believes could be used as measures of the character of our society. In addition, he cited a number of social trends that he believes have impacted these indicators. The following table provides an overview of how these have changed from 1960 to 1990.

Earlier Theoretical Models: Psychoanalysis and Behaviourism

Theories have approached morality differently. Sigmund Freud (1856–1939) described *Oedipus complex* to explain the origins of moral conscience, called the *superego*. The Oedipus complex occurs when a child loves the opposite sex parent and, in order to avoid the anxiety and fear of punishment that this causes, the child identifies with the same sex parent. The child incorporates the same sex parent's prohibitions, starting with "Do not love (sexually) your parent."

For behaviourist theorists, such as Robert R. Sears, Robert Grinder, and Albert Bandura (1982), conscience or morality was considered analogous to the phenomenon of resistance to extinction.

H. Hartshorne and M. A. May, at the end of the 1920s, were pioneers in this line of research. Later, Robert Sears, Eleanor Maccoby, and Harry Levin (1957) and other researchers studied the influence of maternal and paternal disciplines upon development of the conscience.

These studies found that warm and affectionate parents, who reason with their children rather than punish them physically, are more successful in having their children assimilate the moral values of the culture.

Cognitive behaviourists have added other dimensions to this process, such as *expectancies* (what the child expects is going to happen), *incentive value* (how much the child wants something), *hypothesis testing* ("If I do this, then that will happen"), and *self-efficacy* (one's capacity and confidence on doing something).

In the psychoanalytic and behaviourist models, morality seems to be something that comes from outside, from society, which is internalized.

THEORIES OF MORAL DEVELOPMENT

Evaluating theories of moral development is difficult due to lack of a consistent definition. For some, moral development is seen principally as ability to reason about universal principles of justice and fairness (moral judgment). For others, it is a matter of ability to empathize with and act to alleviate others' suffering (compassion). Both reasoning and compassion are necessary in formulating moral actions; however, it is the relative importance of each that distinguishes different theories.

Two of the main modern theories of moral development, Kohlberg's (1984) and Gilligan's (1982), are based on long standing, underlying philosophical arguments about the basis of moral development. Each is a stage theory in which people develop from one stage to the next as they grow in ability to make complex judgments. Where the theories differ is on how people make judgments.

Kohlberg's (1984) theory focuses more on the use of reason to draw conclusions about what ought to be done to achieve justice and fairness in a particular situation. Altruism, compassion and empathy are less important than principles of justice, and are not the main part of the reasoned process of coming to moral decisions. The moral reasoner is one who knows that a moral decision is required, understands that principles need to be applied universally, thinks of the greatest good for the most people, and then makes a decision based on abstract principles of justice and fairness. Kohlberg's theory follows Piaget's and Inhelder's (1969) thinking about the stages of mental development. Because Kohlberg's (1984) theory is based on the ability to reason abstractly, young children are not seen as being able to reason about moral issues yet; they are pre-moral. Another major avenue of exploration of moral issues is based on altruism. Modern philosophers such as Blum (1987) and Matthews (1994) suggested that childhood responsiveness to others is a primary moral characteristic. Responsiveness requires both a cognitive and affective grasp of a situation. It does not require true empathy yet, nor does it require that children be aware of why they act as they do, only that the act has been done. What is required for an act to be moral is a recognition of the emotions of the other, and of the action needed to change the situation. What changes from childhood to adulthood is the amount and type of experience the person brings to the situation. For example, the adult might offer advice the young child might not yet know about. This model of morality has some similarity to the model of care developed by Gilligan (1982). In Gilligan's model it is the interrelationships among people that are important, and these are based on empathic responses between people. Responding to another's pain or difficulty is the basis of moral action. This requires an empathic attitude to others, a sensitivity to others' needs, and a wish to act with these needs in mind. This type of thinking reflects sensitivity towards others rather than a focus on reasoning about what is a principled or unprincipled act.

While Kohlberg's (1984) theory has been directly tested with gifted children, especially through use of the Defining Issues Test, there has been little direct application of Gilligan's (1982) theory to the gifted. Like many other researchers, Gilligan appears to use some data from gifted children, but does not distinguish between data obtained from gifted children and more average subjects. For example, an extensive study at the Emma Willard School illustrated the moral decisions made in the context of relationships with other girls. Many of the girls described appear to be quite gifted.

PIAGET'S THEORY OF COGNITIVE DEVELOPMENT

Jean Piaget (1896-1980) believed that people move through stages of development that allow them to think in new, more complex ways.

Sensorimotor Stage

The first stage in Piaget's Stages of Cognitive Development is the sensorimotor stage. This stage lasts from birth to two years old. During this stage, behaviours lack a sense of thought and logic. Behaviours gradually move from acting upon inherited reflexes to interacting with the environment with a goal in mind and being able to represent the external world at the end.

The sensorimotor stage has been broken down into six sub stages that explain the gradual development of infants at this age.

Birth to one Month

Each child is born with inherited reflexes that they use to gain knowledge and understanding about their environment. Examples of these reflexes include grasping and sucking.

1-4 Months

Children repeat behaviours that happen unexpectedly because of their reflexes. For example, a child's finger comes in contact with the mouth and the child starts sucking on it. If the sensation is pleasurable to the child, then the child will attempt to recreate the behaviour. Infants use their initial reflexes (grasping and sucking) to explore their environment and create schemes. Schemes are groups of similar actions or thoughts that are used repeatedly in response to the environment. Once a child begins to create schemes they use accommodation and assimilation to become progressively adapted to the world. Assimilation is when a child responds to a new event in a way that is consistent with an existing schema. For example, an infant may assimilate a new teddy bear into their putting things in their mouth scheme and use their reflexes to make the teddy bear go into their mouth. Accommodation is when a child either modifies an existing scheme or forms an entirely new schema to deal with a new object or event. For example, an infant may have to open his or her mouth wider than usual to accommodate the teddy bear's paw.

5-8 Months

Child has an experience with an external stimulus that they find pleasurable, so they try to recreate that experience. For example, a child accidentally hits the mobile above the crib and likes to watch it spin. When it stops the child begins to grab at the object to make it spin again. In this stage habits are formed from general schemes that the infant has created but there is not yet, from the child's point of view, any differentiation between means and ends. Children cannot also focus on multiple tasks at once, and only focus on the task at hand. The child may create a habit of spinning the mobile in its crib, but they are still trying to find out methods to reach the mobile in order to get it to spin in the way that they find pleasurable. Once there is another distraction (say the parent walks in the room) the baby will no longer focus on the mobile. Toys should be given to infants that respond to a child's actions to help foster their investigative instincts. For example, a toy plays a song when you push one button, and then a picture pops up if you push another button.

8-12 Months

Behaviours will be displayed for a reason rather than by chance. They begin to understand that one action can cause a reaction. They also begin to understand object permanence, which is the realization that objects continue to exist when removed form view.

For example: The baby wants a rattle but the blanket is in the way. The baby moves the blanket to get the rattle. Now that the infant can understand that they object still exists, they can differentiate between the object, and the experience of the object. According to psychologist David Elkind, "An internal representation of the absent object is the earliest manifestation of the symbolic function which develops gradually during the second year of life whose activities dominate the next stage of mental growth."

12-18 Months

Actions occur deliberately with some variation. For example a baby drums on a pot with a wooden spoon, then drums on the floor, then on the table.

18 - 24 Months

Children begin to build mental symbols and start to participate in pretend play. For example, a child is mixing ingredients together but doesn't have a spoon so they pretend to use one or use another object the replace the spoon Symbolic thought is a representation of objects and events as mental entities or symbols which helps foster cognitive development and the formation of imagination. According to Piaget, the infant begins to act upon intelligence rather than habit at this point. The end product is established after the infant has pursued for the appropriate means. The means are formed from the schemes that are known by the child. The child is starting to learn how to use what it has learned in the first two years to develop and further explore their environment.

These six sub-stages represent the approximate growth a child undergoes during Piaget's sensorimotor stage from birth to age 2. Once the child gains the ability to mentally represent reality, the child begins the transition to the preoperational stage of development.

PREOPERATIONAL STAGE

Lasts from 2 years of age until 6 or 7. It can be characterized in two somewhat different ways. In his early work, before he had developed his structuralist theory of cognition, Piaget described the child's thought during this period as being governed by principles such as egocentrism, animism and other similar constructs. Egocentrism is when a child can only see a certain situation his or her own way. One can not comprehend that other people have other views and perceptions of scenarios. Animism is when an individual gives a lifeless object human like qualities. An individual usually believes that this object has human emotions, thoughts and intentions. Once he had proposed his structuralist theory, Piaget characterized the preoperational child as lacking the cognitive structures possessed by the concrete operational child. The absence of these structures explains, in part, the behaviours Piaget had previously described as egocentric and animistic, for example an inability to comprehend that another individual may have different emotional responses to similar experiences.

Concrete Operational Stage

Lasts from 6 or 7 years until about 12 or 13. During this stage the child's cognitive structures can be characterized by group therapy. Piaget argues that the same general principles can be discerned in a wide range of behaviours. One of the best-known achievements of this stage is that of conservation. In a typical conservation experiment a child is asked to judge whether or not two quantities are the same - such as two equal quantities of liquid in a short and tall glass. A preoperational child will typically judge the taller, thinner glass to contain more, while a concrete operational child will judge the amounts still to be the same. The ability to reason in this way reflects the development of a principle of conservation.

Criticism

Many of his claims have fallen out of favor. For example, he claimed that young children cannot conserve number. However, further experiments show that children did not really understand what was being asked of them. When the experiment is done with candies, and the children are asked which set they want rather than tell an adult which is more, they show no confusion about which group has more items.

CHALLENGES TO PIAGETIAN STAGE THEORY

Piagetians' accounts of development have been challenged on several grounds. First, as Piaget himself noted, development does not always progress in the smooth manner his theory seems to predict. 'Decalage', or unpredicted gaps in the developmental progression, suggest that the stage model is at best a useful approximation. More broadly, Piaget's theory is 'domain general', predicting that cognitive maturation occurs concurrently across different domains of knowledge (such as mathematics, logic, understanding of physics, of language, etc.). During the 1980s and 1990s, cognitive developmentalists were influenced by "neo-nativist" and evolutionary psychology ideas. These ideas de-emphasized domain general theories and emphasized domain specificity or modularity of mind. Modularity implies that different cognitive faculties may be largely independent of one another and thus develop just as to quite different time-tables. In this vein, some cognitive developmentalists argued that rather than being domain general learners, children come equipped with domain specific theories, sometimes referred to as 'core knowledge', which allows them to break into learning within that domain. For example, even young infants appear to be sensitive to some predictable regularities in the movement and interactions of objects (*e.g.* that one object cannot pass through another), or in human behaviour (*e.g.* that a hand repeatedly reaching for an object has that object, not just a particular path of motion, as its goal).

These basic assumptions may be the building block out of which more elaborate knowledge is constructed. More recent work has strongly challenged some of the basic presumptions of the 'core knowledge' school, and revised ideas of domain generality—but from a newer dynamic systems approach, not from a revised Piagetian perspective. Dynamic systems approaches harken to modern neuroscientific research that was not available to Piaget when he was constructing his theory. One important finding is that domain-specific knowledge is constructed as children develop and integrate knowledge.

This suggests more of a "smooth integration" of learning and development than either Piaget, or his neo-nativist critics, had envisioned. Additionally, some psychologists, such as Vygotsky and Jerome Bruner, thought differently from Piaget, suggesting that language was more important than Piaget implied. Sarah Barnes rocks. Another recent challenge to Piaget's theory is a new theory called Ecological Systems Theory. This is based on the contextual influences in the child's life like his/her immediate family, school, society and the world, and how these impact the child's development. The experience of Sudbury model schools shows that a great variety can be found in the minds of children, against Piaget's theory of universal steps in comprehension and general patterns in the acquisition of knowledge: "No two kids ever take the same path. Few are remotely similar. Each child is so unique, so exceptional."

POST-PIAGETIAN AND NEO-PIAGETIAN STAGES

In the recent years, several scholars attempted to ameliorate the problems of Piaget's theory by developing new theories and models that can accommodate evidence that violates Piagetian predictions and postulates.

- The neo-Piagetian theories of cognitive development, advanced by Case, Demetriou, Halford, Fischer, and Pascual-Leone, attempted to integrate Piaget's theory with cognitive and differential theories of cognitive organization and development. Their aim was to better account for the cognitive factors of development and for intra-individual and inter-individual differences in cognitive development. They suggested that development along Piaget's stages is due to increasing working memory capacity and processing efficiency. Moreover, Demetriou's theory ascribes an important role to hypercognitive processes of self-recording, self-monitoring, and self-regulation and it recognizes the operation of several relatively autonomous domains of thought.
- Postformal stages have been proposed. Kurt Fischer suggested two, Michael Commons presents evidence for four postformal stages: the systematic, metasystematic, paradigmatic and cross paradigmatic.
- A "sentential" stage has been proposed, said to occur before the early preoperational stage. Proposed by Fischer, Biggs and Biggs, Commons, and Richards.
- Searching for a micro-physiological basis for human mental capacity, Traill proposed that there may be "pre-sensorimotor" stages—developed in the womb and/or transmitted genetically.

POSTULATED PHYSICAL MECHANISMS UNDERLYING "SCHEMES" AND STAGES

Piaget himself considered the possibility of RNA molecules as likely embodiments of his still-abstract "schemes" (which he promoted as units of action)—though he did not come to any firm conclusion. At that time, due to work such as that of Holger Hydén, RNA concentrations had indeed been shown to correlate with learning, so the idea was quite plausible. However, by the time of Piaget's death in 1980, this notion had lost favour.

One main problem was over the protein which (it was assumed) such RNA would necessarily produce, and that did not fit in with observation. It then turned out, surprisingly, that only about 3% of RNA does code for protein. Hence most of the remaining 97% could now theoretically be available to serve as Piagetian schemes. The issue has not yet been resolved experimentally, but its theoretical aspects have been reviewed.

Information Processing Approach

Cognitive psychology represents the dominant approach in psychology today. A primary focus of this approach is on memory (the storage and retrieval of information), a subject that has been of interest for thousands of years. The most widely accepted theory is labeled the "stage theory," based on the work of Atkinson and Shriffin.

The focus of this model is on how information is stored in memory; the model proposes that information is processed and stored in 3 stages. In this theory, information is thought to be processed in a serial, discontinuous manner as it moves from one stage to the next. In addition to the stage theory model of information processing, there are three more that are widely accepted. The first is based on the work of Craik and Lockhart and is labeled the "levels-of-processing" theory. The major proposition is that learners utilize different levels of elaboration as they process information.

This is done on a continuum from perception, through attention, to labeling, and finally, meaning. The key point is that all stimuli that activate a sensory receptor cell are permanently stored in memory, but that different levels of processing (*i.e.*, elaboration) contribute to an ability to access, or retrieve, that memory. Evidence from hypnosis and forensic psychology provide some interesting support for this hypothesis. This approach has been extended by Bransford (1979) who suggests that it is not only how the information is processed, but how the information is accessed. When the demands for accessing information more closely match the methods used to elaborate or learn the information, more is remembered. Two other models have been proposed as alternatives to the Atkinson-Shiffrin model: parallel-distributed processing and connectionistic.

The parallel-distributed processing model states that information is processed simultaneously by several different parts of the memory system, rather than sequentially as hypothesized by Atkinson-Shiffrin as well as Craik and Lockhart. Work done on how we process emotional data somewhat supports this contention. The connectionistic model proposed by Rumelhart and McClelland extends the parallel-distributed processing model.

It is one of the dominant forms of current research in cognitive psychology and is consistent with the most recent brain research. This model emphasizes the fact that information is stored in multiple locations throughout the brain in the form of networks of connections. It is consistent with the levels-of-processing approach in that the more connections to a single idea or concept, the more likely it is to be remembered.

Even though there are widely varying views within cognitive psychology, there are a few basic principles that most cognitive psychologists agree with. The first is the assumption of a limited capacity of the mental system. This means that the amount of information that can be processed by the system is constrained in some very important ways. Bottlenecks, or restrictions in the flow and processing of information, occur at very specific points.

A second principle is that a control mechanism is required to oversee the encoding, transformation, processing, storage, retrieval and utilization of information. That is, not all of the processing capacity of the system is available; an executive function that oversees this process will use up some of this capability.

When one is learning a new task or is confronted with a new environment, the executive function requires more processing power than when one is doing a routine task or is in a familiar environment. A third principle is that there is a two-way flow of information as we try to make sense of the world around us. We constantly use information that we gather through the senses and information we have stored in memory in a dynamic process as we construct meaning about our environment and our relations to it. This is somewhat analogous to the difference between inductive reasoning and deductive reasoning.

A similar distinction can be made between using information we derive from the senses and that generated by our imaginations. A fourth principle generally accepted by cognitive psychologists is that the human organism has been genetically prepared to process and organize information in specific ways.

For example, a human infant is more likely to look at a human face than any other stimulus. Given that the field of focus of a human infant is 12 to 18 inches, one can surmise that this is an important aspect of the infant's survival. Other research has discovered additional biological predispositions to process information.

For example, language development is similar in all human infants regardless of language spoken by adults or the area in which they live (*e.g.*, rural *versus* urban, Africa *versus* Europe.) All human infants with normal hearing babble and coo, generate first words, begin the use of telegraphic speech (*e.g.*, ball gone), and overgeneralize (*e.g.*, using "goed to the store" when they had previously used "went to the store") at approximately the same ages.

The issue of language development is an area where cognitive and behavioural psychologists as well as cognitive psychologists with different viewpoints have fought many battles regarding the processes underlying human behaviour. Needless to say the disussion continues.

Stage Model of Information Processing

One of the major issues in cognitive psychology is the study of memory. The dominant view is labeled the "stage theory" and is based on the work of Atkinson and Shiffrin.

Sensory Memory

Sensory memory is affiliated with the transduction of energy. The environment makes available a variety of sources of information (light, sound, smell, heat, cold, etc.), but the brain only understands electrical energy. The body has special sensory receptor cells that transduce (change from one form of energy to another) this external energy to something the brain can understand. In the process of transduction, a memory is created. This memory is very short (less than 1/2 second for vision; about 3 seconds for hearing). It is absolutely critical that the learner attend to the information at this initial stage in order to transfer it to the next one. There are two major concepts for getting information into STM: *First,* individuals are more likely to pay attention to a stimulus if it has an interesting feature. We are more likely to get an orienting response if this is present. *Second,* individuals are more likely to pay attention if the stimulus activates a known pattern. To the extent we have students call to mind relevant prior learning before we begin our presentations, we can take advantage of this principle.

Short-Term Memory (STM)

Short-term memory is also called working memory and relates to what we are thinking about at any given moment in time. In Freudian terms, this is conscious memory. It is created by our paying attention to an external stimulus, an internal thought, or both. It will initially last somewhere around 15 to 20 seconds unless it is repeated (called maintenance rehearsal) at which point it may be available for up to 20 minutes. The hypothalamus is a brain structure thought to be involved in this shallow processing of information. The frontal lobes of the cerebral cortex is the structure associated with working memory. For example, you are processing the words you read on the screen in your frontal lobes. However, if I ask, "What is your telephone number?" your brain immediately calls that from long-term memory and replaces what was previously there.

Another major limit on information processing in STM is in terms of the number of units that can be processed an any one time. Miller (1956) gave the number as 7 + 2, but more recent research suggests the number may be more like 5 + 2 for most things we are trying to remember. Because of the variability in how much individuals can work with (for some it may be three, for others seven) it is necessary to point out important information. If some students can only process three units of information at a time, let us make certain it is the most important three. There are two major concepts for retaining information in STM: organization and repetition.

There are four major types of organization that are most often used in instructional design:

- *Component (part/whole)*: Classification by category or concept (*e.g.*, the components of the teaching/learning model);
- *Sequential*: Chronological; cause/effect; building to climax (*e.g.*, baking a cake, reporting on a research study);
- *Relevance*: Central unifying idea or criteria (*e.g.*, most important principles of learning for boys and girls, appropriate management strategies for middle school and high school students);
- *Transitional (connective)*: Relational words or phrases used to indicate qualitative change over time (*e.g.*, stages in Piaget's theory of cognitive development or Erikson's stages of socioemotional development)

A related issue to organization is the concept of chunking or grouping pieces of data into units. For example, the letters"b d e" constitute three units of information while the word "bed" represents one unit even though it is composed of the same number of letters.

Chunking is a major technique for getting and keeping information in short-term memory; it is also a type of elaboration that will help get information into long-term memory. Repetition or rote rehearsal is a technique we all use to try to"learn" something. However, in order to be effective this must be done after forgetting begins.

Researchers advise that the learner should not repeat immediately the content (or skill), but wait a few minutes and then repeat. For the most part, simply memorizing something does not lead to learning (*i.e.*, relatively permanent change). We all have anecdotal evidence that we can remember something we memorized (a poem for example), but just think about all the material we tried to learn this way and the little we are able to remember after six months or a year.

Long-Term Memory (LTM)

Long-term memory is also called preconscious and unconscious memory in Freudian terms. Preconscious means that the information is relatively easily recalled (although it may take several minutes or even hours) while unconscious refers to data that is not available during normal consciousness. It is preconscious memory that is the focus of cognitive psychology as it relates to long-term memory.

The levels-of-processing theory, however, has provided some research that attests to the fact that we"know" more than we can easily recall. The two processes most likely to move information into long-term memory are elaboration and distributed practice.

There are several examples of elaboration that are commonly used in the teaching/ learning process:

- *Imaging*: Creating a mental picture;
- *Method of loci (locations)*: Ideas or things to be remembered are connected to objects located in a familiar location;
- *Pegword method (number, rhyming schemes)*: Ideas or things to be remembered are connected to specific words (*e.g.*, one-bun, two-shoe, three-tree, etc.)
- *Rhyming (songs, phrases)*: Information to be remembered is arranged in a rhyme (*e.g.*, 30 days hath September, April, June, and November, etc.)
- *Initial letter*: The first letter of each word in a list is used to make a sentence (the sillier, the better).

Organization (Types) of Knowledge

As information is stored in long-term memory, it is organized using one or more structures: declarative, procedural, and/or imagery.

Declarative Memory:

- *Semantic Memory*: Facts and generalized information (concepts, principles, rules; problem-solving strategies; learning strategies)
  - *Schema/Schemata*: Networks of connected ideas or relationships; data structures or procedures for organizing the parts of a specific experience into a meaningful system (like a standard or stereotype).
  - *Proposition*: Interconnected set of concepts and relationships; if/then statements (smallest unit of information that can be judged true or false).
  - *Script*: "Declarative knowledge structure that captures general information about a routine series of events or a recurrent type of social event, such as eating in a restaurant or visiting the doctor" Frame — complex organization including concepts and visualizations that provide a reference within which stimuli and actions are judged.
  - *Scheme*: An organization of concepts, principles, rules, etc. that define a perspective and presents specific action patterns to follow.
  - *Programme*: Set of rules that define what to do in a particular situation.

  - *Paradigm*: The basic way of perceiving, thinking, valuing, and doing associated with a particular vision of reality.
  - *Model*: A set of propositions or equations describing in simplified form some aspects of our experience. Every model is based upon a theory or paradigm, but the theory or paradigm may not be stated in concise form.
- *Episodic Memory*: Personal experience.

COGNITIVE PSYCHOLOGY AND BEHAVIOURISM

Cognitive psychology is usually conceived as a revolt against Behaviourism. So is Humanistic psychology. These two revolutions share little in common, thus raising the question of the target of their respective insurrections. That target, for cognitive psychology, appears to be stimulus-response associationism. More specifically, the revolutionary theme is that behaviour cannot be adequately accounted for by stimulus-response connections even when such a conception is enlarged to include chains of internal associations that mediate between the external stimulus and the overt response. Stimulus-response associations, the argument goes, must be discarded in favour of cognitive processes:

"The word cognitive, which is derived from cognition, meaning *knowledge,* emphasises mental activities, not just stimuli and responses. It is precisely this shift of emphasis—away from a passive system that accepts stimuli and automatically produces S-R chains, and toward a notion of mental actions—that characterises cognitive theories. According to Neisser, whose book *Cognitive psychology* (1967) gave real impetus to the approach, the focus of cognitive theory is knowledge—how it is acquired, modified, manipulated, used, stored; in short, how it is processed by the human organism. Thus, information processing (a term cognitive psychologists have borrowed from computer scientists) broadly refers to the human being's active interaction with information about his world. Of central importance in this processing are the mental activities that occur between a stimulus and a response."

An active mental processing of information (knowledge) distinguishes cognitive psychology from a passive stimulus-response associationism. Or does it? Are the distinctions between *active* and *passive, mentalism* and *behaviourism,* and *knowledge* and *S-R associations,* qualitative or one of degree? Do the distinctions represent evolutionary or revolutionary changes?

Active vs. Passive models. Although the active-passive distinction is widely employed, its meaning is not entirely clear. One sometimes gets the impression that the issue is one of whether the organism takes a passive or active role in his own behaviour in the sense that he functions either as a mechanical robot or as a free spirit. Such a distinction reflects more the confusing heritage of the philosophical problem of free will than a meaningful psychological comparison. If we accept a psychological determinism then we cannot conclude that some forms of behaviour are more determined than others.

The passive and active distinction can be equated with the locus of events which initiates behaviour. In a passive model the locus of control resides outside the organism; behaviour is initiated in a machine-like fashion by external stimulation. Behaviour in an active model, in contrast, is self-generated; the organism generates events (e.g., hypotheses) that guide subsequent behaviour. Although the distinction has apparent validity when comparing different kinds of behaviour, such as braking in reaction to a red traffic light as contrasted to searching one's memory for a word that seems to be "on the tip of the tongue", the important question is whether the distinction is theoretically significant. John Watson (1919) in his stimulus-response model, conceptualised food-seeking behaviour of animals as being initiated by stomach contractions which in turn increase the activity level, thus making it more probable that the animal will discover food. Similarly Spence (1952) postulated that rats made observing responses that oriented an organism's receptors toward cues that are correlated with reinforcement. Do these two cases qualify as examples of active behaviour in the sense that they are generated by activities within the organism? Or do they fail to qualify because the S-R model always implies some stimulus, even an unobserved or theoretical one that triggers behaviour? The problem of classifying a theory as active or passive becomes more complicated when mediational processes are considered. One such formulation postulates two modes of behaviour: A "passive" single-unit mode in which an external stimulus triggers a response and a mediational mode in which behaviour is controlled by a covert representational response wherein the representation may entail considerable transformation. Thus, even if the passive-active distinction is accepted as valid, the question remains whether it reliably distinguishes cognitive from stimulus-response formulations.

Mentalism vs. Behaviourism. Watson's initial rejection of all mentalistic terms and final flirtation with the denial of human consciousness, contributed a legacy of confusion from which psychology has still to recover. The major thrust of behaviourism was that psychology is a natural science with behaviour as its dependent variable (Kendler, in press). An important corollary is that the *direct* examination of consciousness, either by rigorous introspection or naive phenomenology, could not produce the reliable knowledge demanded by natural science methodology. What Watson failed to realise, along with many of his critics, is that conscious experience and mentalistic concepts are not excommunicated from methodological behaviourism. They can be incorporated within a behaviouristic research program if the requirements of objectivity (inter-subjectivity) are not violated. This can be accomplished when phenomenological evidence is used as a source of theoretical hypotheses and when mental processes are assumed to operate in a theoretical system that is designed to predict publicly observable behaviour.

The strategy of employing conscious experience as a source of theoretical hypotheses can be justified by the past. One example is the conscious attempt to improve memory by encoding meaningless nonsense syllables into meaningful units. Phenomenological evidence of this sort had strategic value in formulating useful encoding hypotheses for theories of memory. Phenomenological evidence, it should be noted, can also be uninformative as well as misleading. Numerous investigators from the time of the famous imageless thought controversy have reported that thinking can occur without any conscious deliberation: "One does one's thinking before one knows what he is to think about". Other evidence, both psychoanalytic and experimental, indicates that introspective reports can be misleading. Thus, those who believe that introspective evidence can be a rich source of theoretical hypotheses about behaviour must be selective in applying their strategy because of possible discrepancies between the two.

Tolman (1932) demonstrated that a psychological theory could postulate mentalistic activities (e.g., the formation of cognitive maps) without compromising any commitment to methodological behaviourism. By *inferring* the state of a rat's mind from its past experience and its present environment, Tolman was able to make predictions about the rat's behaviour. Cognitive psychology, for the most part, follows the same methodological prescription. The state of the human mind, or more properly its functional organisation, is inferred and then the behavioural output is predicted.

Cognitive psychology, in spite of what some would like to believe, is not at odds with methodological behaviourism. The "revolutionary core" of cognitive psychology is directed against substantive aspects of stimulus-response psychology. But S-R formulations (e.g., Hull-Spence, Skinner, Guthrie) do not share substantive theoretical assumptions; only a commitment to methodological behaviourism and the use of a stimulus-response language (Kendler, 1965) which can be translated into an input-output idiom. The Hull-Spence formulation, it should be noted, rejects the notion that behaviour can be adequately explained solely by stimulus-response associations. Other concepts (e.g., drive) are required even to explain the behaviour of lower animals. When it came to human cognitive behaviour, Spence (1950) proposed a flow-diagram which anticipated later information-processing conceptions, and which radically departed form his own analysis of the discrimination learning of the rat (1936). In his flow diagram he employed concepts (e.g., sense reception, signification, verbal meaning) that referred to the innate organisation of the brain, cognitive expectations, and linguistic meaning. These higher level processes "badly need the attention of all psychologists, cognition, S-R or whatever else" (Spence, 1950).

Knowledge. One of the core concepts of cognitive psychology is *knowledge;* an organism processes knowledge (information) which in turn guides his action. The historical significance of this concept depends upon whether it has an existence independent of conscious experience. If knowledge or information refers to "that which is known" or "familiarity gained by actual experience" then the problem becomes one of defining the procedures for measuring it. Does a rat have knowledge of a maze that it has learned? A methodological behaviourist would ignore such a question if an affirmative answer required experiential evidence. The question would have empirical meaning if "knowledge" is considered analogous to Tolman's 's concept of a cognitive map, an inferred state of mind defined in terms of experimental operations that has observable consequences. In the same sense an animal has "knowledge" of a maze if its anticipatory goal responses guide behaviour toward alleys that lead to the goal box.

6

Social Cognition

Social cognition came to prominence with the rise of cognitive psychology in the late 1960s and early 1970s and is now the dominant model and approach in mainstream social psychology. Common to social cognition theories is the idea that information is represented in the brain as "cognitive elements"—such as schemas, attributions, or stereotypes—and a focus on how these cognitive elements are processed. Social cognition therefore applies and extends many themes, theories and paradigms from cognitive psychology, for example in reasoning (representativeness heuristic, base rate fallacy and confirmation bias), attention (automaticity and priming) and memory (schemas, primacy and recency). It is very likely that social psychology was always a lot more cognitive than mainstream psychology to begin with, as it traditionally discussed internal mental states such as beliefs and desires when mainstream psychology was dominated by behaviourism and rejected them as illusory. A notable theory of social cognition is social schema theory, although this is not the basis of all studies of social cognition. It has been suggested that other disciplines in social psychology such as social identity theory and social representations may be seeking to explain largely the same phenomena as social cognition and that these different disciplines might be merged into a "coherent integrated whole". A parallel paradigm has arisen in the study of action, termed motor cognition. Motor cognition is concerned with understanding the representation of action and the associated process.

Social Schemas

Social schema theory builds on and uses terminology from schema theory in cognitive psychology which describes how ideas, or "concepts" from the world around us are represented in the brain, and how they are categorized. According to this view, when we see or think of a concept, a mental representation or *schema* is "activated", bringing to mind other information which is linked to the original concept by association.

This activation often happens unconsciously. As a result of activating such schemas, judgements are formed which go beyond the information actually available, since many of the associations the schema evokes extend outside the given information. This may influence thinking and social behaviour regardless of whether these judgements are accurate or not.

For example, if an individual is introduced as a teacher, a "teacher schema" may be activated and we might associate this person with wisdom or authority, or past experiences of teachers that we have remembered and are important to us. When a schema is more accessible this means it can more quickly be activated and used in a particular situation.

Two cognitive processes that increase the accessibility of schemas are salience and priming. Salience is the degree to which a particular social object stands out relative to other social objects in a situation. The higher the salience of an object the more likely that schemas for that object will be made accessible. For example, if there is one female in a group of seven males, female gender schemas may be more accessible and influence the group's thinking and behaviour toward the female group member. Priming refers to any experience immediately prior to a situation that causes a schema to be more accessible. For example watching a scary movie at a theatre late at night might increase the accessibility of frightening schemas that affect a person's perception of shadows and background noises as potential threats. Priming happens because of the functions of the reticular cortex.

Social cognition researchers are also interested in how new information is integrated into pre-established schemas, especially when that information is contrary with those pre-established schemas.

Pre-established schemas tend to guide attention to new information. People selectively attend to information that is consistent with the schema and ignore information that is inconsistent. This is referred to as a confirmation bias. Sometimes inconsistent information is sub-categorized and stored away as a special case, leaving the original schema intact without any alterations.

This is referred to as subtyping. Social cognition researchers are also interested in studying the regulation of activated schemas. It is believed that the situational activation of schemas is automatic, meaning that it is outside the control of the individual. In many situations however, the schematic information that has been activated may be in conflict with the social norms of the situation, in which case an individual is motivated to inhibit the influence of the schematic information on their thinking and social behaviour. Whether a person will successfully regulate the application of the activated schemas is dependent on individual differences in self-regulatory ability and the presence of situational impairments to executive control. High self-regulatory ability and the lack of situational impairments on executive functioning increase the likelihood that individuals will successfully inhibit the influence of automatically activated schemas on their thinking and social behaviour. However, when people stop suppressing the influence of the unwanted thoughts, a rebound effect can occur where the thought becomes hyper-accessible.

INFANTS AND SOCIAL COGNITION

Infants are innately interested in, and attentive to, people. Even newborn babies can imitate facial expressions, and older infants prefer to imitate people rather than machines (Meltzoff 1995). Joint attention skills develop by about nine months, and infants probably have a basic notion of agency by the end of the first year. Infants' conscious awareness of their own emotional states and of how they are related to the actions of their caregivers also develops during the first year of life. Although an understanding of *representational* mental states (e.g., thoughts, beliefs, knowledge, ideas, or false beliefs) develops more slowly, a basic understanding of desires and emotions is present relatively early (by around two years). This early focus on other people means that parents and caretakers have an enormously important role to play in cognitive development.

As an illustration, take *pretending,* an early example of the child's symbolic capacity. Children across the world play pretend games, and pretending is important both for the development of the cognitive understanding of the minds of others (Lillard 2002) and for the development of social cognition more generally. Pretence activities focused on objects and props typically begin during the second year of life, and sociodramatic pretending with caretakers and peers typically emerges at around three to four years. Cultural contexts affect children's choice of pretend play topics. For example, the pretend play of U.S. preschoolers shows greater enactment of fantasy themes than the pretend play of Taiwanese children, whereas Taiwanese children spend a lot more time playing games about social routines and "proper" conduct (Haight et al. 1999). Parental attitudes and parental engagement also affect the frequency of pretend play, with more pretend play found in cultures where it is actively encouraged. Thus parents and caretakers act, usually quite unconsciously, in ways that promote and influence cognitive change.

A second illustration comes from research into children's understanding of mental states (*theory of mind*). A basic division between the mental (thoughts, ideas, beliefs) and the physical (substantive, objective objects) is present from early in childhood (Wellman 2002). As they seek causes and explanations for the actions of others, children gradually develop an understanding of mental states such as beliefs, knowledge, and false beliefs. For example, an understanding of false belief, with a consequent understanding of deception and intentional lying, develops at around four years. One important source of individual differences in the development of theory of mind is parent-child and family relationships. Children with brothers and sisters, particularly those with older siblings, typically show earlier psychological understanding, for example passing false belief tasks at earlier ages than children without siblings (e.g., Youngblade and Dunn 1995). Children whose families openly discuss emotions and feelings also show earlier developments in psychological understanding, particularly if the family discussions analyze the causes of emotions. The ways in which we talk to our children and the things that we talk to them about both play key roles in cognitive development.

Earlier Theoretical Models: Psychoanalysis and Behaviorism

Theories have approached morality differently. Sigmund Freud (1856–1939) described *Oedipus complex* to explain the origins of moral conscience, called the *superego.* The Oedipus complex occurs when a child loves the opposite sex parent and, in order to avoid the anxiety and fear of punishment that this causes, the child identifies with the same sex parent. The child incorporates the same sex parent's prohibitions, starting with "Do not love (sexually) your parent."

For behaviorist theorists, such as Robert R. Sears, Robert Grinder, and Albert Bandura (1982), conscience or morality was considered analogous to the phenomenon of resistance to extinction. H. Hartshorne and M. A. May, at the end of the 1920s, were pioneers in this line of research. Later, Robert Sears, Eleanor Maccoby, and Harry Levin (1957) and other researchers studied the influence of maternal and paternal disciplines upon development of the conscience. These studies found that warm and affectionate parents, who reason with their children rather than punish them physically, are more successful in having their children assimilate the moral values of the culture. Cognitive behaviorists have added other dimensions to this process, such as *expectancies* (what the child expects is going to happen), *incentive value* (how much the child wants something), *hypothesis testing* ("If I do this, then that will happen"), and *self-efficacy* (one's capacity and confidence on doing something) (Bandura 1977, 1978). In the psychoanalytic and behaviorist models, morality seems to be something that comes from outside, from society, which is internalized.

COGNITIVE DISSONANCE

Cognitive dissonance is an uncomfortable feeling caused by holding conflicting ideas simultaneously. The theory of cognitive dissonance proposes that people have a motivational drive to reduce dissonance. They do this by changing their attitudes, beliefs, and actions. Dissonance is also reduced by justifying, blaming, and denying. It is one of the most influential and extensively studied theories in social psychology. Experience can clash with expectations, as, for example, with buyer's remorse following the purchase of an expensive item. In a state of dissonance, people may feel surprise, dread, guilt, anger, or embarrassment. People are biased to think of their choices as correct, despite any contrary evidence. This bias gives dissonance theory its predictive power, shedding light on otherwise puzzling irrational and destructive behaviour. A classical example of this idea (and the origin of the expression "sour grapes") is expressed in the fable *The Fox and the Grapes* by Aesop (ca. 620–564 BCE). In the story, a fox sees some high-hanging grapes and wishes to eat them. When the fox is unable to think of a way to reach them, he surmises that the grapes are probably not worth eating, as they must not be ripe or that they are sour. This example follows a pattern: one desires something, finds it unattainable, and reduces one's dissonance by criticizing it. Jon Elster calls this pattern "adaptive preference formation."

Examples

The most famous case in the early study of cognitive dissonance was described by Leon Festinger and others in the book *When Prophecy Fails*. The authors infiltrated a group that was expecting the imminent end of the world on a certain date. When that prediction failed, the movement did not disintegrate, but grew instead. By sharing cult beliefs with others, they gained acceptance and thus reduced their own dissonance. Smoking is often postulated as an example of cognitive dissonance because it is widely accepted that cigarettes can cause lung cancer, yet virtually everyone wants to live a long and healthy life. In terms of the theory, the desire to live a long life is dissonant with the activity of doing something that will most likely shorten one's life. The tension produced by these contradictory ideas can be reduced by quitting smoking, denying the evidence of lung cancer, or justifying one's smoking. For example, smokers could rationalize their behaviour by concluding that only a few smokers become ill, that it only happens to very heavy smokers, or that if smoking does not kill them, something else will. While chemical addiction may operate in addition to cognitive dissonance for existing smokers, new smokers may exhibit a simpler case of the latter. This case of dissonance could also be interpreted in terms of a threat to the self-concept. The thought, "I am increasing my risk of lung cancer" is dissonant with the self-related belief, "I am a smart, reasonable person who makes good decisions." Because it is often easier to make excuses than it is to change behaviour, dissonance theory leads to the conclusion that humans are sometimes rationalizing and not always rational beings.

Other Related Phenomena

There are a great number of phenomena that relate to cognitive dissonance theory: *effort justification*, where working for something causes someone to like it more; *Self-evaluation maintenance theory*, in which the skills or interests that define us can cause dissonance when they appear superior in others close to us; *counter-attitudinal advocacy*, where behaviours supporting a dissonant attitude causes one to adopt that attitude; *post-decision dissonance*, where one justifies an unalterable decision as the right one; *insufficient punishment*, the practice of punishing a person without doing it so harshly that they can tell themselves "I still like the behaviour, but I avoid it because of the devastating punishment"; *overjustification effect*, when an intrinsic (internal) motivation is shifted to extrinsic motivations through external reward; balance theory, a general tendency to seek consonance between our views of others, and our views of their attitudes; *self-handicapping*, avoiding effort in the hopes of keeping potential failure from hurting self-esteem; and finally *justification of altruism*, a habit of attributing kind actions to selfish motivations to avoid feeling committed to being a 'good person', or to thinking the deed was 'the right thing to do'.

Ben Franklin Effect

One situation that may create dissonance is when someone does a favour for a person that they dislike. Here, the dissonance is between those negative feelings for the other person, and the awareness of having expended effort to help them. Cognitive dissonance theory predicts that people will try to resolve this dissonance, by adopting a more positive attitude towards the other person. Several experiments have borne out this prediction. This has been named the *Ben Franklin effect* because it was anticipated by Franklin when he served in the Pennsylvania legislature in the 18th Century. In his autobiography, he explains how he dealt with the animosity of a rival legislator: Having heard that he had in his library a certain very scarce and curious book, I wrote a note to him, expressing my desire of perusing that book, and requesting he would do me the favour of lending it to me for a few days. He sent it immediately, and I return'd it in about a week with another note, expressing strongly my sense of the favour. When we next met in the House, he spoke to me (which he had never done before), and with great civility; and he ever after manifested a readiness to serve me on all occasions, so that we became great friends, and our friendship continued to his death. This is another instance of the truth of an old maxim I had learned, which says, "He that has once done you a kindness will be more ready to do you another, than he whom you yourself have obliged." A counterpart to this effect is when someone's actions hurt another person, whom they regard positively or neutrally. In this case, one way to resolve the dissonance is to think more negatively about that person, so that they seem to deserve what happened to them.

Variants

An overarching principle of cognitive dissonance is that it involves the formation of an idea or emotion in conflict with a fundamental element of the self-concept, such as "I am a successful/functional person", "I am a good person", or "I made the right decision." The anxiety that comes with the possibility of having made a bad decision can lead to rationalization, the tendency to create additional reasons or justifications to support one's choices. A person who just spent too much money on a new car might decide that the new vehicle is much less likely to break down than his or her old car. This belief may or may not be true, but it would reduce dissonance and make the person feel better. Dissonance can also lead to confirmation bias, the denial of dis-confirming evidence, and other ego defense mechanisms. Within this overarching principle, there are two main forms of dissonance: hedonistic dissonance and moral dissonance (Holland, Meertens & Van-Vugt, 2002).

- *Hedonistic dissonance* is elicited when people act in a way which results in negative consequences for themselves. For instance, a person is late for a meeting because of traffic but could have been on time had he taken the subway.
- *Moral dissonance* is aroused when people act in a way that causes negative consequence for others. For instance, cheating and lying.

Theory and Research

Most of the research on cognitive dissonance takes the form of one of four major paradigms. Important research generated by the theory has been concerned with the consequences of exposure to information inconsistent with a prior belief, what happens after individuals act in ways that are inconsistent with their prior attitudes, what happens after individuals make decisions, and the effects of effort expenditure.

The Belief Disconfirmation Paradigm

Dissonance is aroused when people are confronted with information that is inconsistent with their beliefs. If the dissonance is not reduced by changing one's belief, the dissonance can result in misperception or rejection or refutation of the information, seeking support from others who share the beliefs, and attempting to persuade others to restore consonance. An early version of cognitive dissonance theory appeared in Leon Festinger's 1956 book, *When Prophecy Fails*. This book gave an inside account of the increasing belief which sometimes follows the failure of a cult's prophecy. The believers met at a pre-determined place and time, believing they alone would survive the Earth's destruction. The appointed time came and passed without incident. They faced acute cognitive dissonance: had they been the victim of a hoax? Had they donated their worldly possessions in vain? Most members chose to believe something less dissonant: the aliens had given earth a second chance, and the group was now empowered to spread the word: earth-spoiling must stop. The group dramatically increased their proselytism despite the failed prophecy.

The Induced-Compliance Paradigm

In Festinger and Carlsmith's classic 1959 experiment, students were asked to spend an hour on boring and tedious tasks (e.g., turning pegs a quarter turn, over and over again). The tasks were designed to generate a strong, negative attitude. Once the subjects had done this, the experimenters asked some of them to do a simple favour.

They were asked to talk to another subject (actually an actor) and persuade them that the tasks were interesting and engaging. Some participants were paid \$20 (inflation adjusted to 2010, this equates to \$150) for this favour, another group was paid \$1 (or \$7.50 in "2010 dollars"), and a control group was not asked to perform the favour.

When asked to rate the boring tasks at the conclusion of the study (not in the presence of the other "subject"), those in the \$1 group rated them more positively than those in the \$20 and control groups. This was explained by Festinger and Carlsmith as evidence for cognitive dissonance. The researchers theorized that people experienced dissonance between the conflicting cognitions, "I told someone that the task was interesting", and "I actually found it boring." When paid only \$1, students were forced to internalize the attitude they were induced to express, because they had no other justification. Those in the \$20 condition, however, had an obvious external justification for their behaviour, and thus experienced less dissonance.

In subsequent experiments, an alternative method of inducing dissonance has become common. In this research, experimenters use counter-attitudinal essay-writing, in which people are paid varying amounts of money (e.g. \$1 or \$10) for writing essays expressing opinions contrary to their own. People paid only a small amount of money have less external justification for their inconsistency and must produce internal justification in order to reduce the high degree of dissonance that they are experiencing. A variant of the induced-compliance paradigm is the forbidden toy paradigm. An experiment by Aronson and Carlsmith in 1963 examined self-justification in children. In this experiment, children were left in a room with a variety of toys, including a highly desirable toy steam-shovel (or other toy). Upon leaving the room, the experimenter told half the children that there would be a severe punishment if they played with that particular toy and told the other half that there would be a mild punishment. All of the children in the study refrained from playing with the toy. Later, when the children were told that they could freely play with whatever toy they wanted, the ones in the mild punishment condition were less likely to play with the toy, even though the threat had been removed. The children who were only mildly threatened had to justify to themselves why they did not play with the toy. The degree of punishment by itself was not strong enough, so the children had to convince themselves that the toy was not worth playing with in order to resolve their dissonance.

The Free-Choice Paradigm

In a different type of experiment conducted by Jack Brehm, 225 female students rated a series of common appliances and were then allowed to choose one of two appliances to take home as a gift. A second round of ratings showed that the participants increased their ratings of the item they chose, and lowered their ratings of the rejected item. This can be explained in terms of cognitive dissonance. When making a difficult decision, there are always aspects of the rejected choice that one finds appealing and these features are dissonant with choosing something else. In other words, the cognition, "I chose X" is dissonant with the cognition, "There are some things I like about Y." More recent research has found similar results in four-year-old children and capuchin monkeys.

The Effort-Justification Paradigm

Dissonance is aroused whenever individuals voluntarily engage in an unpleasant activity to achieve some desired goal. Dissonance can be reduced by exaggerating the desirability of the goal. Aronson & Mills had individuals undergo a severe or mild "initiation" in order to become a member of a group. In the severe-initiation condition, the individuals engaged in an embarrassing activity. The group turned out to be very dull and boring. The individuals in the severe-initiation condition evaluated the group as more interesting than the individuals in the mild-initiation condition. All of the above paradigms continue to be used in fruitful research. Washing one's hands has been shown to eliminate post-decisional dissonance, presumably because the dissonance is often caused by moral disgust (with oneself) which is related to disgust from unsanitary conditions.

Challenges and Qualifications

Daryl Bem was an early critic of cognitive dissonance theory. He proposed self-perception theory as a more parsimonious alternative explanation of the experimental results. According to Bem, people do not think much about their attitudes, let alone whether they are in conflict. Bem interpreted people in the Festinger and Carlsmith study or the induced-compliance paradigm as inferring their attitudes from their behaviour.

Thus, when asked "Did you find the task interesting?" they decided that they must have found it interesting because that is what they told someone. Bem suggested that people paid $20 had a salient, external incentive for their behaviour and were likely to perceive the money as their reason for saying the task was interesting, rather than concluding that they actually found it interesting.

In many experimental situations, Bem's theory and Festinger's dissonance theory make identical predictions, but only dissonance theory predicts the presence of unpleasant tension or arousal. Lab experiments have verified the presence of arousal in dissonance situations. This provides support for cognitive dissonance theory and makes it unlikely that self-perception by itself can account for all the laboratory findings.

In 1969, Elliot Aronson reformulated the theory by linking it to the self-concept. According to this new interpretation, cognitive dissonance does not arise because people experience dissonance between conflicting cognitions. Instead, it occurs when people see their actions as conflicting with their normally positive view of themselves.

Thus, about the original Festinger and Carlsmith study using the induced-compliance paradigm, Aronson stated that the dissonance was between the cognition, "I am an honest person" and the cognition, "I lied to someone about finding the task interesting." Other psychologists have argued that maintaining cognitive consistency is a way to protect public self-image, rather than private self-concept. However, a recent result seems to rule out such an explanation by showing revaluation of items following a choice even when people have forgotten their choices.

During the 1980s, Cooper and Fazio argued that dissonance was caused by aversive consequences, rather than inconsistency. According to this interpretation, the fact that lying is wrong and hurtful, not the inconsistency between cognitions, is what makes people feel bad. Subsequent research, however, found that people experience dissonance even when they feel they have not done anything wrong. For example, Harmon-Jones and colleagues showed that people experience dissonance even when the consequences of their statements are beneficial—as when they convince sexually active students to use condoms, when they, themselves are not using condoms. Chen and colleagues have criticized the free-choice paradigm and have suggested that the "Rank, choice, rank" method of studying dissonance is invalid.

They argue that research design relies on the assumption that, if the subject rates options differently in the second survey, then the subject's attitudes towards the options have therefore changed. They show that there are other reasons one might get different rankings in the second survey—perhaps the subjects were largely indifferent between choices. Although some follow-up studies have found supportive evidence for Chen's concerns, other studies that have controlled for Chen's concerns have not, instead suggesting that the mere act of making a choice can indeed change preferences. Nevertheless, this issue remains under active investigation.

7

Social Motives

KIND OF MOTIVES

A MOTIVE may be defined as meaning that which acts as an inducement to preference or choice. 'In other words it is a very strong influence toward some object to be attained. Just what these influences are depends entirely upon the nature of the person and on the object to be attained. We often hear the expression, and doubtless use it as often ourselves, "What was your motive in doing this?" meaning what caused you or what influenced you to act in such a manner.

We may state with truth that every wilful act has its inducement or cause. Just as in mathematics there is a reason for every step, so also in every act there is a motive or cause. From the child on up the individual can give a reason for each and every one of his voluntary acts however small and mean the reason may be. Still it is a reason. It may only be a certain state of consciousness which happens to be uppermost in a man's mind as he acts.

Very often Intention and Motive are confused; in fact they are used interchangeably in society. Notwithstanding this fact there is a vast difference in their meaning. Intention is what a man means to do, while Motive is the personal frame of mind which indicates why he means to do it. Therefore Intention has the stronger moral value, while Motive renders the consequences interesting and attractive. Motive is that which makes the difference between one act and another.

As we now know the difference between Intention and Motive, let us examine the different kinds of Motives. Motive may be divided into two classes, Egoistical and Altruistical. Both classes are absolutely necessary in our daily life. Let us first look at egoistic motives or the ones which concern the self only. Our original instincts are such that their objects are to look after the advantages of the self. However everything depends upon the sort of self maintained. What would become of a person if he would not struggle for food and strive against obstacles? What would become of society? Self-preserving instincts must be therefore socially conservative. No one has a right to neglect his own interests, hoping some one else will care for them. The man who takes exercise because he thinks of his health must be commanded, but the one who is thinking continually of his health and excludes other thoughts must be condemned.

The Hierarchal Model of Achievement Motivation

Achievement motivation has been conceptualized in many different ways. Our understanding of achievement-relevant effects, cognition, and behaviour has improved. Despite being similar in nature, many achievement motivation approaches have been developed separately, suggesting that most achievement motivation theories are in concordance with one another instead of competing. Motivational researchers have sought to promote a hierarchal model of approach and avoidance achievement motivation by incorporating the two prominent theories: the achievement motive approach and the achievement goal approach.

Achievement motives include the need for achievement and the fear of failure. These are the more predominant motives that direct our behaviour toward positive and negative outcomes.

Achievement goals are viewed as more solid cognitive representations pointing individuals toward a specific end. There are three types of these achievement goals: a performance-approach goal, a performance-avoidance goal, and a mastery goal. A performance-approach goal is focused on attaining competence relative to others, a performance-avoidance goal is focused on avoiding incompetence relative to others, and a mastery goal is focused on the development of competence itself and of task mastery. Achievement motives can be seen as direct predictors of achievement-relevant circumstances. Thus, achievement motives are said to have an indirect or distal influence, and achievement goals are said to have a direct or proximal influence on achievement-relevant outcomes.

These motives and goals are viewed as working together to regulate achievement behaviour. The hierarchal model presents achievement goals as predictors for performance outcomes. The model is being further conceptualized to include more approaches to achievement motivation. One weakness of the model is that it does not provide an account of the processes responsible for the link between achievement goals and performance. As this model is enhanced, it becomes more useful in predicting the outcomes of achievement-based behaviours.

IMPLICIT AND SELF-ATTRIBUTED MOTIVES

Motivational researchers share the view that achievement behaviour is an interaction between situational variables and the individual subject's motivation to achieve. Two motives are directly involved in the prediction of behaviour, implicit and explicit. Implicit motives are spontaneous impulses to act, also known as task performances, and are aroused through incentives inherent to the task. Explicit motives are expressed through deliberate choices and more often stimulated for extrinsic reasons. Also, individuals with strong implicit needs to achieve goals set higher internal standards, whereas others tend to adhere to the societal norms. These two motives often work together to determine the behaviour of the individual in direction and passion.

PRIMARY AND DERIVED MOTIVES

Primary Motives

There are certain primary conditions which arouse behaviour. Among these are conditions which give rise to thirst, hunger, fatigue, sexual needs, and pain avoidance. It is these primary motives which are employed almost exclusively in the animal laboratory. The strength of these motives may be defined in terms of hours of privation in the case of hunger, thirst, and sex and in terms of hours without rest, for fatigue. Pain avoidance is very difficult to manipulate quantitatively.

While we recognise similar basic motivating conditions in human beings, we have not found it possible, in general, to vary them in experiments with human subjects. In laboratory experiments, the use of electric shock seems to be the only major method of arousing primary motives in humans, and there is even some question as to whether its influence is a direct result of sheer pain.

We do not deprive an adult of food for 24 hours and then offer a filet mignon if he performs a given task it a certain speed, although such a procedure might well be worth trying. The fact is that experiments on motivation with human adults urn at the study of what we choose to call derived motives.

Derived Motives

These motives are so named because unlike primary motives they are believed to be largely learned. These motives have been variously named, have varied greatly in number (in part because of different descriptive dimensions used), and are still subject to considerable controversy, largely because the operations which evoke them are quite obscure.

We may point out some of the *descriptive terms* which have been used to identify these complex motives; motive to preserve self-esteem, to gain prestige, to dominate others, to be gregarious, to achieve one's deepest ambitions, or, for that matter, the motive to see a ball game.

There is nothing sacred about any such list. For the present we need to emphasise only that there *are* complex motives which rather completely prompt adult behaviour.

CONCEPTS OF MOTIVATION

Intrinsic motivation refers to motivation that is driven by an interest or enjoyment in the task itself, and exists within the individual rather than relying on any external pressure. Intrinsic motivation has been studied by social and educational psychologists since the early 1970s. Research has found that it is usually associated with high educational achievement and enjoyment by students. Explanations of intrinsic motivation have been given in the context of Fritz Heider's attribution theory, Bandura's work on self-efficacy, and Deci and Ryan's cognitive evaluation theory. Students are likely to be intrinsically motivated if they:

- attribute their educational results to internal factors that they can control (e.g. the amount of effort they put in),
- believe they can be effective agents in reaching desired goals (i.e. the results are not determined by luck),
- are interested in mastering a topic, rather than just rote-learning to achieve good grades.

Extrinsic motivation comes from outside of the individual. Common extrinsic motivations are rewards like money and grades, coercion and threat of punishment. Competition is in general extrinsic because it encourages the performer to win and beat others, not to enjoy the intrinsic rewards of the activity.

A crowd cheering on the individual and trophies are also extrinsic incentives. Social psychological research has indicated that extrinsic rewards can lead to overjustification and a subsequent reduction in intrinsic motivation. In one study demonstrating this effect, children who expected to be (and were) rewarded with a ribbon and a gold star for drawing pictures spent less time playing with the drawing materials in subsequent observations than children who were assigned to an unexpected reward condition and to children who received no extrinsic reward. Self-determination theory proposes that extrinsic motivation can be internalised by the individual if the task fits with their values and beliefs and therefore helps to fulfil their basic psychological needs.

Self-control

The self-control of motivation is increasingly understood as a subset of emotional intelligence; a person may be highly intelligent according to a more conservative definition (as measured by many intelligence tests), yet unmotivated to dedicate this intelligence to certain tasks. Yale School of Management professor Victor Vroom's "expectancy theory" provides an account of when people will decide whether to exert self control to pursue a particular goal.

Drives and desires can be described as *a deficiency or need that activates behaviour that is aimed at a goal or an incentive*. These are thought to originate within the individual and may not require external stimuli to encourage the behaviour. Basic drives could be sparked by deficiencies such as hunger, which motivates a person to seek food; whereas more subtle drives might be the desire for praise and approval, which motivates a person to behave in a manner pleasing to others.

By contrast, the role of extrinsic rewards and stimuli can be seen in the example of training animals by giving them treats when they perform a trick correctly. The treat motivates the animals to perform the trick consistently, even later when the treat is removed from the process.

MOTIVATION AS A CONSTRUCT

The term *motivation* (or *motive)* is a logical scientific construct.* By this we mean that in its ordinary sense it is not an entity, object, or thing such as a living cell, an eye, or a piece of coal. It has no immediate sensory referent. It is an hypothetical process or state of the organism, the operation of which we infer from 'observations of the behaviour of the organism. *Threshold* is a construct, though in our previous usage of the term we did not indicate specifically that it was. Motivation is a concept like *threshold,* Like *gravity,* or like *intelligence.* You have never seen a threshold. Nor have you ever seen any gravity or intelligence. The term *intelligence* is used to refer to a certain dimension of behaviour manifested in different amounts by different people as measured by the number of items which are correctly answered on a test called an intelligence test. In the same manner, we manipulate a certain class of experimental (stimulus) variables, observe a difference in the responses as a consequence, and infer that we have produced changes in what is called the motivation of the organism. We must, of course, specify the nature of the responses we are to observe as well as the characteristics of the class of stimulus variables which are manipulated. When this is done we have anchored our construct to both the stimulus and response variables.

Response Dimensions Related to Changes in Motivation

We have said that to use motivation as a scientific concept we must specify the nature of the response changes which are associated with motivational changes. We have two response dimensions from which we infer changes in motivation: (i) changes in performance; and (2) changes in muscular tension or energy output.

The most common behaviour from which we infer changes in motivation is a change in performance on standardised tasks. If learning speed is increased we may suspect the motivation has increased; if work output goes up we may suspect that motivation has increased; if output goes down, or if learning is retarded, we may suspect that there has been a decrease in motivation. Note that we may *suspect* that these response changes are a function of motivation. *Change in performance is an unreliable criterion for inferring changes in motivation,* because we may observe changes in performance which are due to stimulus variables not in the class of motivational variables. For example, distributed practice (allowing rest periods) will usually enhance the speed of learning (change in performance), but little credence is given the idea that this is exclusively a function of change in motivation. In short, *whether or not change in performance is to signify a change in motivation depends upon the particular class of stimulus variables being manipulated.* The latter part of this chapter will be devoted to outlining these variables which are believed to be associated with changes in motivation.

The most meaningful response change from which we infer motivation is the amount of energy output or muscular tension exhibited by the organism. This index of change in motivation is used less frequently than the first, largely because of difficulties attending its quantification. Yet, change in activity level is the basic observation associated with motivational changes. The strongly motivated individual is muscularly active or at least muscularly tense; the weakly motivated individual shows signs of ennui, boredom, laziness, or lethargy. When you make an observation that an individual is highly motivated, you usually do it on the basis of the activity level of that individual.

Within certain limits, the two response changes indicating changes in motivation are correlated, but there is not a one to one relationship. If these two measures were perfectly correlated there would be no need for using both. We would work with the one which was least difficult to use in the experimental situation. The fact that they are not perfectly correlated raises some rather difficult problems. How can both performance change and energy change be used as measures of the same process when they are not perfectly correlated? Let us take an illustration. If we announce to an assembly worker that we will give a bonus for every unit produced beyond a certain fixed quantity, and if his production increases following the announcement, we assume that mere has been an increase in motivation.

We may, at the same time, get indices of increased energy being expended as the production goes up. But, suppose there is an increase in energy output and not a corresponding increase in performance? Or, suppose there is an actual inhibition (decrement) of performance accompanying the increased energy output? Are we to say that motivation has increased in spite of the fact that performance decreased? We would have, in such instances, two independent measures of motivation which are not perfectly correlated. Which one is *the* measure of motivation? Neither, of course. We cannot speak of *the* measure of motivation when two measures have been used which are not perfectly correlated in the experimental situation.

It is our belief that we should reserve the term *motivation* for changes in energy output. There are two reasons for this: (i) it would give a clear-cut differentiation between changes in performance due to variables associated with learning and those associated with motivation; and (2) there would be less confusion than is the case when two poorly correlated response measures are used to infer the same process. However, it is unpractical at present to adopt such a criterion for inferring motivation. Many of the data pertaining to motivational changes which are available are based on performance changes. Furthermore, there are many situations in which it is almost impossible to measure the changes in energy level. For the present, then, we cannot use energy changes as the sole index of motivation: we must also use the changes in performance and at the same time recognise that the two are not perfectly correlated.

Why Use the Term?

If you examine the above situation, you might infer that it would not change the nature of the empirical facts obtained by experimentation if we completely eliminated the term *motivation*. For example, when we discover by sound experimental procedure that output goes up as a bonus is given, that stands as a scientific relationship. Why go any further ? Why say that increased output indicates increased motivation? The reason for the use of the term is a scientifically practical one.

Without such a term we have a mass of unrelated facts on our hands. However, if we find that a considerable number of experimental operations will produce a change in performance (or energy output), and if it appears that these stimulus changes are all affecting the same basic process, then our knowledge is integrated by the use of a single term for that process. In this case the term is *motivation.*

Constructs such as this allow for more generalised forms of explanation. Explaining observed phenomena on the basis of the immediate change in the stimulus variable,' a low level form of explanation. Such a procedure does not allow for generalised explanatory concepts. Each fact in and of itself would have to be explained by the change in the stimulus conditions. When, however, there is believed to be communality in the processes produced by those stimulus changes, our explanation becomes more generalised by referring to those processes with a single term. Without such a generalised concept it would be impossible logically to predict behaviour in a new situation. We could only state that such and such *had* happened under such and such highly particular circumstances. Fortunately the scientists isn't content with the level of particulars. He reaches out for the *general* concept, the inclusive formula, the law. So when there is a common basis in experimental manipulations of stimulus variables, and when these manipulations produce similar changes in response, the use of a construct permits explanation at a more general level than does reference to each of the operations individually.

On the conceptual level we may think of motivation as a state which energises the organism. This state is in turn produced and varied by manipulation of environmental conditions by *E.* In animal studies we can give, in most cases, a precise quantitative definition of motivation in terms of the number of hours of privation of food, water, mate, and so forth. Such operational definitions are not easily formulated for human *S*s. In human adult experiments our definition hinges on the instructions we give *S.* In these instructions we may indicate rewards and punishments which *S* may get, or we may try to vary certain aspects of motivation in terms of instructions alone, without threat of punishment or enticement of reward. Strictly speaking, we shall have an operational definition of motivation for each experiment, but we shall find that most of them can be classified under a few general headings. The classes of operations used to produce and measure changes in performance and changes in energy output must remain our operational definition of motivation.

Terminology Troubles

The study of motivation is complicated by the multiplicity of terms which have been used by various writers in referring to what seems to be the same aspect of behaviour. There have been instincts, drives, wants, needs, propensities, appetites, interests, aversions, desires, values, sets, attitudes, valences, forces, and others. All of these terms refer to certain facets of motivation. In most cases each author has defined his own terms for his own writing (which is proper and necessary), but students have had to suffer from a multiplicity of both concepts and vocabularies. We shall limit the number of concepts as much as possible.

CONTEXT OF MOTIVATION

Finally, if we want teachers to apply these constructs in order to develop these motivational patterns in students, it is important to recognize that motivation occurs within a context-the school, the classroom, and the family. We spend a great deal of time discussing individual differences in motivation, treating motivation as a trait, but not enough time attending to how the organization and structure of the classroom shapes and socializes adaptive and maladaptive motivation patterns. Moreover, developing a positive motivational orientation in students is necessarily a matter of dealing with diversity among students in the classroom. Teachers need to know ways of dealing with this diversity, and these methods ought to involve a comprehensive look at the classroom.

Thus, the teacher must first be guided by goals that assign primary importance to developing in students a motivation to learn. Second, we need a framework for identifying those aspects or structures of the classroom that are manipulable. These structures must represent the classroom organization and must relate to instructional planning. Then we need to identify strategies that will serve to enhance the motivation of all students.

These strategies or applications must be grounded in theory and research and evaluated in relation to developmental factors and in relation to other motivation constructs, as well as individual differences. Many educational psychology textbooks describe one or two ideas for application but do not provide a comprehensive view of classroom organization. When we look at the classroom, there are six areas of organization that are manipulable and that involve motivational concerns: task, authority, recognition, grouping, evaluation, and time.

These structures have been described in considerable detail by Epstein. There is considerable research that relates to each area, and there are many motivational strategies that can be extracted from the research; the point is to apply appropriate strategies in all of these areas frequently and consistently. Preservice teachers often learn a great deal about only one area, and practising teachers often focus on one or two areas but do little in the others. As a consequence, motivation becomes restricted to one area of the classroom. Often that area is reward or recognition (providing rewards and incentives), and even in that area inappropriate strategies are used.

This framework offers a starting point for extracting motivational strategies and applications from research and theory, and for relating them to all areas of classroom organization and instructional planning. This is important because motivation enhancement cannot be reserved for Friday afternoons, or be viewed as something to be used during free time or extra time or as superfluous to academic activities. Nor can motivational concerns surface only when a student does not do well. Motivation as an outcome is important to all students in the classroom all the time. This view gives student motivation a central place as an educational outcome, important in its own right. The emphasis is on identifying strategies that will foster a mastery-goal orientation in students and that relate to all aspects of classroom learning and organization. It requires a comprehensive approach to looking at how motivation theory and research interface with classroom learning.

DEVELOPMENT OF MOTIVE-INCENTIVE RELATIONSHIPS

In dealing with motivation we are concerned primarily with its influence on performance phenomena associated with learning. We ask the question: "What roles does motivation play in learning?" In answering this question we shall try to avoid certain problems which are controversial in nature and delay treatment of the difficult questions until we have finished the study of learning later in the book.

We will outline events and interrelationships which we think can be accepted with least hesitation. Following Melton (254), we may recognise three basic roles which motivation plays in the learning process: (i) the energising role, (2) the directing role, and (3) the emphasising or selecting role.

The Energising Role

The motivated organism, when faced with a problem situation—a situation in which a "correct" response is not immediately available—will show variable behaviour. The amount of variable behaviour or general activity is a direct index of the strength of motivation. If the situation is one in which the organism must discover the correct response, it is obvious that the greater the number of responses tried, the greater the probabilities of hitting upon the correct response.

It would appear, then, that Increased energy level may be an important factor in learning just because of the increased likelihood that the correct response will be found. We shall not consider the relationship between energy level and speed of learning at this point; rather, we shall examine the methods which have been used to relate changes in energy output to certain changes in the stimulus conditions.

Animals

The procedure for animal studies is straightforward—deprive an animal of food or water for varying amounts of time and measure the changes in activity. A rotating circular cage mounted on an horizontal axle is one device used to measure activity level A counter is attached to the axle so that the number of revolutions of the cage can be obtained for any desired unit of time. In the cage, as in a treadmill, the animal may run a great distance without getting anywhere.

Another device is the *spring* or *tambour-mounted* cage. Tambours are air tubes with a mouth covered with rubber sheeting. The tubes, joining together from the four legs of the cage, lead to sensitive markers. These markers write on a *kymograph,* a slowly rotating drum covered with waxed or smoked paper. The rat (or other animal), when active, bounces the cage on the tambours, thus changing the air pressure which in turn activates the markers which record the animal's activity.

Still another mechanism is the *tilting cage,* in which slight tilts of the cage (produced by movements of the animal) activate a mechanical or electrical counter (32).

With such devices it has been shown that in general the activity level is related directly to the hours of deprivation of food, water, or mate, these being the three conditions usually studied. Concerning the sex motive, it has been shown that the activity of a female rat is at a maximum every four or five days, (the oestrous cycle), at which time the rat actively seeks a mate (398). Concerning hunger, it is known that the greatest activity of a rat occurs just before eating and the least just after eating (311). If a rat is "deprived of food for several days there is an increase in the amount of activity up to about 96 hours, after which time a gradual reduction (because of weakening) takes place (424). These results are enough to illustrate the point; within limits, as hours of deprivation increase the energy output increases, and we say that this reflects an increase in motivation. The amount of activity is, of course, influenced by many factors such as age, heredity, nutritional balance, and drugs (3°5).

Humans

It is not practical to study human subjects in activity cages, though this technique has been used for other purposes in the case of newborn infants (180). Instead, we must infer from certain findings that the activity level of humans is associated with certain deprivations or unsatisfied states. Our inference relates instructions to perform to changes in energy output. We do not deprive the person of food and measure activity level; rather, we instruct him to learn a task and then measure the difference in tension or energy output before learning (comparative rest) and during learning.

The methods that have been used to measure tension differences between learning and rest have varied, and cannot be said to be highly correlated. Stroud (369) constructed a *hand stylus* so that it would measure air pressure changes produced by the grip of the hand. The stylus was a pencil-like cylinder used to trace the indented path of a maze. Differences in the pressure throughout the stages of learning, or as between one *S* and another, were measured directly.

Reflex responses, such as the knee jerk, may be used as indices of tension. A positive relationship has been demonstrated between the amplitude of the knee jerk and the amount of tension exerted on a *hand dynamometer* (a device for recording grip strength) so that the amplitude of the knee jerk at various times during learning would be indicative of tension changes (68).

The reflex eyelid response (blinking) has been suggested as a measure of tension, with the suggested relationship being: the greater the number of blinks per unit of time the greater the tension. However, results are somewhat contradictory concerning this measure. There is some indication that heart rate is a possible index of tension (27) as is respiration rate also (375), but confirming evidence is needed.

The *galvanic skin response,* with which we are already familiar, has also been used as a measure of tension. It can be shown that the resistance of the skin is inversely related to the amount of tension, but the possibility that factors other than tension may bring about the same change in resistance has also been pointed out Consequently,, we cannot accept without qualification the relationship of the resistance of the skin to tension level (78).

Probably the most satisfactory measure of tension is obtained by direct measurements of electrical changes in the muscles, i.e., the*action potentials* which result from contraction of the muscle fibers. With the great improvements which have been made in amplifying minute electrical changes, this method is probably less ambiguous than any of the others. However, it is not as yet adaptable to certain tasks where considerable overt movement is involved.

Each of the above is presumed to be an index of activity reflecting different energy levels. Since the correlations between the different methods are not perfect, we actually have as many different measures of energy or tension level as we do methods of measurement. These discrepancies may disappear with further research and standardised recording devices. (More detailed accounts of various methods used in measuring tension may be found in Davis, 78.)

With regard to the energy output changes *during* learning, we can make no general statements. Almost all combinations of increases and decreases have been found by various investigators, using various tasks and various methods of measurements. The most common finding has been high initial tension followed by a gradual decrease as learning progressed. Without exception, however, tension is greater during learning than it is during comparative rest. We infer that these changes indicate a state of increased motivation brought on by the attempt to comply with the instructions to learn or to perform a given task.

No *E* has yet made a serious attempt to dimensionalise tension by using judges. It is quite possible that scaling methods would result in reliable measurement, and that certain characteristics of behaviour would be found to vary concomitantly with changes in tension as measured by mechanical devices. Most of our personal estimates of amount of motivation are inferred from such characteristics.

Any instructor who has observed his students while taking examinations can name several responses which seem to increase in frequency and intensity; these responses are such characteristics as the flexing of the ankle of the crossed leg finger chewing, and general exaggeration of tics or twitches of one kind or another. There seems to be no reason why such behaviour could not be quantified by judges rating *S* as he is put through a sequence of experimental conditions.

The Directing Role

Incentives

We seldom deal with organisms which are just plain motivated, without being motivated *toward* something. When an organism is motivated or energised, its behaviour has directive aspects. A hungry rat is active until food is found and the searching behaviour is likely to be directed toward places where food had been found previously. A student, thirsting for knowledge, is almost certain to go to the library and not to the fraternity house. Because of our past experience, we go to restaurants rather than filling stations when we are hungry. The general principle seems to be that we tend, when motivated, to make responses toward a goal which in the past has eliminated or reduced the strength of the motivational state. Learning has established a relationship between the motivating state and the goal-objects which reduce that motivational state. Thus, certain objects (real or symbolic), or classes of objects or states, are perceived as being satisfying to a given motivational condition. Such goal objects are called *incentives*. In studying the influence of motivation on performance we must usually include an incentive as part of the motivation complex.

In the case of animals the motive and the incentive are fairly clear-cut. A rat is deprived of food for a period of time and the food is placed at the end of a maze as an incentive. In the case of human *Ss* the incentives of laboratory experiments are as obscure as the motives. What, for example, is the motive-incentive relationship when a student volunteers to serve in an experiment? All we can say is that the student has agreed to cooperate. What is the incentive? What is it that the student "gets out of the experiment" which brings about satisfaction in the sense that food reduces the motivation of a hungry rat? If he has a motive to cooperate, then cooperation is the satisfying incentive. This, however, is just so much naming, and scientifically is quite unsatisfying. Because of this unsatisfying state of affairs, psychologists are motivated to know more about these problems. We might, of course, ask *S* what the motive was that prompted him to volunteer for the experiment, and we might ask him what provides the source of satisfaction, if the latter is apparent. However, clinical psychologists and psychiatrists have taught us to be skeptical of the reasons people give us for their behaviour, since their underlying motives may be unconscious or unreported.

The facts of the case are that we know very little about the motive-incentive relationships in *Ss* upon whom the overwhelming proportion of our data has been collected. This will come out more clearly when we start to examine in detail the conditions which *Es* have manipulated in an attempt to vary motivation. In most human experiments the directive function is supplied in part by the instructions to *S* along with the past experience of *S* with similar problems.

Illustrations of incentives considered thus far have all been *positive* in nature. In everyday life,as well as in the laboratory learning is thought to be influenced by the administration of punishment or *negative incentives.* It is an "If-you-don't-do-this-you-will-get-this" type of situation. Electric shock has been used most often in the laboratory as a from of negative incentive. The influence of shock, as well as other negative incentives, may be both directive and energising in function.

With human *Ss* especially, there are many instances in which in incentive itself appears to have the power to energise as well as direct behaviour. Most of our complex psychological motives appear to be long-term in nature and are relatively non-cyclical as is the case with hunger or thirst. Let us assume that *S* has a long term motive to make money. He is sitting, relaxed in an arm-chair listening to the ratio, when a friend enters the room and offers him ten dollars if he will write a term paper for him. With the exhibition of the ten dollars, *S's* behaviour changes markedly. He is now highly energised or activated to start work. It is as if the presentation of the ten dollar incentive "set off" or tapped a motive; or, it is as if a motive were "waiting around" for an incentive. It appears that the receipt of money has served to satisfy a motive in the past, a motive which we have probably simplified by calling it a motive to make money. Therefore the incentive is now perceived as being potentially satisfying to the motive which must have been present in some sort of latent and long-lasting form. Thus, incentives may not only provide the basis for the acquisition of direction to motivated behaviour, but may "set off" motives also.

Experimental Demonstration of the Directive Nature of Motivation

Animal experimentation is somewhat more difficult than it might seem at first. One doesn't *just* drop a rat in a maze and record the time it takes the rat to reach the food at the end of the maze. Many preliminary steps and controls are necessary. We shall follow a study through in some detail in order to understand some of the problems faced by the animal psychologist.

An experiment by Kendler (193) was designed to investigate the directive function of physiologically motivating stimuli. Rats were trained in a simple T-maze, under two motivating conditions, hunger and thirst, each defined by hours of deprivation. During training, food was found at one end of the *T*, water at the other. On test trials the rats were made *either* hungry or thirsty, one or the other of the motive conditions having been satiated. The question is whether or not the rat, after training under both motivating conditions, will go to the appropriate end of the *T* when either hungry or thirsty, e.g., if thirsty, will he go to the end where he has previously found water?

Preliminary training of naive rats usually involves two steps. First, the rats must become adjusted to being handled. Kendler did this by handling each of his 20 rats for several minutes each day for a week. The second step involves adjustment to the apparatus. In this Experiment, two days were allowed for the second objective. On the first day the rats explored the maze for an hour. None of the doors was closed and neither food nor water was available in the food boxes. On the second day, *E* gave each rat two trial runs by placing the animal in the starting box and, as the rating moved down the alley, closing the doors behind him to prevent retracing.

Rats may have biases for making left or right turns. Kendler recorded the turns made by each rat on the preliminary trials and discarded any rat which consistently made the same turn at the junction. Moreover, during the regular training series, *E* forced half the rats to go to the left for food and to the right for water, and reversed the positions of the incentives for the other half. All rats were under 21-hour deprivation at the time of the raining series, and were believed to have bene satiated nearly equally on water and food before the 21-hour period started.

The training series consisted of four trials daily for seven days. The initial run of each day was a free choice, the second was a forced trial to the side opposite that chosen on trial one, the third was a free choice while the fourth was a forced run to the side opposite that chosen on trial three. Thus, the animals had equal experience with the contents of both goal boxes. Forced runs were accomplished by lowering Door Three or Door Four. Test trials consisted of four runs, each run being given on a different day. On the first and fourth days of the test series the *Ss* were motivated for one goal object (food or water), while on the second and third day they were motivated for the other goal object. This *abba* order was utilised to avoid any possibility of building up an alternation pattern of responding in successive test trials.

Since many animals had acquired preferences for one of the two alternative sides, the last four free choices on the sixth and seventh days of raining were noted, and half the animals were motivated, on the first test trial, against the side for which they had a preference, while for the other half the opposite was true. Thus, on any one test trial the preference factor was approximately equated.

On the four test trials the rats chose the appropriate alley 68 per cent of the time when motivated for water, and 73 per cent of the time when motivated for food. The two groups combined gave 85 per cent correct choice. Chance would be 50 per cent. It is clear from these results that the animal's behaviour is directed on the basis of internal motivating stimuli. It is presumed that this directive function is acquired as a consequence of the learning trials, where the rats were rewarded by incentives appropriate to only one of the two motivating conditions present at the time. The directive function of motivating stimuli may be inferred from certain other animal data. Rats prefer bran mash to sunflower seed as a reward or incentive. Elliott (88) gave bran mash as a reward while rats were learning a maze until the tenth trial, at which time he substituted sunflower seed. On the eleventh trial the number of errors made in running the maze greatly increased. It was as if the rats were running to a specific incentive and the change La the incentive disrupted their performance.

The Emphasising or Selecting Role

We have seen that following the awarding of incentives for performing a certain task, the behaviour sequence preceding the reward tends to be strengthened—learning has taken place. When given precise statement this is known as the *law of effect,* which we shall accept as established for the present. The principle assumes that reduction in motivation, through interaction with an incentive appropriate to the motivating condition, tends to strengthen or select the responses which brought about this state of affairs. Indeed, the emphasising or selective function of motivation develops the directive function, since it is only by such strengthening of responses that the organism's behaviour shows less variability and greater efficiency as successive trials are given. Furthermore, it can be seen, the receipt of an incentive which reduces the motivating condition must necessarily affect the energy level of the organism, within certain limits. Thus, all three roles are closely intertwined.

Symbolic Incentive or Reward

We have said that the incentive or reward received at the end of a behaviour sequence will tend to strengthen or reinforce that sequence. If a rat is allowed to eat food in the goal box at the end of the maze after each run, the number of errors made, and the time required to ran the maze, are gradually reduced. Now let us inqire into the situations in which incentives are symbolic in nature, i.e., when they do not have direct reinforcing power as such. For example, how does it happen that money is avidly received as an incentive? We can't eat money, we can't drink money—it has no power to satisfy primary motives directly. If we assume, as most psychologists do, that our derived motives are built on primary motives as a consequence of learning, any information we can get concerning the origin of derived motives and the incentives which touch them off and satisfy them, will add to our knowledge of the motivation of human adults. We shall examine several animal duties to show a few basic mechanisms by the operation of which it is probable that our complex motive-incentive conditions are derived.

Token experiments. Studies by Wolfe (418) and Cowles (71 with chimpanzees have shown that tokens—poker chips—can become incentives and acquire reinforcing power. In the beginning the chimpanzees were taught to insert the chips into a slot machine to get grapes, which were considered to have direct or primary incentive value. The animals learned to differentiate between colours of the chips so that a certain colour was found to be worth 1 grape, another 5 grapes, and so forth. Then the chimpanzees were put to work, doing manual tasks in some instances, for which they were given poker chips periodically, but they were not allowed to cash them in immediately for grapes. The animals might continue to work for chips alone for as long as 20 minutes before they would leave the work to try to cash the chips for primary incentive (grapes). Furthermore, not only would the animal work for tokens, but it would learn new tasks also, with only the chips serving as incentives. Clearly, the chips had gained incentive value for the animals. The analogy with human behaviour is obvious.

"Click" experiments. Experiments by Skinner (356) and Bugelski (40) have demonstrated symbolic incentives in rats. The device used in these experiments

has become standard equipment in one form or another and has come to be known as the *Skinner box*. We shall refer to it frequently throughout this book. A small bar projects from the end of a box. Immediately below the bar is a small food box (or water orifice). Pushing was *hungry* when placed in the experimental situation and no food was given after the response.

Ten test periods were given, 20 trials per period, each period on successive days. Each trial consisted of ringing the bell once. Group I had only slight decrement in response over the 200 trials. At the end of this period, 73 per cent of the bell presentations were still being followed by flexion responses even though no food was ingested. Both of the other groups showed rapid extinction, i.e., the response died out so that it no longer occurred to the bell. Since Group II was not presented food following the response and Group I was, this variation in treatment must account for the differences in frequency of response. It would appear that the *sight* and *smell* of food have incentive properties so that the response continues to be evoked. Thus we have another kind of symbolic reward in which the stimulus which normally serves to reduce the strength of motivation, and hence bring about learning, will continue to perpetuate learned behaviour even though the dog cannot be said to be getting direct motive reduction. This type of symbolic incentive needs to be produced in a situation where a new response has to be acquired, although setting up such a situation would be difficult.

There are many other illustrations of the development of symbolic rewards in the literature, but these are enough to illustrate the point—the emphasising function of incentives need not come from objects with direct physiological value.

From the considerations in this section we must grasp, in addition to the understanding of the various methods of experimentation, the three following systematic relationships:

1. *Primary reinforcement.* Achievement of an incentive appropriate to the motivation serves to select or emphasise the behaviour sequence which precedes the obtaining of the incentive.
2. *Secondary reinforcement.* If other stimuli occur consistently with an incentive which is appropriate for the reduction of a motivating state, these stimuli may gain incentive value to the extent that they will perpetuate behaviour for a period of time, and under certain conditions, will act as incentives for the acquisition of new responses. Such stimuli we have called symbolic incentives or rewards.
3. *Primary incentive with symbolic characteristics.* From Brogden's experiment we may make the tentative generalisation that a primary incentive will perpetuate a given response for a much greater period of time than will

a symbolic incentive, even though that primary incentive does not reduce a primary motivational state. It may be that the visual and olfactory aspects of food in and of themselves are largely symbolic incentives, having gained such reinforcing properties by being consistently present when eating has taken place.

Now we may see somewhat more clearly how it is possible for complex symbolic or derived motives to develop in humans. II we take into consideration the vastly greater symbolic power of humans as compared with animals (this is a human's opinion), it seems quite feasible that our highly symbolic motive-incentive relationships could have developed by processes of learning stemming originally from incentives which satisfied basic physiological motives. We have, however, no experimental evidence other than the type presented here to show how this comes about. We have attempted to set up guides for thinking about the complex topic of motivation. We have organised this material around the roles which motivation plays in performance phenomena which are associated with learning.

ENHANCING MOTIVATION

In most of our foundational courses, we stop once we have covered the basic theories or motivational constructs. We cannot assume, however, that teachers are prepared to translate these ideas into classroom practice. This is a major problem for foundations courses. We give too little attention to how motivation concepts interface with the instructional programme, too little attention to how the social context of the classroom can undermine or facilitate the development of students' motivation to learn, and too little attention to how motivation principles relate to each other. What we do is cover the basics, highlight a few principles, maybe even review a case study or two, and then hope that the teacher's intuition has somehow been enlightened and that the teacher will be able to apply this knowledge. Many textbooks, when it comes to dealing with applications, rely on conventional wisdom.

There are several major texts that present a problem (*e.g.*, how to deal with a child who exhibits poor motivation) and then present teachers' solutions. These solutions are not linked to any conceptual framework. There is even an implicit endorsement of these ideas and solutions as credible, viable, and conceptually sound because the source is practising teachers.

Unfortunately, it is often the case that this is not so. The problem is that many strategies for enhancing student motivation involve the use of principles that are counterintuitive. Let me illustrate this point with examples that are related to the motivation constructs described in the preceding section.

- If children lack confidence in their ability to succeed, we might infer that these low-confident children should receive a heavy dose of success experience. The considerable literature on learned helplessness and attribution retraining, however, has shown that success alone does not alleviate a helplessness syndrome. In contrast to what we might surmise, providing or ensuring successful outcomes or feedback does not necessarily bolster children's confidence in their abilities. Such a prescription ignores the role of cognitive motivational factors in determining how children interpret their classroom experiences. For many children success is not sufficient to create or maintain a belief that they have the ability to reverse failure. Children who are convinced that they lack the necessary ability to do school tasks do not take responsibility for success and even underestimate their performance when they do well. Thus, it is not a matter of persuading them they can do well or even guaranteeing it; instead, practice should involve giving them short-term goals and strategies for making progress towards the goals." Once students understand how to reach a goal and focus on strategies, rather than outcomes, they are more likely to "own" the outcome.
- Related to an emphasis on success is the prescription "try to find something positive to say about a child's work." Reinforcing children's work even if it involves some small aspect of the total effort should be a step in the direction of giving the child more confidence. Unfortunately, for the very children who most need positive feedback, the "something positive" is often something unimportant and irrelevant to the task requirements. For example, if the task is to write a book report in a certain format, commenting positively on the child's neat handwriting is not likely to have the intended effect. On the one hand, the generous use of praise would seem to be an obvious and salient way of encouraging children who generally perform poorly, but as Brophy has shown, the way praise is often used in elementary school classrooms can undermine the achievement behaviour of these children. The praise children receive is often on irrelevant aspects of a task; in these instances, children discount the praise. Praise on easy tasks or praise that is non-contingent on children's effort or performance quality can be interpreted by children as evidence that they lack ability; it can, therefore, have unintended negative effects on children's self-confidence. The effects of praise must also be considered from a developmental perspective. Praise can be interpreted quite differently by younger and older children. Praising young children's effort conveys to them a positive expectation that they can do the work and can enhance their perceptions of their

the admonishment to try harder is to no avail to the student who believes he or she is already trying hard. This is a very likely scenario for young children, who believe they always try hard because it is not smart not to try. Telling these children that they did not work hard enough may actually decrease their sense of efficacy. Second, problems arise when we put too much emphasis on effort. We do not want to impress on students that sustained maximal effort is what leads to success. Students may feel very satisfied when they have worked very hard and achieved success, but this is usually accompanied by the feeling that "I don't want to work that hard again." Conveying the expectation that a maximized effort is necessary may spark a child's investment once in a while, but over time students are more likely to become discouraged. In classrooms where the goal is to demonstrate one's ability over the long term, continuously maximizing one's effort is not desirable.

- Finally, in most classrooms, students do not perceive the classroom hierarchy as effort-determined. As Nicholls suggests, students at the bottom of the hierarchy are not there because they are not effortful; convincing students that this is, in fact, the case has little credence. If we want teachers to apply attribution theory to classroom practice, they need to know that whether they convey to students that effort is important depends on how they structure tasks, evaluate students, and give recognition and rewards. These examples illustrate the complex nature of classroom learning and motivation. One of the major problems in our training of teachers is that we do not adequately address how motivation theory, constructs, and principles relate to practice: How can teachers develop in students a motivation to learn? As the preceding five examples illustrate, we currently rely on the wisdom of experience or derive applications without regard to the complexities involved. We need to consider how motivation constructs relate to each other, to developmental changes, to individual and culturally related differences, and to the context or structure of the classroom itself when we apply motivation theory and research to practice.

8

Psychology and Social Groups

SOCIAL GROUP

Social group, any set of human beings who either are, recently have been, or anticipate being in some kind of interrelation. The term *group*, or *social group*, has been used to designate many kinds of aggregations of humans. Aggregations of two members and aggregations that include the total population of a large nation-state have been called groups.

One of the earliest and best-known classifications of groups was the American sociologist C.H. Cooley's distinction between primary and secondary groups, set forth in his *Human Nature and the Social Order* (1902). "Primary group" refers to those personal relations that are direct, face-to-face, relatively permanent, and intimate, such as the relations in a family, a group of close friends, and the like. "Secondary group" (an expression that Cooley himself did not actually use but that emerged later) refers to all other person-to-person relations but especially to those groups or associations, such as work groups, in which the individual is related to others through formal, often legalistic or contractual ties.

Cooley felt that primary groups were the fundamental agencies through which the individual's character or personality was formed. American sociologist Talcott Parsons distinguished five factors that differentiate primary groups from secondary groups: relations between members of primary groups, as contrasted with secondary groups, tend to be (1) diffuse, rather than specific or delimited, (2) particularistic, rather than universalistic, (3) ascription-based (*i.e.*, based on who or what you are), rather than achievement-based (*i.e.*, based on what you do or have done), (4) other-oriented or group-oriented, rather than self-oriented, (5) affective or emotion-laden, rather than emotionally neutral. Secondary groups are those in which relations between members tend to fit the opposite poles of the five factors.

Historically, many other pairs of terms have been used to classify groups. The German sociologist Ferdinand Tönnies coined the now-famous distinction between *Gemeinschaft* ("community") and *Gesellschaft* ("society," or "association"), which for all practical purposes reflect the same distinction as that between primary and secondary. The American anthropologist Robert Redfield distinguished between folk society and urban society. The English jurist Sir Henry Maine talked of societies of status and societies of contract. All of these categories are virtually coterminous with the primary-group–secondary-group distinction. There is also a close correspondence between these pairs of terms and the distinction between mechanical solidarity and organic solidarity, which was emphasized by the French sociologist Émile Durkheim.

Still other sets of terms are used, not as bases for distinguishing types of groups but as bases for describing the individual's relationship to different groups. Thus, the terms *we-group* and *they-group,* as well as the terms *in-group* and *out-group,* are used in order to contrast a group of which the referent, or focal person, is a member (often, a primary-type group) and some other group—not necessarily different in kind—of which the focal person (and other members of his in-group, or we-group) is not a member and towards which he feels some degree of animosity or negative affect.

Another set of distinctions based on the individual's relationship to the group is expressed by the terms *membership group* and *reference group*. The former has the obvious meaning of a group of which the individual is a member, here and now, by reason of one characteristic or another (such as being a member of a particular family or a member of the sixth-grade class in Jefferson School). The term *reference group* has been used in two ways, to mean either a group for which the individual aspires to membership or a group whose values, norms, and attitudes serve as points of reference for the individual. In either case, the crucial feature is that the individual adapts his attitudes and behaviour to model those of the members of the reference group. Obviously, membership groups andreference groups are not mutually exclusive.

The term *group,* or *social group,* has been used to refer to very divergent kinds of aggregations of people. Indeed, the term has been used so broadly as to threaten its fruitfulness as a focal concept. For one thing, the word *group* has sometimes been used to designate the members of a social category based on possession of a common attribute, even when the members have no meaningful degree of interrelation. Thus, it has been used to refer to such collections as persons of a particular age, all persons having similar incomes or occupations, and all persons with similar reading habits. These are what might be called statistical groups, as distinct from actual groups, the latter being characterized by interrelatedness of the members.

Virtually all efforts to classify social groups result in a certain degree of artificiality. Because of these and other problems of definition and classification, sociologists have attempted to distinguish between various kinds of social aggregates, some to be considered groups and others to be identified by other terms—audiences, publics, and the like; there is, however, no generally accepted classification at this time.

THE ROLE OF GROUPS

Do you think you act differently when alone than when other people are around? The answer to this question is typically a resounding 'yes.' We are concerned with our social image or how other people see us; some more than others, but very few people see no difference in their behaviour. The various theories relating to our behaviour in group settings or when others are present.

Social Facilitation

Lets start with one of the most simple theory related to social psychology. When alone, we tend to be more relaxed, less concerned with the outward expression of our behaviour, and are basically 'ourselves.' Add just one other person, even if we don't know that person, our behaviour tends to change, and not always for the better. Research has found that when others are present, our level of arousal is increased (Zajonc, 1965). In other words, we are suddenly more aware of what's going on around us. Because of this, we tend to perform better at tasks that are well learned or simple (Guerin, 1993). When completing a difficult or new task, however, our performance level decreases and we tend to do more poorly.

This phenomenon is called Social Facilitation (Guerin, 1993), and as we try harder due to the presence of others, our performance actually decreases for difficult or unlearned tasks. Think about learning to play basketball for the first time. If you are alone, you will likely be more relaxed, and better able to concentrate. When others are watching you, however, you are more likely to be self-conscious, and therefore make more mistakes. Professional basketball players, however, because the task is so well learned, perform better when others are watching and they are able demonstrate their confidence and ability.

Group Think and Group Polarization

If you've ever been involved in a group decision making process, you've probably seen one of two things happen: either the group agrees on all of the major issues, or there is significant dissent that splits the group. If the group is cohesive; if they agree on most issues, they tend to stifle dissent because group harmony is the anticipated outcome (Janis, 1972). When we all agree, and are happy with that agreement, we typically do not want to hear opposing arguments. This phenomenon is referred to as Group Think. It can lead to impulsive decisions and a failure to identify and/or consider all sides of an argument. Some classic examples of group decisions going bad include lynch mobs, actions of the Ku Klux Klan, discrimination among hate groups, and mass riots. Similar to this, Group Polarization refers to a groups tendency to talk itself into extreme positions. In this case, a group gets so focused and energized about a decision that it creates an internal fuel, so to speak, which pushes itself forward faster than originally intended. Imagine a group of protesters, all agreeing and deciding to picket. You can see how this could get out of hand because opposing views (Group Think) are not considered and the push to move forward for the cause is fueled internally (Group Polarization).

Social Loafing

Another phenomenon that occurs in groups is referred to as Social Loafing. This theory states that as a group gets larger, the individual contribution decreases disproportionate to the group size. This is due to the diffusion of responsibility created as the size of the group increases. Imagine being assigned a project to complete by yourself. Most likely you would complete 100% of it. Now if two people are involved, the percentage will typically not be 50/50. As more people are added to the group, you will end up with a small percentage doing a large portion of the work and a large percentage doing a much smaller proportion.

Bystander Effect

This last phenomenon is an unfortunate reality which has been observed far to many times in groups and in larger cities. We've all heard stories of people getting mugged, or beaten, or raped in broad daylight while people around offered no assistance. We have found that the internal push to help a person in need decreases as the group gets larger, very similar to Social Loafing. In this instance, however, people tend to be followers and will only get involved if they witness another person getting involved. What results is a group of people witnessing a crime and wondering why nobody is helping. This does not occur if you are the only person witnessing the crime. If nobody else is around, a person will tend to help the victim. The more people, however, the less likely someone will offer assistance.

TYPES OF GROUPS

Primary groups According to Charles Horton Cooley (1864–1929), a primary group is a small social group whose members share personal and lasting relationships. People joined in primary relationships spend a great deal of time together, engage in a wide range of activities, and feel that they know one another well. In short, they show real concern for one another. In every society, the family is the most important primary group. Groups based on lasting friendships are also primary groups.

Secondary groups, in contrast to primary groups, are large groups involving formal and institutional relationships. Secondary relationships involve weak emotional ties and little personal knowledge of one another.

Most secondary groups are short term, beginning and ending without particular significance. They may last for years or may disband after a short time. The formation of primary groups happens within secondary groups.

Primary groups can be present in secondary settings. For example, attending a university exemplifies membership of a secondary group, while the friendships that are made there would be considered a primary group that you belong to.

Likewise, some businesses care deeply about the well being of one another, while some immediate families have hostile relations within it.

Individuals almost universally have a bond towards what sociologists call reference groups. A reference group is a social group that serves as a point of reference in making evaluations and decisions.

Development of a Group

If one brings a small collection of strangers together in a restricted space and environment, provides a common goal and maybe a few ground rules, then a highly probable course of events will follow. Interaction between individuals is the basic requirement. At first, individuals will differentially interact in sets of twos or threes while seeking to interact with those with whom they share something in common: *i.e.*, interests, skills, and cultural background. Relationships will develop some stability in these small sets, in that individuals may temporarily change from one set to another, but will return to the same pairs or trios rather consistently and resist change. Particular twosomes and threesomes will stake out their special spots within the overall space. Again depending on the common goal, eventually twosomes and threesomes will integrate into larger sets of six or eight, with corresponding revisions of territory, dominance-ranking, and further differentiation of roles. All of this seldom takes place without some conflict or disagreement: for example, fighting over the distribution of resources, the choices of means and different subgoals, the development of what are appropriate norms, rewards and punishments. Some of these conflicts will be territorial in nature: *i.e.*, jealousy over roles, or locations, or favoured relationships. But most will be involved with struggles for status, ranging from mild protests to serious verbal conflicts and even dangerous violence.

By analogy to animal behaviour, sociologists may term these behaviours *territorial behaviours* and *dominance behaviours*. Depending on the pressure of the common goal and on the various skills of individuals, differentiations of leadership, dominance, or authority will develop. Once these relationships solidify, with their defined roles, norms, and sanctions, a productive group will have been established.

Aggression is the mark of unsettled dominance order. Productive group cooperation requires that both dominance order and territorial arrangements (identity, self concept) be settled with respect to the common goal and with respect to the particular group.

Often some individuals will withdraw from interaction or be excluded from the developing group. Depending on the number of individuals in the original collection of strangers, and the number of hangers-on that are tolerated, one or more competing groups of ten or less may form, and the competition for territory and dominance will then also be manifested in the intergroup transactions.

COMMON NEEDS AND GROUP ORIGINS

The social group has a variety of origins. The interaction of physical factors and human beings as well as interaction between human beings themselves are among the main causes. *Common needs* lead to group organization. The need for food prompts wolves to hunt in packs; and the need for security partly explains why sheep graze in droves. Among human beings, the "gang" resembles the animal group, in that it is often an expression of elemental needs. In organized society, people slowly learn that by putting away their egocentric beliefs and prejudices, sprung from immature thought and judgment, and by working together, they can multiply the results of their labours. The whole idea is included in the simple illustration of ten men making chairs independently of each other as compared with the same ten, dividing up the process of chair-making and each working at a specialized but coÿrdinated task.

Geography and Aggregation

Physical and geographic factors sometimes account for groups. The sparse resources of deserts and steppes draw peoples out into small marauding bands, while rich, fertile valleys throw them together in vast masses. Mountains hold peoples apart, while river systems tend to concentrate them. Geographic influences produce what Giddings has called aggregation, that is, the physical proximity of peoples. Aggregation may be either *genetic* or *congregate.* If it comes from the birth-rate it is genetic, but is thereby in danger of stagnating through lack of new stimuli, or of degenerating through inbreeding. Congregate grouping is the product of immigration. Individuals are attracted to some point because of reports of oil or gold discovery or some other physical feature, and establish primitive relationships. A congregate group is usually made up first of foot-loose individuals, impelled by wanderlust. Men generally preponderate in the founding of a congregate group, and hence the refining influence of women is missing. The congregate group is apt to be unorganized, restless, and anarchistic since it is composed of individualistic pioneers.

Genetic and Congregate Grouping

The ideal group is both genetic and congregate with genetic factors predominating. The combination gives needed organization and new stimuli, stability and mobility; but in all cases organization may well preponderate over new stimuli, and stability over mobility, or else social gains will be dissipated. If the preponderance is very great, however, mental interaction is likely to be paralyzed. Organization is needed in order to maintain law and order. Since these may easily be synonymous with injustice, freedom is needed for the play of new stimuli. Free speech and a free press governed by rules of fair play and good faith are essential to group progress.

A variety of elements, unless too widely different in nature, is a boon to social progress for it makes interaction lively and furnishes that wealth of social contacts out of which stimuli are born and nurtured. But when the population elements are greatly different there is likely to be a surplus of conflict that is uncompromising and intolerant.

Temporary Grouping

Much grouping is for the moment. A conversational group may consist of two strangers met by chance on a street corner, whose contacts may consist of a few minutes of the simplest and most perfunctory talk. Still these persons are not wholly "strangers"; they probably know one another's language, dress more or less similarly, have an elemental confidence in one another, and a mutually social spirit. Their conversation is made possible by the social elements in their common human nature and experiences.

Temporary groups may spring up primarily on *feeling* and *emotional bases.* The *crowd* is the best known type of temporary grouping. A crowd is any number of persons in the physical presence of one another who have common objects of attention and who are governed more by their feelings than by careful thinking. Feeling is easily excited and the crowd quickly mobilizes itself into a mob or experiences a panic. The mob seeks some person or object upon which to wreak vengeance; in a panic the group flees from something which has aroused fear.

Temporary groups may exist on the basis of rational thought. The *assembly is* an illustration. In an assembly ideas are in conflict. A classroom recitation, a scientific conference, a committee meeting are samples of assemblies. There is no clear line of demarcation between them and crowds; in fact, they may easily degenerate into crowds. Occasionally in the sessions of the United States Senate members come to blows or even a grave-mannered church congregation breaks out in applause.

Modern means of communication have brought people together mentally without congregating physically. The *public,* or the group *without physical presence, is* an entity of increasing proportions. The number and variety of publics, of people who are made to feel and think alike because of reading more or less simultaneously about the same occurrences are on the increase, and public opinion gyrates with greater speed than ever before.

The transition from temporary to permanent groups is gradual, for the terms "temporary" and "permanent" are relative. In one sense there are no permanent groups, although it is common to refer to the family or nation as such. A given family may die out or scatter. Nations rise and fall. There is no reason, however, why groups might not live on permanently, for it seems as though they are not subject to the biological laws of birth, maturation, and decay. If their constituent members are wise enough, that is, if they have social knowledge and foresight, or social telesis, to use an excellent term that Lester F. Ward originated, they may eliminate their destructive tendencies before these destroy them.

There are at least fourteen different important types of permanent groups, ranging from an association of two persons by marriage to the world group. These types are the family, the play group, the neighbourhood group, the school group, the occupational group, the employees' and the employers' groups, the fraternal, the political and governmental, the religious, the racial, and the sex groups, and the human species group.

Permanent groups are the outgrowth of temporary groupings. The order of development is as follows : first, human needs; then a temporary group, sometimes a committee, to meet those needs; finally, if the needs remain active, the evolution of a permanent group or social organization. Out of countless temporary groupings, a few permanent types have attained historical prominence, but are continually subject to the laws of change and evolution. A permanent group, such as an occupational one, by way of example, shows a history of the following order: human needs, crude ways of meeting these needs, the invention of methods and tools, the rise of specialization, the conscious, unconscious, or accidental line of activity, the appearance of a definite occupational or caste culture, ethics, and organization. In primitive days men were hunters and fighters, and later, herdsmen; women were untrained home-makers, crude hoe-culturists, and crass manufacturers. Under settled social conditions men transferred their attention to hoe-culture and changed it into agriculture; and to manufacture and turned it into machino-facture with its elaborate development of skilled, clerical, and entrepreneural positions. The higher needs of life, freedom from manual toil, the development of science, and the demand for specialization created the professions.

Permanent groups vary from *purely instinctive* to *socially purposive.* The best illustration of purely instinctive groups is found among animals, for instance, insect societies. The primitive horde and the family are less instinctive than a hive of bees or a nest of wasps. The modern family including courtship is often instinctive, although showing signs of conscious purpose that are worthy of these institutions. The modern state is largely instinctive, although Germany in 1914 showed a powerful national purposiveness. Economic organizations, such as corporations and labour unions, are formed for definite purposes. Educational associations are strikingly telic. Purposive groups vary from organizations which struggle vigorously for their own advancement irrespective of the welfare of other groups or of society to those which wholeheartedly and unselfishly endeavor to serve wherever they may. Permanent groups, thus, begin with the purely instinctive aggregations at the lowest extremes of the social scale, include transitional types, and end with the purely telic groups with highly socialized purposes.

Primary Groups

The most significant type of group is that originally called the *primary group* by Cooley, whose contribution in this connection to social psychology is of first magnitude. The primary group is one "characterized by intimate face-to-face association and cooperation," such as the family, play, and neighbourhood groups. It is of primary importance, because it is fundamental "in forming the social nature and ideals of the individual," because individuals live in the feeling of the whole group, and because it is from the group of the face-to-face type that one receives most of his social contacts, especially in the formative years. One's life of mental interaction is spent largely in primary groups. One's standards are usually those which will give one "some desired place in the thought of others." The parent who can choose the primary groups for his children to grow up in can forecast their future. Their development and ultimate achievements are concealed not only in their inherited natures but equally in the nature of their primary groups. To choose constructive and wholesome groups for children to mature in is one of the greatest achievements of successful parenthood.

The Larger Permanent Groups

The larger grand divisions of permanent groups may be classified as either sects, castes, classes, or states. The *sect is* a group of persons who differ markedly but who are united by a common ideal and faith—such as religious denominations and political parties. A sect, freed from its narrower religious sense, arises frequently in the form of propaganda movements. It is likely to be intense; and its leaders, to be motivated by determination and courage. Because of its feeling and emotional bias, a sect is apt to be characterized by narrow-mindedness and intolerance, at least, until it becomes socially recognized. The *caste is* a group set apart by occupation or responsibility or legal privilege or wealth so that its members show themselves non-associative and non-intermarrying with respect to outsiders. In India, for example, custom and heredity autocratically put people into castes where they must stay. In England, for example, many of the wealthy have established virtual castes for themselves. In both illustrations, purity of stock is maintained: in one case by objective and custom fiat, and in the other by intracaste control.

Wealth establishes castes, which are exclusive except as outsiders acquire wealth. The hereditarily rich caste, however, remains suspicious for a long time of the newly made or fortune-made rich. The "four hundred" maintain a strict code that keeps out all except those who by wealth can qualify, and which forces its membership to assume an air of superiority towards all outsiders, thus doing violence to the basic principles of democracy within which it may operate.

The older professions have developed a semblance of the caste principle. Consider how difficult it is for a man to change from one recognized profession to another line of activity, and what criticism falls upon the clergyman who changes to the insurance business, upon the lawyer who shifts to bricklaying, upon the teacher who becomes a dairyman. It is disgraceful to change from a higher to a so-called lower calling, even though a mistake was made in the initial choice of an occupation. It is even a questioned procedure for a person who has reached middle life to shift from a lower to a so-called higher calling. Nevertheless, this inelasticity in public opinion is on the whole justifiable, despite the fact that in the broad sense it creates castes.

The *class* possesses a psychological bond that is found in a unity of interests. The class is less precise in its limits, but more "formidably belligerent" in its attitudes than the caste. Observe the outstanding class divisions of the day, such as the distinction between the labouring and capitalistic classes, with their bickerings, strifes, intrigues, and underlying hatreds. Segregation and sense of superiority characterize the "class." The recent rise of "blocs" in Congress illustrates well the competitive nature of classes as compared with the more non-competitive castes. With classes, conflict is "inter;" while with a caste, it is chiefly "intra." In very old countries of the monarchical type a class may become deeply intrenched in the customs and develop a caste-like nature. Nation *states* are the most extensive group organizations with powerful prerogatives that have yet evolved. A state is characterized by common bonds of language, national values, and national prestige. The natural climax of the state idea is now taking form in a world association which among large permanent groups will ultimately perhaps attain the most prominent place.

Social Self-consciousness

By interstimulation the members of a group develop, not only a self-consciousness, a social consciousness, but also a social self-consciousness, which is one of the culminating points of socialization. Each individual not only becomes aware of himself and of his group and develops personal opinions like those of his fellows, but each becomes aware of his fellows' opinions and feelings, and thus may help to swell the rising tides of public opinion and emotion.

New means of communication enable persons a thousand miles apart to think and feel alike, but far more important, to know that everyone is thinking and feeling just the same at that particular time about particular occurrences. It is this outstanding fact which distinguishes groups, even the largest groups, and makes of them subjects of fascinating study; they afford an amazing interplay of leadership and social control.

Community Spirit

Social self-consciousness is partly synonymous with community spirit. Community means common attitudes, a common understanding of different attitudes, common social values, and communion. It involves participation and the rise of social responsibility. The community organization movement is psychologically sound because of its emphasis upon participation as the chief means of expanding the ethical responsibility of individuals, and at the same time of magnifying the spirit of democracy. Community may easily arise where a few congenial persons are gathered together, but it is difficult to secure in a city where millions live. The concept of world community is even more idealistic, but is scientifically sound, judging by the trend of social evolution.

Group Quotients

Since a person is indebted so fundamentally to groups, since the number and quality of his social stimuli are determined by them, it would be important to measure the creative influence of different groups upon him. One might divide the amount of time he gives in a week to each of the various groups in which he participates weekly by the total amount of time that he gives to all groups in the same period of time. The result would be a rough quantitative group quotient. By taking a large number of people and finding out their group quotients for any particular group, such as the religious group or family, it would be possible to work out quantitative norms, with which any given person could compare his own quotient for that particular group. F. Stuart Chapin suggests finding out the average attendance at a group's meeting for a term of years, distribution and average financial support of the members, active membership on committees, on how many committees, for how many years, and active committee chairmanships as a basis of measuring personal relationship to group life. He advances this hypothesis: "There is a direct correlation between the number of groups that the average person may belong to and the intensity of his participation in each group activity as indicated by such objective facts as regularity of attendance, membership on committees, and financial support." The suggestion is also made that group participation for each person has its saturation point. Dr. Chapin believes that this saturation point rests upon a person's range of elasticity for group participation which can be measured. Such data would help in working out a quantitative group quotient.

Qualitative group quotients for a person would be more worth while and also far more difficult to obtain. An approach might be made by determining a rating for the various offices in groups as well as active and passive membership and then "scoring"a large number of representative persons in a given community. A person could divide his own score by the medium score for representative persons in order to obtain a qualitative quotient. The real group quotient that is needed is one showing the quality of social contacts and stimuli afforded a person by each of his groups. The relationships between a person's intelligence quotient and his group quotient represent another field of research.

NATION-GROUP LOYALTIES

The members of a nation-group may be classified under one or more of several headings regarding their national loyalty. There are many brands and grades of nationalism, or nation-group loyalties. *Pugnacious patriotism* is an over-development of the combative impulses. There are persons who are habitually on the lookout for trouble. As some are fussy about their personal dignity, and imagine themselves slighted under almost any circumstances, so there are those who are provincial in imagining or magnifying national provocations. Many persons are willing to rush their country into war upon the slightest excuse. If an American in a foreign country has been insulted or killed—regardless of his guilt—these pugnacious persons would have their country declare war immediately. Jingoists abound. Combative patriotism does not wait for an investigation of causal circumstances. It works continuously for an aggressive foreign policy; it is impatient with negotiation, and is prejudiced and irrational.

Professional patriotism characterizes many of the military and naval classes. It is valuable in a society where force predominates. Its weakness is its tendency towards arrogance, hard-heartedness, and an exaggerated desire for recognition. The promotion ambition is illustrated in the extreme case of the officer who some years ago expressed a hope that the United States would declare war upon Panama, after Panama had committed a slight breach of courtesy. When asked for his reasons, he candidly replied : "Because my chances for promotion would be greatly increased."

Profiteering patriotism raises its blas features in spite of the need for war sacrifices. After the entry of the United States into the World War, the cry was raised, "Business as usual." But everyone knew that if the war was to be won, business could not go on as usual. Before the United States declared war, the dividends of certain companies which were manufacturing war materials rose rapidly, and after our war declaration, the war profits of these firms created millionaires. One American openly and shamelessly boasted : "This war has surely been a fine thing for me. If it lasts two years, I will have made enough money to live in leisure the rest of my life." While 70,000 American soldiers were giving up their lives during the war, it is estimated that 18,000 American millionaires were made. Another profiteering patriot sold to the government shoddy clothing for the soldiers and sailors. Still another set up wooden images of the Kaiser, and playing upon the war feelings of the passers-by, invited them to "Swat the Kaiser"—for ten cents a throw. A theatre owner subscribed heavily to one of the war funds and then advertised that fact widely. His theatre drew unusually large crowds of people, who felt that they should patronize such an unusually generous proprietor and "patriot." The profiteer hoists the flag, but locks up coal in his mines while women and children suffer from the cold. He buys up foodstuffs and holds them while prices rise and people starve.

Faddish patriotism gives benefit "teas" in war time, despite the fact that such affairs provide an unnecessary fourth meal. A young woman who wore a service star was found to have no nearer relative in the World War than a cousin whom she had never seen. She easily justified to herself this action on the grounds that "all the other girls were wearing service stars." In certain cases the carrying of flags upon the front of automobiles is faddish patriotism. Shortly after the United States declared war in 1917, as high as forty per cent of automobiles in some communities carried flags, but six months later the proportion fell to less than five per cent. In the meantime, however, the real patriotism of the people had greatly increased.

Patriotism is sometimes *adveuturesome.* It appeals to the desire for new experience. The slogan "Join the navy and see the world," recognizes this adventuresome element. In the World War there were many young men who volunteered, stating that they were moved strongly by the desire to go abroad and see "the sights," and who were willing to risk returning alive.

Conspicuous patriotism exhausts itself in applauding the flag or in patriotic statements, but whines when asked to observe meatless days and to refrain from using wheat bread. It carries the flag, but secretly encourages profiteering and self-indulgence. It is generally hypocritical; it evaporates in patriotic statements. The conspicuous patriot loudly abuses others for not going to war—when he knows that he can remain safe at home.

Pacific patriotism is two-fold. There are group members who believe in peace at any price. As practical citizens they are mistaken and sometimes dangerous. It is necessary in times of group crises to be willing to fight to save those social values which the group through the slow process of time has acquired. As long as powerful national wolves are loose in the world, it is folly to believe in peace at any price. In such a case a nation may be called on to fight not only for itself but for the values which civilization has slowly and painfully constructed. Peace-at-any-price individuals possess a willingness to undergo hardships and even to die for the principles they represent. They frequently possess those fine moral qualities which cannot be found in the loyal but truculent chauvinist. The other type of pacifist patriot tries all honourable methods of solving international controversies before resorting to war. In ordinary peace times most Americans would come within this category. Such persons believe in the principles of peace rather than of war as means of progress. In time of war, however, such a declaration is likely to be grossly misunderstood. At such a time any type of pacifist is anathema.

Provincial patriotism magnifies and places the interests of one section of the country ahead of the welfare of the whole nation. It measures long distances with the yard-stick that it uses in its own provincial area. It opposed the

Louisiana Purchase and the acquisition of the Philippines. It would settle the Japanese problem in the United States irrespective of international justice. It would prevent our nation from functioning fully in the League of Nations. Today, as in the time of Epaminondas, there are too many provincial patriots.

Chauvinistic patriotism is boastful loyalty; it is dominated by watchwords and phrases. It is the direct descendant of the boastful attitudes of lower races. It wildly shouts "My country, right or wrong," when its country may be already on the rocks of greed and injustice. It forgets that the slogan, "My country, right or wrong," made Germany a menace to the world. It does not possess the courage to face national evils and to assist constructively in righting maladjustments, thereby strengthening the nation.

True national patriotism, is based on the belief that there must be nation-groups as necessary intermediate structures between the family and the community on one hand and the world order on the other. One comes to love his native land, even though its faults may be many. Wherever one finds food and shelter and kindly ministrations, one feels patriotic. True national patriotism is national love divorced from all narrow desires. It urges that one's nation group play a rle of wholesomeness in the world. It is expressed not only in exciting war times, but in the most monotonous days of peace. True patriotism functions in both peace and war, but it is far more difficult to be patriotic in peace than in war. In the routine days of the work-a-day world, private interests press forward and command attention. As a result, a person forgets to go to the polls, neglects to study the merits of candidates, fails to keep in touch with his representatives in legislative and administrative positions—in short, to be fully patriotic.

Super-patriotism is a high order of true national patriotism. It gives all for the sake of its nation when the nation is fighting righteously. Super-patriots include the Joan of Arcs and the Nathaniel Hales, the heroes of Zeebrugge and the Argonne, and the unknown, brave mothers and fathers who have given up sons and daughters anywhere in a worthy cause.

World Loyalties

Besides loyalty to family, to community, to nation-state, the trend of social evolution is producing another type of group loyalty—internationalism. The world is on the verge of forming an international consciousness and a sense of planetary values. President Wilson's famous pleas for world-wide democracy and the organization of the friendship of the world are forerunners of the rise of a new world society.

International loyalties are illustrated by two leading types. *Industrial internationalism* holds that the industrial classes throughout all countries should organize in a world order and renounce the existing national governments as being the tools of capitalism. Industrial inter-nationalism is an outgrowth of Marxian socialism and is closely allied to Communism. Industrial internationalism fails to recognize that its programme runs counter to the laws of social evolution and of democratic growth. No stable international order can be built on class consciousness alone. A permanent world structure cannot be suspended in mid-air, supported chiefly by personal, familial, or communal units.

Democratic internationalism is scientifically founded. Upon persons, the family rests. Upon family groups, the community, city, or province depends. Upon persons, families, and communities, the nation relies. Upon all these constituent elements, and only so, an enduring world organization can be constructed. Ordinarily family loyalty fits harmoniously into national loyalty, without disrupting or weakening the former. Similarly, there is no reason why national loyalty should suffer by locating it properly within the boundaries of democratic internationalism. A person who has learned rational loyalty to his nation will be no less a national patriot by catching a vision of the larger internationalism.

Democratic internationalism is built upon the highest virtues and the best moral characteristics of the nation. It recognizes that points of view naturally vary in different national habitats. It promotes the principles : Come, let us reason together. Democratic internationalism would dignify nationalism and make it a nobler sentiment. It would end economic conflict between nations for the same reason that such conflicts were stopped between the colonies when the United States was formed. It would eventually raze military and naval harriers between nations on the same basis that it has never been necessary to separate the United States from Canada by fortifications and dreadnoughts.

Planetary good feeling will develop concomitantly with an enlarged means of communication and a world-wide cultural uniformity. While commerce and religion have strong international organizations, education is still represented on a world scale only by international congresses on various subjects.

Hyphenism

Hyphenism is double loyalty or loyalty to two groups in the same class, such as national groups. If a person is living in and being protected by one nation group but feels more loyalty to some other nation, he is guilty of hyphenism. Immigrants from advanced countries often find it difficult to give up their loyalty to the homeland. The loyalty of an English or German immigrant to his native land is apt to persist for many years. His problem of giving up a loyalty to one country is one of the hardest that faces any person.

He probably cannot give up wholly the homeland loyalty, especially if his childhood days in the home country have been happy, and if his parents or other loved ones lie buried there. When a man marries he does not give up his loyalty to his mother, and should not. The loyalty to the original home group may remain in the form of a sacred memory.

National hyphenism is likely to take dangerous forms in war times. The loyalty to an "enemy" country may lead one to furnish valuable information to that country. Hyphenism easily produces spies. It leads to treason, which is owing loyalty to one group, while surreptitiously supporting an opposing group. The pretense of a loyalty which is false makes treason especially despicable. A modified form of treason is shown by the profiteer, by the revolutionary propagandist in a democracy, by anyone who publicly professes a love for democracy and justice but who in business or privately violates laws or connives at exploitation.

Universal Loyalties

Philosophy and religion have formulated still more comprehensive group loyalties. Philosophy has often projected a loyalty to the universe, but this loses its richest quality when it becomes materialistic or impersonal. When personality is entirely removed from any set of group values it fails to possess a wide appeal.

9

Social Feeling

It is our task to help such people develop the social feeling demanded of a socially well-adjusted human being. How is this to be done? The great difficulty with individuals behaving this way is that they are overstrained and always looking for confirmation of their fixed ideas. It thus becomes impossible to change their ideas unless somehow we can penetrate their personality in a way that will question their preconceptions. To accomplish this it is necessary to use both skill and tact. And it is best if the counsellor has no close relationship to or interest in the patient, for if one is directly concerned in the case, one will find that one is acting in one's own interest and not in the interest of the patient. The patient will not fail to notice this and will become suspicious.

The important thing is to decrease patients' feelings of inferiority. These cannot be eliminated entirely, and in fact we do not want to do so because feelings of inferiority can serve as useful foundations on which to build. What we have to do is to change patients' goals. We have seen that their goal has been one of escape because someone else is preferred, and it is around this complex of ideas that we must work. We must decrease their feelings of inferiority by showing them that they really undervalue themselves. We can show them the mistakes in their actions and explain to them their tendency to be over-tense, as if they were standing before a great chasm or as if they were living in enemy territory, in constant danger. We can indicate to them how their fear that others may do better than them is standing in the way of their doing their best work and making the best impression.

If such people could act out the role of a host at a party, making sure their friends have a good time, being friendly with them and thinking of their interests, they would improve tremendously. But in ordinary social life we see that they do not enjoy themselves, do not have constructive ideas, and as a result say: 'Stupid people-they cannot enjoy being with me, they cannot interest me.' The trouble with people suffering under these misconceptions is that they do not understand their situation because of their reliance on private logic and their lack of common sense.

Overcoming Depression and Fear

Let us now look at another specific case — the case of a man afflicted with depression. This is a very common illness, but it can be cured. People susceptible to depression can be identified very early in life. Many children, in their approach to new circumstances, show signs of suffering from depression. The man in this case had about ten bouts of depression, and these always occurred when he started a new job. As long as he was in a familiar job he could be described as nearly 'normal', but he did not want to go out and he wanted to rule over others. Consequently he had no friends, and at fifty he had never married.

Let us look at his childhood in order to study his life style. He had been very sensitive and quarrelsome, always dominating his older brothers and sisters by emphasising his pains and his weaknesses. When playing on a couch one day, he told us, when he was only four or five years old, he pushed all the other children off. When his aunt reproached him for this, he said, 'Now my whole life is ruined because you have blamed me!'

Such was his life style — always trying to rule over others, always complaining of his weakness and of how much he suffered. This characteristic led in his later life to depression which in itself is simply an expression of weakness. Many depressed patients use almost the same words: 'My whole life is ruined. I have lost everything. Frequently, such people have once been pampered and are so no longer, and this influences their life style.

For the most part, human beings have a tendency to be afraid. This timidity, when expressed in a social situation, is one of the most frequent causes of poor social adjustment. There was a man from an aristocratic family who never wanted to exert himself, but always wished to be supported and looked after. He appeared weak, and of course he could not find a job. His brothers turned against him, saying, 'You are so stupid that you cannot even find a job. You don't understand anything.' So he turned to drink. After some months, he was a confirmed alcoholic and was put in a treatment centre for two years.

The treatment helped him but did not benefit him permanently, for he was sent back into the community without any preparation. He could find no work except as a labourer, even though he was a scion of a well-known family. Soon he began to have hallucinations. He thought a man appeared before him to tease and torment him so that he could not work. First he could not work because he was an alcoholic, and then because he had Hallucinations. And so we can see that it is not appropriate treatment merely to make alcoholics stop drinking; we must find and correct the errors in their life style. This man had been a Pampered child, always wanting to be helped. He was not pre-pared to work alone.

We must help all children to become independent, and this can be done only if we get them to understand the mistakes in their life styles. In this case, the child should have been trained to do some useful work, and then he would not have had to be ashamed before his brothers and sisters.

FEELINGS OF INFERIORITY

The key to the social process is the fact that people are always striving to find a situation in which they can excel. Thus, children who have a strong feeling of inferiority want to exclude bigger children and play with the younger or weaker ones whom they can dominate. This is an abnormal and pathological expression of the feeling of inferiority, for it is important to realise that it is not the sense of inferiority itself that matters but its degree and expression.

An abnormal feeling of inferiority has acquired the name of ' inferiority complex'. But 'complex' is not the correct word for a feeling that permeates the whole personality. It is more than a complex; it is almost a disease whose severity varies under different circumstances. Thus we sometimes do not notice someone's feeling of inferiority when they are at work because they feel sure of their ability, but they may not be sure of themselves in the company of others, particularly in their relations with the other sex, and there we are able to discover their true psychological situation. Mistakes are more evident in a tense or difficult situation. The prototype appears more clearly when an individual is in a difficult or new situation; a difficult situation being more often than not a new one. When we send children to school we may observe their social interest in seeing whether they mix with their fellow pupils or avoid them. If they respond to other children only conditionally or hesitantly, we must be on the lookout for the same characteristics being revealed later on in society and marriage.

There are many people who say, 'I would do that in such-and-such a way', 'I would take that job', 'I would take on that man,... *but...!*' All such statements indicate a strong feeling of inferiority, and if we interpret them in this way we get a new insight into certain emotions, such as doubt. A person who feels in doubt usually remains in doubt and accomplishes nothing.

The psychologist can often see hesitations and contradictions in people, which may be considered signs of a feeling of inferiority, but we must also take into account the physical movements of the subjects. Their approach, or way of dealing with other people, may be poor; perhaps they approach hesitantly or with an awkward bodily posture. This hesitation will often be expressed in other situations in life. Many people habitually take one step forward and one step backward — quite literally.

Our whole task is to train people away from this hesitant attitude. The proper treatment is to encourage them — never to discourage them. We must make them understand that they are capable of facing difficulties and solving the problems of life. This is the only way to build self-confidence, and this is the only way the feeling of inferiority can be treated.

ACCENTUATIONS OF FEELINGS AND EMOTIONS

Feelings and emotions are accentuations of what we have previously described as character traits. Emotions express themselves in a sudden flow under the pressure of some conscious or unconscious necessity. Like character traits, they have a definite goal and direction. We might call them psychological developments within a definite time limit.

Feelings are not mysterious phenomena that defy interpretation; they occur wherever they are appropriate to the given life style and predetermined behaviour pattern of individuals. Their purpose is to modify the situation of the individuals in whom they occur, to their benefit. They are accentuated, vehement movements that occur in individuals who have abandoned other mechanisms for achieving their purpose, or have lost faith in any other means of attaining their goal.

We are dealing again with individuals who, burdened by a feeling of inferiority and inadequacy that forces them to gather all their powers together, make more strenuous efforts than would otherwise be necessary. By the force of these exertions they believe they can get into the limelight, and prove themselves victorious. We cannot have anger without an enemy; we cannot conceive of the emotion of anger without considering also that its purpose is a victory over this enemy. In our culture it is still possible to achieve our aims by means of this exaggerated behaviour. We would have fewer outbursts of temper if it were not possible to achieve some goal in this way.

Individuals who do not have sufficient confidence in their ability to achieve their goal tend not to give up their aim because of their feeling of insecurity, but rather to approach it with greater efforts and with the aid of additional feelings and emotions. In this way individuals, stung by a sense of their inferiority, gather their powers together and attempt to win a desired objective in a manner reminiscent of a brutal, uncivilised savage. Since feelings and emotions are closely bound up with the very essence of personality, they are not the unique characteristics of a few individuals, but are to be found more or less uniformly among all people. All individuals are capable of showing some particular emotion if they are put into an appropriate situation; we might call this capability the faculty for emotion. The emotions are such an essential part of human life that we are all capable of experiencing them.

As soon as we have gained a fairly good understanding of human beings, we may well be able to imagine their usual feelings and emotions without ever having actually come into contact with them. It is quite natural that so deeply rooted a phenomenon as a feeling or emotion shows its effect upon the body, since body and mind are so intimately allied. The physical phenomena that accompany feelings and emotions are indicated by various changes in the blood vessels and in the respiratory apparatus, for example in the appearance of blushing, pallor, rapid pulse rates and variations in breathing.

FEELING REACTIONS

Feeling is the nominalization of the verb *to feel*. The word was first used in the English language to describe the physical sensation of touch through either experience or perception. The word is also used to describe experiences, other than the physical sensation of touch, such as "a feeling of warmth".

In psychology, the word is usually reserved for the conscious subjective experience of emotion. Phenomenology and heterophenomenology are philosophical approaches that provide some basis for knowledge of feelings. Many schools of psychotherapy depend on the therapist achieving some kind of understanding of the client's feelings, for which methodologies exist. Some theories of interpersonal relationships also have a role for shared feelings or understanding of another person's feelings.

Perception of the physical world does not necessarily result in a universal reaction among receivers, but varies depending on one's tendency to handle the situation, how the situation relates to the receiver's past experiences, and any number of other factors. Feelings are also known as a state of consciousness, such as that resulting from emotions, sentiments or desires.

Human nature possesses *a tonal quality,* somewhat after the fashion perhaps of a musical instrument, only far more complex and significant. If all goes well the human organism experiences a pleasant tone or feeling. If the environment impinges harshly upon the organism, then a disagreeable tone is experienced. An unbroken continuance of favourable or unfavourable circumstances may cease to bring out the organic tonal quality. If the environment has few new stimuli and arouses no new responses then the human organism lapses into a chronic state of disagreeableness, or ennui. If the environmental factors repeatedly defeat the organism at every turn then an essentially unpleasant organic tone becomes chronic and is accompanied by cynicism and fatalism. If circumstances present new problems from time to time the organism is likely to be stimulated to its highest efficiency.

The tones of psychic nature are as old as psychic nature itself. They appear almost simultaneously with the causal stimuli. They are the first or advance responses of the organism to specific stimuli. A type of stimuli which as a rule has been favourable in the past to the organism or to the race or to both produces an agreeable tone in the organism. If some one were to suggest to me a visit to the dentist's chair, I should experience an unpleasant tone, providing my previous experiences have been exceedingly painful.

The stimulus releases an habitual reaction that has been built up on the basis of painful dental experiences, and I experience disagreeable feelings again. On the other hand if some one were to suggest to me a beefsteak fry in the Rockies, I should experience a highly agreeable psychic tone, providing I have enjoyed several such occasions.

This tonal character of one's nature seems to give a quicker-than-thought evaluation to a proposed activity upon the basis of past experience. It was this which Plato undoubtedly had in mind when he said that there are two counsellors in one's bosom, one is pleasure and the other is pain. A pleasurable feeling is the beginning of a whole response of the organism and indicates that in the history of the organism or the species, the act which the given stimulus is calling forth has been helpful. The pleasurable tone is a blind guide, implying but not necessarily proving the present value of a proposed response. The fact that a certain type of responses has been helpful or harmful in the past indicates that in all probability this type will continue to be helpful or harmful. If, however, conditions have changed, the tonal voice may prove a misleader. Before he responds to his tonal or feeling guidance, it is necessary, therefore, for a person to notice whether or not the main factors in a given social situation have changed.

People are alike in their tonal responses because they have had about the same fundamental experiences of gain and loss. In the history of the human species, certain ways of doing have proved favourable to race development; and others, unfavourable. Advantage is accompanied by agreeable tones or feelings, and disadvantage by a disagreeable tonal quality, ranging from a sense of complete loss (sorrow) to one of complete energization (angry determination). Upholders of race prejudice and race pride should observe that all races irrespective of colour are characterized under similar circumstances by the same psychic tones or feelings. Social traditions have developed variations, but after all, the white, yellow, and black races alike experience joy, sorrow, and anger when responding to the respective types of stimuli. The feeling or tonal qualities developed earlier than thinking in the species. The feelings have longer roots than ideas. They are more definitely a part of the inner core of personality. They have helped to make personality, long before thinking reached its full development, either in the individual or in the race. It is difficult to argue down the feelings.

Again, feeling is not on the plane of thinking. It is not in the same class of phenomena. Thinking is superior in quality to feeling in that it can describe and analyse feeling, but it is inferior in that it can rarely overcome feeling. If one has been taught throughout the earlier years of life that thirteen is an unlucky number, it is with difficulty in later years that one can throw off the feeling response that thirteen had better be avoided. Years of thinking to the contrary do not always succeed in overcoming feeling. An idea which is thrown against the feelings by way of argument does not meet them on their plane. It would seem that the best way to cope with the feelings is to stimulate counter feelings.

Emotional Reactions

Our desire to be free of emotional suffering and pain is real and authentic. However, when we express our desire for change with an attitude laced with judgment, rejection, disdain, or frustration, it now becomes another emotional reaction. We are now having emotional reactions about our emotional reactions. Another type of inherited response is the emotional. An emotion, may be considered a *complex of feeling responses.* It is usually accompanied by marked activity of the glandular system and hence is related to the autonomic neural system as well as to the central neural system. It may be accompanied not only by muscular responses but also by special activity of both the duct and the ductless glands, that is, in the case of anger, for example, there may be not only clenched fists, but also perspiration, and marked activity by the adrenals. An emotion is a complete organic disturbance.

It arises when the organized inherited impulses or the habitual responses are blocked. Whenever an obstacle appears in the path of a human tendency a disturbance occurs, accompanied by affective manifestations. In a way, an emotion is a heightened affective phase of a mental crisis. Whenever a conflict in the central neural system takes place, an emotional disturbance occurs; when no conflict exists, ennui is likely to ensue.

Emotions and ennui are the opposite feeling poles of personality. It may also be said that ennui is the dead centre between the extremes represented by the joyful and the sorrowful feeling responses. *Angry emotion* accompanies the conflict stages of a crisis when an individual is struggling against obstacles.

The function of anger is apparently that of energizing the individual so that he may overcome obstructions in the path of his tendencies. Anger is clearly a combatant emotion, but it becomes transformed into joyful or sorrowful responses when the given conflict begins to eventuate into gain or loss for the individual as judged by the individual.

A joyful response full of animation and expressions of surplus energy marks the more or less sudden realization of some important personal desire. *A sorrowful* response indicates the individual's realization of defeat, at least temporary, in some of his aims; while remorse, forlornness, pessimism, fatalism are permanent expressions of defeated desires. The joyful tone of the human organism accompanies a general expansion of the individual's powers—his heart beats faster, circulation and respiration increase, and the organism is actually larger; while a sorrowful tone accompanies a general organic shrinking. Joyfulness is accompanied by a reckless organic offensive type of attitude; while sorrowfulness is paralleled by a retiring defencelessness.

Fear is an emotional response, which occurs whenever the individual realizes that his life, his possessions, or his loved ones are in great danger. Fear is an emotional response of a defensive nature and is closely associated with the desire for security. Fear may easily be acquired and developed into a standard set of habitual responses. That which is peculiarly strange naturally causes the individual to shrink away or to assume a defensive attitude. As concentrations of feeling tones, the emotions often run to extremes and are expressed in wild, blind discharges of energy or possibly in a more or less complete paralysis of organic activity. For example, anger results in concentrated but irrational outbursts of activity or it may completely block all motor activity; while sorrow usually tends to produce only impotence.

One of the most elemental of emotional responses, basic to joy, sorrow, and even anger, is *sympathy.* As the term implies, sympathy means "feeling with," and it may be regarded as a generic social tone of all higher organic life. An example of the expression of an elemental form of sympathetic emotion is the immediate and appropriate response of the brood of chickens to the warning cry of the mother hen. As a result of sympathetic emotion, the vigorous crying of a baby is followed often by the simultaneous wailing on the part of all nearby infants, even when they apparently cannot have the slightest conception of the cause of the crying of the first child. For the same reason a scream of terror on the part of an adult evokes a similar pang on the part of bystanders, although the latter do not know the cause of the scream. By virtue of sympathetic emotion, anger provokes anger. If the parent or teacher spoken to angrily is able only by a great effort to keep angry feelings from arising, how much less is a child able to control angry response when spoken to in an angry tone. The wise parent, or teacher speaks authoritatively, but not angrily. The characteristic of "feeling with" others varies in degree with individuals and circumstances. In an extreme form it often decreases personal efficiency. It is unfortunate, for example, for a surgeon to be over-sympathetic. At the other extreme a want of sympathy permits one's egoistic, selfish impulses to run riot. Sympathy enables the individual to understand the experiences, attitudes, and behaviour of other people. While its generic nature contributes to self-sacrifice and unselfish living, it may be used by the shrewd in highly selfish ways. Through sympathy one can learn to understand other people, and then by playing upon their sympathy, gain their confidence and take advantage of them. Courtship is often characterized by this abuse of sympathy, and many hasty and unwise marriages are to be explained in this way. Politicians often acquire an unsavory reputation by overmuch appeal to the sympathy of people.

When an important issue is to be settled, the party which is successful in enlisting the sympathies of the public possesses a great advantage. The sympathies often lead to erratic behaviour. Inasmuch as they, like the feelings, are not always in accord with the cognitive phases of mental life, they may be expressed in strange, irrational, and at times in unreliable ways. Sympathy does not always connote dependable conduct. Perhaps the most conspicuous social characteristic of sympathy is its tendency to go out to the under dog in a conflict. It is also commonly allied with the old, the tried, and the true. It is a gigantic stabilizing force, but oftentimes it adds too much stability. Occasionally it is so closely attached to outworn habits and customs that it constitutes a stumbling block to progress. Nevertheless every new reform measure tries to win the permanent sympathy of the people. In fact, it must win these, if it is to achieve real success. Sympathetic feelings "always follow activities, and if the new activities can be established long enough feeling is sure in time to give them sanction. In this way new social values may be established and social attitudes changed and improved.

Sentiments

Sentimentality originally indicated the reliance on feelings as a guide to truth, but current usage defines it as an appeal to shallow, uncomplicated emotions at the expense of reason. Sentimentalism in philosophy is a view in meta-ethics according to which morality is somehow grounded in moral sentiments or emotions. Sentimentalism in literature is both a device used to induce a tender emotional response disproportionate to the situation at hand, (and thus to substitute heightened and generally uncritical feeling for normal ethical and intellectual judgments), and a heightened reader response willing to invest previously prepared emotions to respond disproportionately to a literary situation. Emotions tend to become organized in relation to personal values, and may then be referred to as *sentiments.*

For example, there is the sentiment of *admiration,* or a certain extension of one's personality towards another person who manifests fine qualities of behaviour. It always involves admirer and admired; it implies the expression of a measure of curiosity and wonder, or self-abasement, and also of being responsive to the person for whom admiration is experienced. A leader who is genuinely, successful must gain the permanent admiration of other persons. Admiration plus fear constitutes awe; and awe with the sense of indebtedness leads to reverence—the highest religious sentiment. Closely allied to admiration is *respect.* It involves more judgment and less emotion, and hence is more permanent than admiration. Respect is perhaps the most rationalized sentiment. Self respect means that one has given thought to his behaviour and has justified it in the light of social standards. Without self respect it is almost impossible for one to maintain the respect of other persons, for by suggestion one's attitudes towards one's self influence the attitudes of others. Respect for another person means that one has analysed the activities of the other person and approved them. The available evidence seems to show that McDougall may be mistaken in assuming that we always respect those who respect themselves and that our respect for other persons is always a sympathetic reflection of their self respect. It is usually true that others must respect themselves before we will truly respect them, but if the social standards of others are below our own or if their dependableness falls short of our own ideal of dependableness, respect for them fails to develop.

There is a mild sentiment which arises out of sympathy for other persons but which does not result in positive sacrifice for others; this sentiment is commonly known as*pity.* The person who pities usually feels that he is definitely separated by some barrier from the one who is pitied. Pity may be regarded as a differentiated form of sympathy which is held in check by a feeling of superiority, of inability to render aid, or of the impractability of giving aid. Pity rarely instigates activity but it may stay ruthless or vengeful action. When a person finds himself depreciated or when he falls below the standards which others expect of him, his normal reaction *is shame. To* protect himself from such an experience, he is apt to submit unflinchingly to severe discipline. The group or the leaders in the group will often capitalize a person's aversion to shame in order to secure his otherwise unattainable support of either a worthy or unworthy cause.

When native impulses are closely organized and egoism has become standardized, an exaggerated sense of self-feeling easily becomes stimulated into the emotion of*jealousy.* Wherever invidious comparisons are made in one's own field of activity, jealousy easily flares up. The suitor is "jealous" of all rivals, because somebody whom he is willing to die for is in danger of being won by other persons. The egoistic parent is sensitive regarding the success of the companions of his children, for he does not want *his* children to be outshone. He is especially jealous of those persons whom his children listen to more than to him, for thereby his own opinions are being flouted. The egoistic jealousy of artists, dbutantes, prima donnas, and others, "painters of the limelight and wooers of public favour," comes from their having hinged their lives on applause. When that applause is transferred, their lives are flattened out entirely, except as jealousy blazes up. As a rule jealousy narrows personality, lowers one's social standing, and cuts down one's usefulness. In the long run one is justified in being "jealous" only for his character, for the character of other persons and of social institutions.

A more aggressive but often subtler type of sentiment than jealousy is *revenge.* It arises when a person feels that he or someone in whom he is interested has been grievously injured and when the alleged offender does not make what is considered adequate amends. It is fitful, flaring high and dying down quickly, or it may smolder for years and break out in unexpected ways. It demands at least "an eye for an eye," and because of its emotional nature it is likely to overrun its goal and to exact a double portion of atonement. Furthermore it invites retribution, arousing furious emotional reactions on the part of the persons against whom it is directed. Thus when the vindictive attempt to secure justice, they use methods which prolong the justice-securing processes indefinitely and inflict serious injustices.

Revenge easily becomes generalized, and organized into group reactions which assume socially deep-seated and long term proportions, as in the case of blood feuds. The development of courts of justice has met the general need which is served by vengeance; and consequently the overt and group-organized expressions of the sentiment are losing their original function, although still persisting tenaciously. Vengeance blazes up as in the case' of lynchings; it also holds a concealed place in many lives as evidenced in class and race prejudices.

Sentiments, diametrically opposed, are *hate* and *love.* Hate is an organization of emotional energy against a person or a group believed to be hostile. It differs from revenge and jealousy in containing less pure feeling, and in being more rationally organized. It is also more openly expressed; it does not cover itself up, except for conventional reasons. It stages open warfare and declares publicly its reasons. It is a long-lived, ingrained sentiment that functions unfortunately in behalf of narrow loyalties as distinguished from larger ideals. It hinders the progress of both its subject and its object. It is an ominous element in race prejudice. Its constructive value appears when it is directed not against people as such, but against evil behaviour of any person and any group.

Love is a conserving, stabilizing, and yet tumultous sentiment of unmeasured power. In its more primitive, elemental nature it may be made up largely of sex impulses, and consequently it may easily lead to license. A higher form is romantic love, which prompts one to great undertakings and sacrifices in behalf of the one who is loved. The primitive nature of romantic love is demonstrated by its fickleness. It may lead, however, to conjugal love which possesses remarkable qualities of endurance.

The strength of conjugal love develops out of the fact that husbands and wives have common experience of great joys and sorrows. It is particularly in the suffering together of husband and wife that fitful romantic love becomes transformed into strong, deep, and abiding conjugal love. Maternal love is the keenest, deepest, and most concentrated form of the love of one person for another.

The love of a mother for her child is the most enduring; it persists despite continued gross neglect and even of utterly despicable conduct on the part of the son or daughter. Paternal love is far less intense and permanent than maternal; it is more akin to fraternal love. Filial love is often strongly expressed in childhood and adolescence; it may then subside but be revived in the later years of life and assume its earlier strength, gladdening parental hearts.

Consanguineal love ranges from the close attachment that is characteristic of fraternal love, to the affective elements in the brotherhood-of-man principle. It frequently takes on idealistic forms, and easily extends beyond blood relationships, producing the highest bonds of friendship, as of him "who sticketh closer than a brother." Consanguineal love leads to the most dependable types of loyalty. In it lies the energizing power for socializing the world.

Desire

Desire is a sense of longing for a person or object or hoping for an outcome. Desire is the fire that sets action aflame. The same sense is expressed by emotions such as "craving" or "hankering". When a person desires something or someone, their sense of longing is excited by the enjoyment or the thought of the item or person, and they want to take actions to obtain their goal. The motivational aspect of desire has long been noted by philosophers; Hobbes (1588–1679) asserted that human desire is the fundamental motivation of all human action. In Buddhism, for an individual to effect his or her liberation, the flow of sense-desire must be cut completely; however, while training, he or she must work with motivational processes based on skilfully applied desire.

The Buddha stated, according to the early Buddhist scriptures, that monks should "generate desire" for the sake of fostering skilful qualities and abandoning unskilful ones.

While desires are often classified as emotions by laypersons, psychologists often describe desires as different from emotions; psychologists tend to argue that desires arise from bodily structures, such as the stomach's need for food, whereas emotions arise from a person's mental state. Marketing and advertising companies have used psychological research on how desire is stimulated to find more effective ways to induce consumers to buy a given product or service. While some advertising attempts to give buyers a sense of lack or wanting, other types of advertising create desire associating the product with desirable attributes, either by showing a celebrity or model with the product.

The theme of desire is at the core of the romance novel, which often create drama by showing cases where human desire is impeded by social conventions, class, or cultural barriers. As well, it is used in other literary genres, such as gothic novels such as *Dracula* by Bram Stoker, in which desire is mingled with fear and dread. Poets ranging from Homer to Toni Morrison have dealt with the themes of desire in their work. Just as desire is central to the written fiction genre of romance, it is the central theme of melodrama films, which use plots that appeal to the heightened emotions of the audience by showing "crises of human emotion, failed romance or friendship", in which desire is thwarted or unrequited.

Repeated inability to respond to moderate environmental stimuli creates in time a somewhat turbulent state known as *desire.* If the organism is unable after repeated attempts to secure the object of desire, then a chronic unpleasant tone results. Desire, declared Lester F. Ward, is painful. He asserted that the sensation must be a disagreeable one because the organism struggles to end it. The reasoning is hardly complete. Many of the objects of desire involve an expansion of the organism in definitely sought directions. The desire for wealth if once gratified maintains itself, not because it is painful but rather because wealth gives a person increased control over things and people. This control results in an expansion *of* the person's sense of the "me" and particularly of the "mine." It secures him an increased degree of attention from and perhaps admiration of other persons. Desire itself may contain a painful element, because the individual is temporarily unable to respond the way he has been stimulated to do. The agreeable psychic tone which results from the gratification of desire more than offsets a temporarily painful element. It is this aroused but temporarily unsatisfied condition of psychic nature, or desire, that Ward believed to be the dynamic force in individual life and hence in social life. To point simply to an unsatisfied state of the psychic organism as the dynamic social agent is to overlook the factors conditioning desire. Desire is a complex of affective and cognitive mechanisms resulting from the interplay of environmental stimuli and innate tendencies. It is in part an habitual seeking after objects, which thereby become values that give the organism a pleasant reaction tone but do not entirely satisfy it, and thus act as stimuli for further search after the desired objects or values.

All the natural impulses, the feelings, emotions, sentiments may become organized into what W. I. Thomas calls "wishes;" he classifies four : (1) the desire for new experience, (2) the desire for security, (3) the desire for recognition, (4) and the desire for response. The last mentioned should perhaps be put first, for it appears to be basic to all the others. The simpler forms of life, even the most elementary, are characterized by response to stimuli but cannot be said to have desires, with attention fixed on remote objectives. We therefore may refer to the fourth mentioned desire as a basic mechanism of organic life. In a higher form it appears as a desire for social response. The desire for recognition definitely reflects the stimuli which come from social life; it expands into the desire for power. The desire for security is evidently elemental and primary; it is made up largely of the self-preservation impulses. The desire for new experience leads out into the desire to do, to achieve. Thomas' fourfold classification seems to be primarily individualistic. There may be also a fundamental desire to aid, to help. Its objective is not primarily the individual's satisfaction, but rather the growth and satisfaction that others experience. This ultimately becomes an ethical attitude.

Repressed Feelings and Emotions

When a neuro-muscular mechanism is stimulated the natural tendency is for the neural process to run its course and issue in some form of motor activity. This process being largely physiological and psychological takes place in accordance with the nature of the environmental stimulus and not necessarily in harmony with socially derived standards of conduct. The child cries for candy when it would be bad for him; he wishes to stay up beyond his regular bedtime, but regularity in sleeping hours is decreed; he wants a bicycle when in the judgment of his parents the dangers of bicycle riding are great, and the request is denied: in these illustrative instances, which might be multiplied without end, environmental factors have served as stimuli to perform actions that better adult judgment cannot permit. The ordinary adult reply to the child is "don't", and the stimulated activity in the child is repressed before reaching its fruition. This released but "blocked" energy wells up and acts as a drive to emotional mechanisms, and thus may be expressed in harmful ways. Sometimes an individual after suffering bitter disappointment threatens to take his own life. Crying often serves as a means of discharge of energy that is blocked by some objective "don't" to a desire that is in process of being fulfilled. Occasionally when a desire mechanism has been thwarted, the individual is "too angry" to express himself or to secure emotional satisfaction. In cases such as these repression may do great and lasting harm. The released but undischarged energy is held up in "mid-air" as it were, producing a fundamental disturbance of the whole organism. It is to complexes of this type that psychotherapy has offered considerable aid. It is important that the resentment which commonly follows repression be dissipated quickly and not be allowed to assume chronic forms, such as a permanently "balked disposition."

A boy or girl who possesses a high degree of energy naturally responds to countless environmental stimuli to activity, and his parents find themselves unwittingly "sitting on the lid." Through ignorance or sheer lack of ingenuity, they fail to keep the boy's energies engaged in constructive enterprises, and sooner or later find him guilty of destructive mischief. In rural life, there are wholesome opportunities for expressions of energy in field and farmyard, but in the city, these opportunities are cut off, one by one. Vacant lots disappear, and the streets become increasingly dangerous playgrounds until city ordinance forbids all play upon them. Houses encroach on all available yard space until dark hallways and alleyways alone are left as spaces in which the normal energies of youth may be released, but in these remaining places of rendezvous the stimuli are too often of a vicious and evil nature. Cities, through their encroachment upon the playgrounds of youth act as crass repressive agents, meanwhile letting loose influences, which prey upon the repressed energies of untrained human nature. It is well to remember that psychic energy cannot be abolished. "If it is neither exploded nor converted, it is turned inwards, to lead a surreptitious, subterranean life."

The Puritanic attitude, being repressive with reference to childhood, often produced a rooted hatred of the Sabbath, of church, or of other religious institutions or practices. Repression does not destroy, but causes a "welling up" of psychical energy which too frequently takes the form of sullenness, hatred, or even recalcitrancy. In its worthy aims of discipline, Puritanism neglected to study the psychology of repressed desires. Many church bodies have likewise neglected the psychology of repression and sublimation in their emphases upon the "Thou shalt pots" of religious discipline as related particularly to the play impulses of young people.

The "only" child has received a considerable amount of attention on the part of the Freudians and other psychoanalysists. The repression is that of the gregarious impulses and is produced indirectly by an absence of proper environmental stimuli of the gregarious and playful types, The "only" child has a normal social nature but possessing limited opportunities for expression of his social traits in the company of other children, his energies are not released. They well up until they force themselves over the void into non-social or anti-social directions. They may turn into organized moroseness, selfishness, sexual self-abuse, or other unfortunate channels. Such a child may receive a surplus of attention from parents, and hence develop a chronic expectation of receiving attention.

A child with a large endowment of energy may react to repression by "contrariness." He often makes requests which cannot be granted; his environment as he sees it impinges upon him at nearly every turn. Being continually repressed, his energies express themselves in beliefs that the world is against him, that all is wrong. Sometimes these beliefs may lead to murder or suicide. Most phenomena of the last mentioned type have been preceded by long periods of repression of certain dominant desires, although occasionally life is taken as a result of an abrupt repression, as in the case of the jilted lover, or the jealous spouse.

Repression often leads to a super-development of imagination. Balked impulses may seek satisfaction in religious imagery. In fact one of the chief constructive phases of religious beliefs is that they are often sublimated opportunities for broken hopes and defeated ambitions. Of course the imagery results of repression may easily take harmful trends as well as helpful ones. Then there is wise repression, *i.e., rational discipline.* Without repression, the developing child succumbs to pernicious stimuli, and anti-personal as well as anti-social habits result. Youth cannot have the discretion of age, and thus many tendencies are repressed by parent or by society. This process is basic to *self control,* without which there can be no dependable conduct. But where repression is resorted to, the disciplinarian normally will provide for adequate sublimation. This need may often be met by a simple explanation of the dangers in the given stimulus, but if the stimuli are strong and insistent, then an alternative activity, future or present, will need to be provided.

Discipline is essential to both personal and social progress, but it cannot be achieved without obliging the individual to run the gauntlet of the psychical dangers incident to repression. As a youth cannot well safeguard himself from these evils, the major responsibility rests on his elders, or those who have his training in charge. Since these persons may be unversed in the psychology of repression, they perpetrate all kinds of blunders upon relatively helpless children.

The importance of disseminating the available knowledge concerning the nature of repression and sublimation is seen in the cases of lenient parents who, dismayed by the effects of repression in their children, find themselves baffled. Oftentimes they have neglected to provide sublimated opportunities until repression produces such a storm of angry opposition, based on untoward habits, that they lose all control over their children.

Undue repression of the feelings and emotions has led to warped personalities, insanity, and social radicalism. Psychiatry offers valuable data for social psychology when it reveals case after case in which the impingement of social conditions or personal insult and injustice has upset an individual's feeling and emotional nature and thrown it into a distorted condition. The life histories of revolutionists in various countries would doubtless reveal that their revolutionary attitude arose out of feelings distorted by genuine or imagined injustice. Affective human nature is evidently the most delicately adjusted and at the same time the most dynamic of all the factors involved in intersocial stimulation. It operates now subtly, now rashly, now without control, but always significantly in the formation of all social attitudes and values, while being at the same time the colourful dynamo of personal achievement and social progress.

DISJUNCTIVE FEELINGS

Anger

Anger is the feeling that most typifies the striving for power and domination. Its purpose is the rapid and forceful destruction of every obstacle in the way of the angered person. Previous research has shown us that angry individuals are those who are striving for superiority by every possible application of all their powers. The striving for recognition occasionally degenerates into real power-madness. Where this occurs we expect to find individuals who respond with violent outbursts to the slightest occurrence that might detract from their sense of power. They believe (perhaps as a result of previous experiences) that they can best get their own way, thus conquering their opponents, by this method. This procedure does not stand on a very high intel-lectual level, yet it works in a majority of cases. It is not difficult for most people to remember how they have won back their prestige or got their own way through an occasional outburst of fury.

There are occasions when anger is largely justified, but we are not considering such cases here. In discussing the use of anger we are referring to individuals in whom this feeling is always present and is a habitual, well-marked response. Some people systematically use their anger for their own ends, because they have no other way of approaching a problem. They are usually haughty, highly sensitive people who cannot bear anyone to be their superior or even their equal, who must themselves be superior in order to be happy. Consequently they are continually on guard in case anyone comes too close to them or does not value them highly enough. Distrust is the character trait most frequently allied with this kind of sensitivity. They find it impossible to trust their fellow human beings.

Other, closely related character traits go along with their anger, sensitivity and mistrust. In extreme cases one might find, for example, exceptionally ambitious individuals shying away from every serious task, incapable of ever adjusting to society. Should they be denied anything, they only know one method of response. They announce their protest in a manner that is usually very painful for everyone else. They may, for instance, shatter a mirror or destroy an expensive vase. We cannot really accept their apologies if they afterwards attempt to excuse themselves by saying that they did not know what they were doing. The desire to express themselves by destructiveness is plainly evident, for they always destroy something valuable and never confine their rage to worthless objects. A plan of some kind must have been behind their action.

Although this method achieves a certain success on a small scale, as soon as the context becomes wider it loses its effectiveness. Consequently, these habitually angry people soon find themselves in conflict with the whole world. The external signs of anger are so common that we have only to think of the word 'fury' to call up a mental picture of an irascible people.

Their hostile attitude towards the world is clearly evident. The feeling of anger signifies an almost complete negation of social feeling. The striving for power is so bitterly expressed that even killing an opponent is not too difficult to imagine. We can practise our knowledge of human nature by analysing the various emotions and feelings we observe, since feelings and emotions are the clearest indications of character. We must classify all irascible, angry, acrimonious individuals as enemies of society and enemies of life. We must again call attention to the fact that their striving for power is rooted in their feeling of inferiority. No human beings confident of their own power need to show these aggressive, violent reactions and gestures. This fact must never be overlooked. In paroxysms of rage, the whole pattern of inferiority and superiority appears with utter clarity. It is a cheap trick whereby one person's self-esteem is raised at another person's expense.

Alcohol is one of the most important triggers of rage and anger. Very small quantities of alcohol are often sufficient to produce this effect. It is well known that the action of alcohol deadens or removes the inhibitions of civilisation. Intoxicated individuals act as if they had never been civilised. In this way they lose control of themselves and all consideration for others. When they are not intoxicated they may, with great effort, be able to hide their hostility to humanity and inhibit their unfriendly tendencies. Once they are intoxicated their true character is expressed. It is by no means coincidental that people who are out of tune with life often take to alcohol. They find in this drug a certain consolation and forgetfulness, as well as an excuse for their failure to attain what they desire.

Temper tantrums are much more frequent among children than among adults. Sometimes an insignificant event is sufficient to throw a child into a temper tantrum. This arises from the fact that children, as a result of their greater feeling of inferiority and their lack of experience, show their striving for power in a more transparent manner. Angry children are striving for recognition because every obstacle they meet appears exceptionally difficult, if not insurmountable.

A deep-seated feeling of anger, when it goes beyond the usual behaviour of swearing and rage, may cause physical as well as psychological injury to the person who is angry. It is worth adding a note in this connection on the nature of suicide. Suicide is often an attempt to hurt relatives or friends, and to avenge oneself for some perceived defeat.

Grief

Grief occurs when individuals cannot console themselves for a loss or deprivation. Grief, along with the other feelings, is a compensation for the experience of displeasure or weakness, and amounts to an attempt to secure something better. In this respect its value is identical with that of a temper tantrum. The difference is that it occurs as a result of other stimuli, is marked by a different attitude, and uses a different method.

The striving for superiority plays a role in the excesses of grief, just as in all other feelings. Whereas anger is used to raise the self-esteem of individuals while degrading their opponents, and is thus directed against someone, grief amounts to an actual shrinkage of the psychological horizons, which is a prerequisite to their subsequent expansion in which the grieving individuals achieve their personal elevation and satisfaction. But this satisfaction takes the form of a kind of outburst, a reaction against the social environment, although in a different manner from that of anger. The grieving individuals complain, and with their complaint express their opposition to their fellows. Natural as sorrow is in the nature of humanity, its exaggeration is a hostile gesture against society.

The elevation of grief-stricken individuals is achieved through the attitude of those around them. We all know how these individuals find their position alleviated by the way others hurry to help them, sympathise with them, support them, encourage them and otherwise contribute to their welfare. If people feel relieved after crying, it is because they have achieved a kind of elevation by setting themselves up as plain-tiffs against the existing order of things. The more plaintiffs demand of their environment because of their grief, the more obvious their claims become. Grief becomes an irrefutable argument that places a binding duty upon the friends, neighbours and family of these individuals. This feeling clearly indicates the struggle to pass from weakness to superiority, and the attempt to retain one's position and evade a feeling of powerlessness and inferiority.

Disgust

The affect of disgust is socially disruptive too, although less so than the other feelings. Physically, disgust occurs when an unpleasant sight or smell causes a certain stimulus in the stomach walls. Mentally, disgust consists of tendencies and attempts to 'vomit' matter out of the psyche. It is here that the disruptive nature of disgust becomes apparent. Disgust is a feeling of aversion. The grimaces that accompany it signify contempt for everything and everyone, and an attempt to solve a problem by a gesture of rejection.

This feeling can easily be misused by being made an excuse or removing ourselves from an unpleasant situation. It is easy to simulate a feeling of nausea, and once it is conjured up we must, of necessity, escape from the particular situation in which we find ourselves. No other feeling can be artificially produced as easily as disgust. With a little practice, anyone can learn to feel nauseous to order. Thus a harmless feeling becomes a powerful weapon against society, or a reliable excuse for withdrawing from

Fear

Fear is one of the most significant phenomena in the life of human beings. This feeling is complicated by the fact that it is not only a disjunctive emotion, but like sorrow it is capable of creating a one-sided bond with one's fellows. A child escapes from a situation because of fear, and runs to the protection of someone else.

The mechanism of fear does not directly demonstrate any superiority-indeed, it seems to denote a defeat. When we are afraid, we try to make ourselves as small as possible, but it is at this point that the other side of this feeling, involving a simultaneous thirst for superiority, becomes evident, Fearful individuals flee to seek the protection of others, and attempt to strengthen themselves in this way until they feel capable of meeting and triumphing over the dangers to which they feel exposed.

With fear, we are dealing with a phenomenon that is a deeply rooted organic function. It is a reflection of the primitive fear that seizes all living creatures. Humans are especially subject to this fear because of their weakness and insecurity in the natural scheme of things. So inadequate is our inborn knowledge of the difficulties of life that children can never reconcile themselves with it unaided. Others must contribute whatever they lack. Children sense these difficulties as soon as they come into the world and the world begins to make its demands on them. There is always a danger that they will fail in striving to compensate for their insecurity, and develop a pessimistic philosophy as a result. Their most significant character trait becomes, therefore, a certain thirst for the help and consideration of those around her. The farther they are from solving life's problems, the more cautious they are. If ever such children are forced to do something on their own, they carry with them everything they need for their retreat. They are always poised for flight, and naturally their most common and obvious character trait is the feeling of fearfulness.

We see the beginnings of confrontation in the way fear is expressed, perhaps indirectly and without open aggression. We sometimes gain a particularly clear insight into the workings of the psyche when pathological degenerations of this feeling occur. In these cases we see clearly how fearful individuals reach out for a helping hand, and seek to draw other people towards them and chain them to their side.

Further study of this phenomenon leads us to considerations we have already discussed when looking at anxiety. In this case, we are dealing with individuals who demand support from someone, who need someone to pay attention to them at all times. Their relationship becomes similar to that of a master and slave, as if someone else had to be present to aid and support the anxious person. If we investigate this further we find many people who go through life demanding special attention. They have lost their independence to such an extent (as a result of inadequate and defective contact with life) that they demand exceptional privileges with extraordinary vehemence. No matter how much they seek out the company of others, they have little real social feeling. Let them show fear and fright, and they can establish their privileged position again. Fear helps them to both evade the demands of life and enslave all those about them. Finally fear worms its way into everyday relationships, and becomes an individual's most important instrument of domination.

The Misuse of Emotion

No one understood the meaning and value of feelings and emotions until it was discovered that they were valuable instruments to overcome a sense of inferiority and to elevate the personality and obtain recognition. The faculty of showing emotion has a wide application in the life of the psyche. Once children, feeling neglected, learn that they can tyrannize their environment through fury or tears or fearfulness they will test this method of obtaining domination again and again. In this way they will fall easily into a behaviour pattern that allows them to react to insignificant stimuli with their typical emotional response. They use their emotions whenever they suit their needs. Preoccupation with emotion is a bad habit that occasionally becomes pathological.

When this has developed in childhood we find adults who constantly misuse emotions. Such individuals utilise anger, grief and all the other feelings in a dramatic way, as though they were puppets. This valueless and often unpleasant behaviour robs emotions of their true value. Play-acting with emotions becomes a habitual response whenever such an individuals are denied anything or whenever the dominance of their personality is threatened. Grief may be so violently expressed that it becomes distasteful: it is too loud, too showy, too histrionic. We have seen people who give the impression that they are competing with everyone in the amount of grief they can display. The same misuse can be made of the physical accompaniments of emotion. It is well known that there are people who allow their anger to react so strongly upon their digestive systems that they vomit when they are angry. This mechanism expresses their hostility all the more transparently. The emotion of grief is similarly associated with a refusal to eat so that the grieving person actually loses weight and really looks 'the picture of sadness'.

HELPING THE CHILD BECOME SOCIALLY ADEQUATE

The child's style of life, which includes his basic attitudes toward others, is formulated early in life. The early interaction between parent and child is most significant in setting up the child's self image. The child gets his picture of self from the appraisal of others.

With the very young child, undesirable behaviour can be eliminated by distracting the child from antisocial activities. If, instead, the adults become excited and overly absorbed in the "bad behaviour," the child's tendency to respond in this manner may only be strengthened.

It is important to avoid giving a reward to socially undesirable behaviour. At the same time, the parent can support the child's attempts to engage in social relationships. They should avoid experiences which make the child fearful or skeptical about his ability to be accepted socially.

Social adequacy is fostered as exploration is stimulated. The child who is interested in visiting children or participating in social activities should be supported. For the child who does not readily find social experiences, it may be necessary to analyse his interests and try to put him in contact with children of similar interests.

However, it is important to recognise that the concept of readiness is as relevant to social growth as it is to reading. Recognise the individual differences in the primary reaction patterns and the social maturity of children. Avoid forcing children into social experiences, because of parental concern.

The child can easily interpret this concern as a belief that he is socially inadequate; the result is more inadequate social behaviour. Instead, try to develop experiences that provide social success by giving the child access to children with similar social skills or children who may complement each other's social needs.

A child's social adequacy is also influenced by people's beliefs in his sense of social responsibility. A variety of leadership opportunities enabling the child to take on responsibility should be made available both within the home and the school. The assumption by both parents and teachers that the child must first be responsible in order to be given responsibility is faulty. We must not require a sense of responsibility as a prerequisite for permitting or selecting a child to function. Often the child who most needs to find a new social place within the group is denied it, because an adult does not feel that he is responsible.

Parents and teachers, to an extent, should avoid projecting their goals and expectations on the child. If we recognise individual differences, we will certainly accept that not all children are outgoing, friendly, and eager for social contact. while focusing on an atmosphere designed to foster the growth and development of such traits, our acceptance of their lack lends support which may eventually make the child feel more adequate socially. Valuing and accepting the child as he is, even without the skills that you hold to be important, is vital for social development. The child who cannot immediately relate to other adults, who appears shy, who tends to hang on the edge of crowds, cannot change if he is rejected because of these traits,

The child's social development will best be promoted through encouragement of his social contacts. We should look for the positive elements in the way in which he relates to others and point them out to him. We should be concerned about building his self-respect and self-image in social areas. If he is not immediately ready to function socially, our faith that he is operating in the way which makes most sense to him at this time, enables him to develop socially. Give examples of specific ways in which forcing the child socially may actually produce more inadequate behaviour. How would you deal with the shy, socially withdrawn child?

THE FORMATION OF SOCIAL ATTITUDES

It is increasingly evident that both parents and schools need to be concerned about the social perceptions and attitudes of children. In a culture that is increasingly diverse, we must understand one another and be able to accept differences.

Research indicates that children acquire a considerable amount of their social prejudices toward other racial and religious groups, not through direct experience, but through contact with prejudiced peers, parents, and socially biased adults. Yarrow, Trager, and Davis made a study of children in kindergarten, first, and second grade, which reveals that attitudes toward racial and religious groups are learned early in childhood. Children are instructed in such a way that attitudes are formed toward a group; seldom is differentiation made among members of the group.

The social learning of the child is most frequently a reflection of his subcultures and the social relationships which exist in his neighborhood. In acquiring their values, children reflect their own interpersonal experiences with members of other groups, and not the adult values which exist about them. As the child's chronological age increased, Yarrow found evidence that he became more aware of group conflicts, patterns of exclusion in society, and the forms of stereotyping of attitudes became more set. This study also revealed that at an early age children develop negative self feelings based on their group membership. Thus, membership in the group tends either to abase or enhance the child's image of self.

This study indicates a definite need for information and for the acquisition of social techniques for adjusting in a society that is becoming more socially diverse all the time, Human relations groups in a number of the large cities have been taking direct steps to provide information and techniques that can have an effect on the development of attitudes.

THE SCHOOL AND SOCIAL DEVELOPMENT

The school represents one of the first major challenges to the child in the social area. He must engage in new relationships with an adult figure, the teacher, and with a large group of peers who are not of his choosing. There are new expectations about getting along with others, and school offers the first intensive contact with children who represent a variety of subcultures.

The school, for the child, becomes an important source of status, some of which derives from the child's ability and willingness to deal with the work tasks. Children who are not readily successful in this area may find other methods of attracting the teacher's attention. The cute, charming, and even the socially withdrawn child may find that their behaviour gives them a special place with the teacher.

The child also has to meet with the expectations of the peers in a new setting. While the children are in academic competition, with one another, they are also involved in just as significant a search for a place within the group.

They must understand the various points of view that exist within the group and must learn to consider the rights of others as well as their own. Social acceptability is frequently related to the capacity of the child to understand the needs of others.

Schools are becoming increasingly aware that children develop at various rates in academic and intellectual areas, but this same recognition has not been granted to differences in social development.

It is fundamental that a child's social development proceeds at a faster or slower pace according to his experiences with significant others in the group.

Developmental psychology has made us aware of some of the "ages and stages," hut it is interesting to contemplate whether these stages would be so apparent in children if their social needs were met more adequately. When the child is understood and his social needs are provided for some "stages" may not necessarily develop.

There is considerable evidence that the social climate of the group has a significant effect on the attitudes developed by members of the group. Perhaps the most significant studies in this area were conducted by Ronald Lippett and Ralph White. In a classic study that is often quoted and that should be examined in detail by serious students, Lippett and White investigated the effects on group and individual behaviour of providing three pure styles of leadership—"democratic," "authoritarian."' and laissezfaire" for clubs of eleven-year-old children.

The authoritarian leaders decided practically all policies and procedures. They took responsibility for assigning tasks and companions in any group activities. They remained aloof from group participation.

The democratic leader was interested in developing policies through group decision. He encouraged discussion and frequently provided alternative procedures so that the group might make a choice. The group made decisions about partners in projects and the division of responsibility. The laissez-faire leader played a comparatively passive role and allowed complete freedom to the group for individual decisions on group procedures. He made no attempt to evaluate and merely supplied information and help when asked.

The groups organised on a democratic basis were motivated to engage in self-and group-sustained activities. They participated whether the leader was present or not. The groups which experienced authoritarian leadership either tended to become aggressive or apathetic. The children in the laissez-faire situation were generally the least efficient and became increasingly confused and unhappy with their growing lack of accomplishment. There is significant evidence that the group atmosphere has a considerable effect on the convictions, attitudes, and progress of the individuals and the group. Evidence indicates that the democratic style of leadership, as defined by Lewin and his co-workers, is most productive.

In considering these studies it is important to recognise that the leaders played distinct roles which resulted in individuals who were as completely democratic or authoritarian in their leadership as it is humanly possible to be. The typical teacher will not be a pure type but more frequently a blend of these behaviours'. It is probably quite important that the teacher have some flexibility in roles so that she can meet various personality needs.

The teacher in training is frequently impressed with the importance of recognising individual differences and meeting these individual needs in the instructional process. However, it is just as important that she recognise her role in working with a group. The school is a social setting. This is an opportunity for children, under the supervision of a group leader, to develop socially.

The goals of group work in the classroom center around the development of cooperation among students. It is important that they develop an interest in the needs of others and a willingness to participate in give-and- take relationships. The group also provides an opportunity for identification, and here the teacher must strive to encourage each child to identify with the group. The group also can fill each child's need to belong.

One technique available to all teachers is group discussion. There should be a regular opportunity in the classroom for the child to express himself and to listen to others. This can only come about in an atmosphere in which individuals feel free to express their opinions and make suggestions.

This implies that the teacher is socially mature and able to accept criticism of procedure. When the teacher helps the group to participate in developing group plans, and eventually to evaluate group progress, he is helping the children to mature.

Group discussion is based upon mutual acceptance, and the leader shares in the positive interpersonal relationship that develops within the group. To be effective in the classroom, group discussions should not be used to lecture or to get over a point. The goal is not to get the class to confirm the leader's opinion. At the same time, group leaders need to be careful to set limits for the discussion, so that members of the group can take responsibility for the nature of their comments and contributions.

Teachers soon learn that the group can either be an obstacle to the instructional process or a help in the children's development.

However, the child's behaviour must always be viewed as part of his social interaction with other children. Group discussion time can be used to deal with emergencies, but it definitely should not be construed only as an emergency measure.

Group discussion should be planned on a regular basis, and the discussion should relate to topics that are pertinent to the concerns, interests, and goals of the students.

Every teacher works in relationship to strong peer-group loyalties. One job is to help integrate the group so that a group cohesiveness develops. Jennings established experimentally that an improved social climate resulted in higher achievement. A considerable portion of classroom work can be organised on a group basis, and a teacher conserves energy when he assists children to acquire the social skills necessary for group cooperation. Observe a classroom where group discussion takes place. Is the teacher merely devising methods for the children to confirm her point of view? How can the group be an obstacle to educational progress?

Co-curricular activities are an important part of the school experience and are basic to the socialisation process. These activities must be managed in such a manner that the" permit maximal social adjustment. Supervision of co-curricular activities is needed to implement the long-range purposes and goals of this programme.

Belonging to the group, then, meets certain specific needs of the child. It gives the individual support which frees him to act. It also helps him to face reality and test his abilities with his peers.

Supervised group experience helps him to appreciate and develop the social skills fundamental for human relationships. It is in this setting that he can comprehend tasks of leading and following. The effective group leader can help point out to the group, and at times to individuals in the group, their purposes in certain kinds of social interactions.

Improved social relations have an effect on the learning of the individual. As the child becomes more secure, he is able to concentrate on the tasks at hand.

The importance of group acceptance can increase a child's motivation to learn. In a well-knit class, group loyalty can be a strong motive for success. The general morale of the group also provides opportunity for the development of favourable attitudes toward learning experiences. Finally, the exchange of ideas in group discussion provides the opportunity for clarification.

The teacher should be involved in the utilisation of sociometric results in the classroom. Sociometrics can help promote group solidarity, and committee work can be assigned in such a manner as to promote social growth. The teacher needs to be aware of the interpersonal relationships which exist in the group and the ways in which new relationships can be used to promote social growth.

The child who is rejected by the peer group requires special understanding. The behaviour of rejected pupils is frequently designed to gain the attention of peers, rather than to antagonise the teacher. This does not mean that the teacher must accept a pupil's antisocial behaviour, but it does indicate that the behaviour should be handled without a display of personal feelings or possible resentment toward the pupil.

The rejected child usually does not feel secure or adequate. He is frightened by new learning situations, and resists change. Any possibility of failure is usually avoided. This child reacts strongly to teacher criticism, and his self-esteem is injured as his sense of inadequacy increases.

While it is important that the teacher provide an accepting atmosphere for these children, certain specifics can develop out of sociometric evaluation. For example, in the arrangement of seating in the classroom and the development of committees, it is important that children who are isolated or rejected by the group be given their first choices. These children require the greatest opportunity to establish satisfying social relationships. Students who do not accept the isolated or rejected student should not be placed in the same work groups. In working with the isolate, the child who is not chosen by others, the teacher should note whether this child attempts to make social contacts or whether he regularly withdraws from social interaction. This will give some measure of the extent of feelings of discouragement and inferiority. These children can be nurtured back into the group as certain assets which they have are made apparent to other children. A good device is to conduct an inventory of some of the strengths of children who are isolates and place them in positions within the group which permit them to contribute to group life.

STABILITY OF SOCIAL DEVELOPMENT

Considerable research has been directed at investigating the long-term stability of personal and social behaviour. Martin did a study to investigate the stability, individuality, and continuity of psychological development. The study was done with children of nursery school age. Over a two-year period of observation, he found that children tended to demonstrate the same relative amount of aggression, dominance, dependency, autonomy, achievement, and friendship-affiliation traits.

The study demonstrated both constancy and change, while the frequency of behaviour increased with age; constancy occurred in such a way that the child tended to maintain his position in the group in regard to frequency of behaviour. There is adequate evidence of unique social behaviour patterns of the children studied.

These individual behaviour profiles were unique both in content and form. Martin concluded that 80 per cent of the children's behaviour profiles were stable over a two-year period at the nursery school level. In referring to the unchanged and emerging individualised pattern, Martin states, "It is as if each child has his own 'behavioural economy,' which persists through time. Admittedly, he modifies his behaviour but only in search of enduring goals."

Anderson also reported findings of consistency in personality traits. However, the fact that behaviour at the nursery school level was predictable over a two-year period of time does not mean that behaviour could be predicted from this level to adulthood. The Kagan and Moss studies indicate that very few of the behaviours observed between ages three and six were predictive of related behaviours in early adulthood. Kagan and Moss did stress that all behaviour is patterned and underscored the importance of comprehending the patterns.

STAGES IN THE SOCIAUSATION PROCESS

A number of the schools of psychological thought have formulated stages in the process of socialisation. Psychoanalysts have described a system in which the child is striving to reduce biologically based drives and adjust to the world about him to achieve pleasure and avoid pain. In their model, the child's interest is focused on himself, and he is well-adjusted to the extent that he finds release from his internal tensions without causing conflict with others in the environment.

Erikson's Stages in the Development Socialisation

Erikson has developed a concept of eight stages through which man progresses in his development. His premise is that the individual is well-adjusted to the extent that he possesses the positive rather than the negative characteristics of each stage.

The first stage is one of trust as contrasted with mistrust. If the child is well-nurtured he develops trust and security. If the infant can endure the mother's absence without becoming anxious because he can depend upon his mother's satisfying his needs, he has passed through this stage successfully. If the child is inadequately handled, he becomes insecure and mistrustful.

The second stage, autonomy versus shame and doubt, is reached during the Freudian's anal stage. The child is being toilet trained. If he is well managed, he comes out of this stage certain, rather than ashamed. This is the period in which the child learns to assert his will. The next stage, initiative versus guilt, is when the healthy child learns to broaden his skills, to cooperate, and to lead as well as follow. If he is fearful, he will continue to be dependent on adults and be restricted in the development of social skills and imagination.

Entrance into school coincides with the stage labeled industry versus inferiority. It is at this time that the child learns to win recognition by being productive. Work becomes pleasurable, and he learns to persevere. If the child does not feel competent in his skills or satisfied with his status among his peers in work skills, then he may develop a sense of inadequacy and inferiority.

The stage of identity versus role diffusion is reached at the time of puberty when childhood is left behind and the transition to adulthood The individual has to find a place for himself, an identity, a self concept, that corresponds with others' ideas of him. He is seeking answers to the question "Who am I?" Role diffusion implies an uncertainty of one's place in his world, with an accompanying uncertainty of appropriate behaviour.

When the individual has ascertained his identity, he is ready for the sixth stage, intimacy versus isolation. He is now capable of experiencing the intimacy of an enduring friendship or marriage. He is sure of his own identity so that he can completely abandon himself in situations that call for it, without being afraid of losing that identity. Fear of self-abandonment results in a feeling of isolation,

The seventh stage in which a conflict occurs is an outgrowth of the sixth. It is generativity versus stagnation, in which generativity has been defined as parental responsibility, the interest in producing as well as guiding the next generation. The individual is able to work productively and creatively. When this interest is lacking, the individual stagnates and may regress. The last stage of development which Erikson calls ego integrity versus despair is the culmination of successful completion of the preceding seven stages. Integrity, as he uses the word, means facing reality, recognising it, and accepting it. The mature individual has developed a self concept he can accept, and he is pleased with his role in life and what he produces.

A Social Interpersonal Theory of Development

Sullivan developed a description of the stages of development which did not relate directly to Freud's emergent biological needs. Sullivan's system was based on the interpersonal relationships which the individual experiences as he pursues security. These stages were infancy, childhood juvenile era, preadolescence, early adolescence, and late adolescence.

Infancy. The infant organism enters the world helpless and unable to deal with its needs directly. In this stage the infant reacts to the significant adults about him with what Sullivan called empathy—a direct reflection of the mood of the parent. For example, if the parent is anxious, the infant also is uncomfortable.

The anxious mother, then, is very likely to have an anxious, crying infant, even though needs are cared for and she is indulgent The child's states of equilibrium win approval from the parents. Because the infant is unable to make fine discriminations as to what he specifically does to bring about parental responses, he cannot evaluate the approval and disapproval he receives. He seems to be continuously between equilibrium or distress, which, for the child, results in the concept of "good" or "bad" mother. According to Sullivan, this emerges in a self system known as either the "good me" or the "bad me."

As the infant becomes capable of differentiating between others and his own bodily limitations, he also develops the need for security. At this time the child first experiences "anxiety" as a consequence of his relationship with significant adults, Anxiety is an interpersonal phenomenon which develops as the infant learns that his comfort is based primarily on the actions of the mother. The child's opinion of self conies out of this early "empathic" relationship with "mothering" individuals.

Childhood. As the child develops motor and language skills which enable him to go about and interact more freely, he becomes the target for education and training. In this period the child learns the dimensions of his culture. As he matures, language becomes a means of communication. He also learns ways of manipulating people to help him achieve security. The child now becomes able to determine certain impulses which provoke anxiety and those which can be discharged without anxiety.

Juvenile Era. The juvenile stage is usually closely associated with entry into school. The child is beginning to see himself as distinct from other entities, to identify the self. He is surrounded by peers, and is now first coming into contact with significant adults other than his parents. In this period the child begins to look at himself objectively and to develop an, internal critic who tests his impulses. This internal critic, which might be compared to the superego, is really a reflection of the appraisals of significant adults. Attitudes of competition, rivalry, and eventually more or less realistic compromise begin to appear. The child is engaged in defining his own status and his own self in relationship to the broader culture with which he is daily interacting.

Preadolescence. If the individual is to mature psychologically in preadolescence he must move from egocentric achievements and take his first steps toward believing that satisfactions experienced by others are as significant to him as his own. At this stage he is capable of a more mature love that goes beyond the pursuit of his own security. In preadolescence concern for others is usually expressed toward a friend of the same sex, whose pattern of behaviour may be similar to his own. The child's consensual validation is developed as he becomes free to express his thoughts and feelings to this friend. This more expansive concern is similar to the development of social interest in the Adlerian theory. The child is familiar with the tasks and responsibilities of home and school; as he comes to accept them, he is moving toward the basic attitudes necessary for mature psychological development.

Adolescence. There is a shift in interest from a person of the same sex to one *of the* opposite sex. *This* is the time when *the* child must come to terms *with* the sex drive. Due to the attitudes toward sex in our culture, the adolescent is frequently faced with new problems in integrating his personality.

THE DYNAMICS OF ATTRACTION

Let us turn now to the special preparation necessary for a committed relationship. This involves, as we have seen, the training of social feeling in conjunction with the instinct of sexual attraction. As a matter of fact we know that everyone creates in his own mind from childhood onwards an ideal picture of a partner. In the case of a boy it is very probable that the mother provides the model for the ideal woman, and that the boy will look for a similar type of partner. Sometimes there may be a state of unhappy tension between a boy and his mother, in which case he may look for a completely different type of partner. So close is the correspondence between a child's relationship with his mother and the person he afterwards marries that we can observe it in such little details as eye colour, figure, colour of hair, and so on.

We know, too, that if a mother is domineering and represses her son, he may not want to act courageously when the time comes for becoming emotionally involved, for his sexual ideal is likely to be weak and obedient, or, if he is aggressive, he will fight and want to dominate his partner.

We can see how all the characteristics manifested in childhood are emphasised and magnified when people face the problem of love. We can imagine how people suffering from an inferiority complex will behave in sexual matters. Perhaps because they feel weak and inferior they will express their feelings by always asking for support from other people. Often such types have the motherly character as an ideal. Or sometimes, by way of compensating for their inferiority, they may take the opposite direction in love and become arrogant and aggressive. Then they may select a stubborn or quarrelsome partner, finding it more honourable to be the conqueror in a difficult battle.

Neither sex can act successfully in this way. It is ridiculous to have the sexual, relationship reduced to the satisfaction of an inferiority or superiority complex, and yet this happens very frequently. If we look closely we see that in seeking a partner many people are really looking for a victim. They do not understand that sexual relationships cannot be exploited for such ends. For if one person seeks to dominate, the other will do likewise. As a result, a shared life becomes impossible.

The observation that some people are attempting to satisfy their complexes illuminates certain peculiarities in their choice of a partner which are otherwise difficult to understand. It tells us why some people choose weak, sick, or old partners: they choose them because they believe they will have an easier time with them. Sometimes they choose someone already married: here it is a case of never wanting to make a commitment. Sometimes we find people falling in love with two people at the same time, because, as I have already remarked, 'two people are less than one'.

We have seen how people who suffer from an inferiority complex change their job, refuse to face problems, and never finish things. When confronted with the problem of love they act similarly. Falling in love with a married person or with two people at once is a way of perpetuating habitual indecisiveness. There are other ways, too, such as overlong engagements that never result in marriage.

The Spoilt Child

Spoilt children show up in relationships and marriage true to type: they want to be pampered by their partners. Such a state of affairs may exist without danger in the early stages of a relationship or in the first years of marriage, but later it will bring about complications. We can imagine what happens when two such persons develop a relationship. Both want to be pampered, and neither of them wants to play the pamperer. It is as if they each stood around expecting something from the other and giving nothing. Both have the feeling that they are misunderstood.

When people feel misunderstood and thwarted, they feel inferior and want to escape. Such feelings are extremely bad in a relationship or marriage, particularly if a sense of hopelessness arises. When this happens the desire for revenge begins to creep in; one person wants to disrupt the life of the other. The most common way to do this is to be unfaithful. Infidelity is always an act of vengeance. True, partners who are unfaithful always justify themselves by speaking about love and feelings, but we know the value of such feelings and sentiments — they always agree with the goal of superiority, and should not be regarded as anything but excuses.

As an illustration we may take the case of a certain pampered woman. She married a man who had always felt in the shadow of his brother. The man was attracted by the mildness and sweetness of this girl, an only child, who in turn expected always to be appreciated and the centre of attention. The marriage was quite happy until a child came along. We can predict what happened then: the wife still wanted to be the centre of attention but was afraid that the child might take her place, and so she was not very happy. The husband, on the other hand, also wanted to be number one and was afraid that the child would usurp his place. As a result, husband and wife became suspicious of one another. They did not neglect the child and were quite good parents, but they were always expecting that their love for each other would decrease. Such a suspicion is dangerous, because if one starts to measure every word and every action, it is easy to find, or to appear to find, a decrease in affection. In this case, both parties found it. The husband went on a holiday to Paris and enjoyed himself while his wife recuperated from childbirth and looked after the baby. He wrote exuberant letters from Paris, telling his wife what a good time he was having, how he was meeting all sorts of people, and so on. The wife began to feel neglected, became depressed and soon began to suffer from agoraphobia. She could not go out alone any more. When her husband returned he had to accompany her everywhere. On the surface at least, it would seem that she had attained her goal, and that she was now the centre of attention. But nonetheless she had the feeling that if her agoraphobia, disappeared, her husband would disappear, too, so she continued to suffer from agoraphobia.

During her illness she found a doctor who gave her considerable attention. While under his care she felt much better, and all the feelings of friendship she had she directed towards him. But when the doctor decided that she was better, he stopped seeing her. She wrote him a letter thanking him for all he had, done for her, but he did not reply. From this time on, her illness became worse.

At this time she began to have ideas and fantasies about liaisons with other men in order to revenge herself upon her husband. However, her agoraphobia, which meant she could not go out alone, prevented her from being unfaithful to him.

METHODS MODERN OF INTERPRETATION

Modern interpretation of dreams dates from the early part of the twentieth century. Dreams were first regarded by Freud as the fulfilment of infantile sexual desires. I cannot agree with this, inasmuch as if dreams are such a fulfilment then everything can be regarded as a fulfilment. Every idea behaves in this way— going from the depths of the subconscious up into consciousness. The formula of sex-fulfilment thus explains nothing in particular.

Later Freud suggested that the desire for death was involved. But surely our last example could not be explained very well in these terms, for we cannot say that the father wanted a child to get lost and die, or to die himself.

The truth is that there is no specific formula that will explain all dreams, except the general principles we have discussed about the unity of mental life and about the special emotional character of dream life. This character, and its accompanying self-deception, is a theme with many variations. It is also expressed in a preoccupation with comparisons and metaphors. The use of comparisons is one of the best means of deceiving oneself and others, for we may be sure that if people use them they do not feel sure that they can convince others with facts and logic. They always want to influence others by means of useless and farfetched comparisons.

Poets use these devices to deceive, but pleasantly, and we enjoy being entertained by their metaphors and poetic comparisons. We may be sure, however, that they are meant to influence us more than we would be influenced by plainer words. If Homer, for example, speaks of an army of Greek soldiers overrunning a field like lions, the metaphor will not deceive us when we think sharply but it will certainly intoxicate us when we are taken by the poetic mood. The author makes us believe in a marvellous power, but he could not do this if he were merely to describe the clothes the soldiers wore, the arms they carried, and so on.

We see the same thing in the case of people who are in difficulty explaining something: if they see they cannot convince you, they will use comparisons. This use of metaphors and comparisons, as we have said, is self-deceptive, and this is the reason it is so prominent in dreams, in the selection of symbolic images. It is an artistic way of intoxicating oneself.

Dreamers and Non-Dreamers

The fact that dreams are emotionally intoxicating offers, curiously enough, a method for *preventing* dreams. If people understand what they have been dreaming about and realise that they have merely been intoxicating themselves, they will stop dreaming. To dream will have no more purpose for them. At least, this is the case with me; I stopped dreaming as soon as I realised what dreaming meant. This realisation, to be effective, must be a thorough emotional conversion. This was brought about, in my case, by my last dream. The dream occurred during the First World War. In connection with my duties I was making a great effort to keep a certain man from being sent to the front. In the dream the idea came to me that I had murdered someone, but I did not know whom. I got myself into a bad state wondering, 'Who have I murdered?'

The fact is, I was simply intoxicated with the idea of making the greatest possible effort to keep the soldier in a safe place. The dream emotion was meant to be conducive to this idea, but when I understood the subterfuge of the dream, I gave up dreaming altogether, since I did not want to deceive myself in order to do the things that, for reasons of logic, I should either do or leave undone. This may be taken as an answer to the question that is frequently asked, 'Why do some people never dream?' These are people who do not want to deceive themselves. They are concerned with action and logic, and want to face up to problems. People of this sort, if they dream, often forget their dreams very quickly, so quickly, in fact, that they believe they have not been dreaming.

There is a theory that we always dream but forget most of our dreams. If we accepted such a theory it would shed a different light on the fact that some of us never dream: we would become people who always forget their dreams. I do not accept this theory. I rather believe that there are people who never dream, and there are also dreamers who sometimes forget their dreams. In the nature of the case such a theory is hard to refute, but perhaps the burden of proof should be put on the propounders of the theory.

Why do we sometimes have the same dream repeatedly? This is a curious fact for which no definite explanation can be given. However, in such repeated dreams we are often able to find the life style expressed with greater clarity. Such a repeated dream gives us a definite and unmistakable indication as to where the individual goal of superiority lies. In the case of long, extended dreams we must believe that the dreamers are not ready and are looking for the way out of their problem to the achievement of their goal. For this reason, the dreams that can best be understood are short dreams. Sometimes dreams consist of only one image, or a few words, and this shows that dreamers are really trying to find an easy way to deceive themselves.

Sleep and Hypnotism

We may close our discussion with the question of sleep. A great many people ask themselves needless questions about sleep. They imagine that sleep is the direct opposite of being awake, and that it is akin to death. But such views are erroneous. Sleep is not the opposite of being awake, but rather a degree of wakefulness. We are not cut off from life during sleep. On the contrary, we think and hear in our sleep, and the same tendencies are generally expressed in sleep as in waking life. Thus, there are mothers who cannot be awakened by any noises in the street, but if the children make the slightest sound they immediately jump up. We see from this how their interest is always awake. Also from the fact that we do not fall out of bad we can see that we are conscious of limits during sleep.

An individual's entire personality is expressed in both sleeping and waking. This explains the phenomenon of hypnotism. What charlatans have represented as a magical power is for the most part nothing more than a kind of sleep. But it is a sleep during which people wants to obey another and know that the hypnotist want to make them sleep. A simple from of the same thing is when parents say, That's enough-now go to sleep! and the children obey. Hypnotism, too, works because the subjects are obedient. The ease with which individuals may be hypnotised is in proportion to their obedience.

In hypnotism we have an opportunity to make people imagine scenes, ideas, or memories that would be blocked by their waking inhibitions. The only requirement is obedience. By this method we can often discover early memories that may have been forgotten before.

As a method of treatment and cure, hypnotism has its dangers, however. I do not like hypnotism, and use it only when a patient responds to no other method. One will find that hypnotised people can be rather vengeful. In the beginning they appear to overcome their difficulties, but they do not really change their life style. Hypnotism is like a drug or a mechanical aid: the individual's true nature has not been touch. What we have to do is to give people courage, self confidence and better understanding of their mistakes, if we are really to help. Hypnotism does not do this, and should not be used except in rare case.

DETERRENTS TO SOCIAL DEVELOPMENT

Social development is hampered by overprotection and pampering by the parent, which produces in the child a desire to be noticed, even if negatively. Too many controls make the child dependent upon the parents for his social satisfaction. An autocratic atmosphere in the home, characterised by parental domination, does not permit the child to recognise the choices in social behaviour that are available to him. Children from an autocratic atmosphere tend to be more quarrelsome, unstable, and inhibited. These children are literally afraid to try. They are overimpressed with the dangers in life. The child has much to learn from firmness and must experience limits, but the atmosphere must be kind as well as firm.Social development is hampered by mistake-centered training; which emphasises what is wrong. If a child is too frequently confronted with a continual series of negative commands, he comes to believe that there is something wrong with him and that he dare not try, because things do not work out. In this connection, physical punishment tends to retard social development in the sense that it moves the child away from reality and makes him more dependent on adult affection. The child who is a recipient of physical punishment tends to set the standards for conduct external to the self and hence is extremely handicapped in interaction with peers where no adult is available to set limitations.

A child's social maturity can also be hampered by unrealistic expectations on the part of the parent. Too high expectations that he adhere to the model of the well-adjusted child" or that he become socialised more rapidly than his readiness dictates, discourage the child. when parents force and punish a child in a social direction the message the child receives is, "You are not what you should he." This attack on the child's self concept inhibits functioning in a social area.

Considerable conflicts between the various socialisation forces and expectations will deter social growth also. The family, the peers, the significant adults, and the school should try to reinforce each others' values as much as possible. In order for social standards to be set, the other social institutions of the community should be supported by the home.

Bibliography

Asch, M : *Abnormal and Developmental Psychology*, Ivy Pub, Delhi, 2003.

Bandura, A.: *Psychological modeling: Conflicting theories.* New York: Aldine-Atherton, 1971.

Cohn, Bernard S.: *India: The Social Anthropology of a Civilization*, New Jersey: Prentice-Hall, 1971.

Deepesh Chandra Prasad and Rinu Prasad: *Applied Educational Psychology*, KSK Pub, Delhi, 2006.

Dewald, P.A.: *Psychotherapy: A Dynamic Approach*, New York, Basic Books, 1971.

Festinger, L.: *A Theory of Cognitive Dissonance*, Row, Peterson, Evanston, IL, 1957.

Flavell, J. *H. The developmental psychology of Jean Piaget.* New York: Van Nostrand Co., 1963.

Gedo, J. E. & Goldberg, A.: *Models of the Mind: A Psychoanalytic Theory*, Chicago, University of Chicago Press, 1973.

Gedo, J. E. & Goldberg, A.: *Models of the Mind: A Psychoanalytic Theory*, Chicago, University of Chicago Press, 1973.

Georgi, A. : *Psychology as a Human Science*, Harper & Row, New York, 1970.

Goldberg, A.: *The Psychology of the Self: A Casebook*, New York, International Universities Press, 1978.

Jafar Mahmud: *Abnormal Psychology*, APH, Delhi, 2005.

James. W.: *The Principles of Psychology.* New York: Henry Holt & Co., 1896.

Kagan, J. *Change and continuity in infancy.* New York: John Wiley & Sons, 1971.

Kalpana Banerjee: *An Introduction to Comparative Psychology*, Indian Publishing House, Delhi, 2010.

Kaur, Rajpal : *Developmental Psychology : New Trends and Innovations*, Deep and Deep, Delhi, 2006.

Kendler, H.H.: *Psychology: A Science in Conflict.* New York: Oxford, 1981.

Klatzky, R.: *Human Memory: structure and processes.* San Francisco: Freeman, 1975.

Lee, R.& Martin, C.: *Psychotherapy after Kohut: A Textbook of Psychology*, Hillsdale, The Analytic Press, 1991.

Leo Postman: *The Psychology of Rumour*, Rinehart & Winston, Holt, 1947.

Luria, Z., & Rose, M.: *Psychology* of *human sexuality.* New York: John Wiley & Sons, 1979.

MacDonald, S.: *Evolutionary Perspectives on Human Development,* Thousand Oaks, CA: Sage Publications, 2004.

Madhu Jain: *Comprehensive Objective Psychology*, University Book House, Delhi, 2006.
Mead, G. H.: *Mind, self, and society*. Chicago: University of Chicago Press, 1934.
Michaels, J.J.: *Handbook of Psychiatry*. Mew York: basic Books, 1959.
Mischel, W.: *Personality and assessment*. New York: John Wiley & Sons, 1968.
Mittal, Sujata : *Experimental Child Psychology*, Isha Books, Delhi, 2005.
Moberly, E.: *Homosexuality: A New Christian Ethic*. Cambridge: James Clarke, 1983.
Moustakas, S. : *Existential Psychotherapy and the Interpretation of Dreams*, J. Aronson, C., Northvale, NJ, 1994.
Nisbett, R. E.: *Social Psychology*, Norton & Company, New York, 2006.
Nitesh Kumar Singh: *Human Deformities and Abnormal Psychology*, Signature Books International, Delhi, 2011.
Parens, H.: *The Development of Aggression in Early Childhood*, New York, Aronson, 1979.
Prasad, Deepesh Chandra : *A-Z Handbook of Child Psychology*, Khel Sahitya Kendra, Delhi, 2006.
Pratt, C.C.: *The Logic of Modern Psychology*. New York: MacMillan, 1948.
Rachana Sharma: *Advanced Applied Psychology*, Atlantic, Delhi, 2004.
Ram Nath Sharma and Rachana Sharma: *Advanced Applied Psychology*, Atlantic, Delhi, 2004.
Rogers, A. : *Adults Learning for Development*, London, Cassell, 1992.
Rose, M.: *Psychology* of *Human Sexuality*. New York: John Wiley & Sons, 1979.
Ross, E. A.: *Social control: A survey of the foundations of order*. Cleveland: Case Westem Reserve University Press, 1969.
Rotter, J. B.: *Social learning and clinical psychology. New* York: Prentice-Hall, 1954.
Saks, M.J.: *Advances in Applied Social Psychology*, Erlbaum, Hillsdale, NJ, 1980.
Sam Vaknin: *A Textbook of Applied Clinical Psychology*, Dominant, Delhi, 2010.
Sen, Anuradha : *An Introduction to Developmental Psychology*, Indian Pub, Delhi, 2010.
Sharma, R. N. : *Child Psychology and Child Development*, Shubhi Pub, Delhi, 2006.
Shen, Zheng : *Organizational Psychology: Foundations and Applications*. New York: Oxford University Press, 1998.
Snow, C.P.: *The Two Cultures and the Scientific Revolution*. Cambridge: Cambridge University Press, 1961.
Stepansky, P. E. & Goldberg, A.: *Kohut's Legacy: Contributions to Self Psychology*, Hillsdale, Analytic Press, 1984.
Sydney Ellen Schultz: *Psychology and Work Today*. Upper Saddle River, NJ: Prentice Hall, 1998.
Vaknin, Sam : *A Textbook of Organizational Psychology*, Dominant Pub, Delhi, 2010.
Verma, R.B. : *Developmental Psychology and Human Development*, Alfa, Delhi, 2006.
Watson, J.B.: *Psychology from the Standpoint of a Behaviourist*. Philadelphia, PA: Lippincott, 1919.

Index